WATER IN THE MACRO ECONOMY

I dedicate this book to my parents,
my brother Ghassane,
and my sisters Mouna, Soundouss and Nibrass

Water in the Macro Economy

Integrating economics and engineering into an analytical model

HYND BOUHIA

Routledge
Taylor & Francis Group

LONDON AND NEW YORK

First published 2001 by Ashgate Publishing

Reissued 2018 by Routledge
2 Park Square, Milton Park, Abingdon, Oxon OX14 4RN
711 Third Avenue, New York, NY 10017, USA

Routledge is an imprint of the Taylor & Francis Group, an informa business

Publisher's Note
The publisher has gone to great lengths to ensure the quality of this reprint but points out that some imperfections in the original copies may be apparent.

Disclaimer
The publisher has made every effort to trace copyright holders and welcomes correspondence from those they have been unable to contact.

A Library of Congress record exists under LC control number: 00109567

ISBN 13: 978-1-138-71159-4 (hbk)
ISBN 13: 978-1-138-71158-7 (pbk)
ISBN 13: 978-1-315-19974-0 (ebk)

Contents

List of Figures

List of Tables

Acknowledgements

This book is based on graduate research at Harvard University and work at the World Bank. I am grateful to many people for teaching and support which made it possible. Firstly, I thank my doctoral advisor, Prof. Peter Rogers, who has been a true mentor; his creative vitality and intellectual honesty have been an inspiration throughout our work together. I also had the pleasure of working with Prof. Karen Polenske, head of the Department of International Development and Regional Planning at MIT, who guided me throughout my research. Other Harvard professors whom I would like to thank are Richard Wilson, Charles Harvey and Joseph Harrington, as well as several colleagues at Harvard, in particular Nagaraja Rao Harshadeep. Susan Miller and Thomas Mullins of the Harvard Center for Middle Eastern Studies gave me helpful advice on making a technical study accessible to those in other disciplines.

A large amount of data and factual information was required to develop this research, especially to apply my model to the case of Morocco. I would like to thank the government of Morocco, and the Middle East and North Africa Region department at the World Bank for their help in bringing together the necessary data and statistics. At the World Bank, I must mention, in particular, John Hayward for his support and encouragement, and Van Tuu Nguyen for his valuable assistance.

I have valued the opportunity to present this work in several international conferences, occasions which clarified my project's significance beyond the case of Morocco. In particular, I would like to thank the Global Water Partnership for including me in their international meetings.

I thank Peter Lydon, my editor, for his precision and patience, and greatly appreciate the skill of Marc Kaufman and his colleagues at Desktop Publishing and Design Co. in giving form to the book. Several colleagues have been extremely generous with their advice and insights during the writing, especially Franklyn Ayensu. The warm support of a circle of friends, particularly that of my best friend, Lisa Lawrence, has meant a great deal to me through a long project.

Finally, mere words cannot convey the depth of my gratitude to my family for its love, encouragement and support. My parents have been my inspiration all my life. My sisters, Mouna, Soundouss and Nibrass, and my brother Ghassane, have offered immense moral companionship during the writing of this book and throughout my life, as has my entire extended family.

Preface

Because it is essential to human life and has a rich symbolic history, individuals and countries have used water without close regard to its economic value. This practice was acceptable as long as there was enough water to satisfy all demands. Recently, due to population and economic growth, however, per capita fresh water availability has dropped precipitously. Conflicting users and uses have emerged at both the national and the international level, and great concern has been expressed over water availability in terms of both quantity and quality. Today water concerns are high on many national and international agendas.

Developed countries are facing increased pressure on the quality of their supplies and developing countries are mainly concerned about the renewability of existing supplies given the increased demands placed upon them by burgeoning populations and their increased affluence. Unfortunately, the link between the management of the water sector and national economic planning remains ambiguous. Despite billions of dollars expended annually on water by governments, industries, and individuals, the level of technical and economic analysis has rarely reached beyond the project level, or on occasion the river basin level. Water planning is now on the verge of an evolution like that of energy planning two decades ago. Before 1973, energy was considered cheap and plentiful; only with the impending oil crisis did national planners make energy a central component of economic policy. It is to be expected that current and future water crises will highlight the need to integrate water into economic planning.

There are few reported cases of serious studies of the macroeconomic impacts of water investments. The cases that are reported rely upon the use of classical macroeconomic models that do not treat the issues of the water sector in all of its physical, technical, and intersectoral economic complexity. Hynd Bouhia's book is a landmark study in the analysis of development projects generally, and waters projects specifically. For the first time, the entire water sector of a country has been correctly embedded in a macroeconomic model in a way that reflects the physical, technical, and economic interactions.

Specifically Bouhia has modified the classic Leontief Model of the economic relationships between all of the sectors of an economy to include water. Water is not, of course, by itself a single sector in the economy, but rather water is a resource that is used by all sectors of the economy and which has sources and sinks which are themselves connected by the annual water cycle. Hence, water accounting needs to be done at many levels, which include the sources of precipitation and the sinks of return flows and evaporation. Traditionally, Leontief and his followers computed the value of water transactions between the sectors in monetary terms. They then related the transactions to a hypothetical "water sector." Industries and consumers, however, get and dispose of water in many ways, few of which involve cash payments to another sector. Much of the water comes in directly un-priced from the environment and is disposed of directly to the environment without payment to other economic actors. Also, the water that cycles through the economy can be transformed from fresh to polluted, and from available to evaporated, and, hence, lost to the economy. In order to keep track of these physical and economic transformations, Bouhia has devised a very clever system whereby the water is tracked through the economy both as economic transactions and physical quantities. In this way, she is able to maintain an overall annual water balance as well as the annual economic balance. To my knowledge, this is the first time that this has been accomplished for water resources although in the 1970s a group at Brookhaven National Laboratory accomplished a similar feat for energy flows throughout the economy.

The availability of both the water balance and the economy balance is extremely useful. It enables the analyst to compute the direct and indirect multiplier effects of changes in the economy. Of particular interest to water planners is the ability to predict the total impact of investments in the water sector on total income, employment, and water use in the entire economy. The reverse is also true; it allows the macroeconomic planners the option of assessing where in the economy marginal investments should be placed to maximum effect. It also allows the computation of the economy-wide value of water. Under current planning approaches all of these computations would have to be guessed at or derived in roundabout ways. This new approach allows for direct computation of them.

In order to modify the original input-output model which does not include water, Bouhia made a water resource allocation model that computes the optimal levels of sectoral water demands, the supply by source, costs of production and distribution, effluent discharges, return flows, and water losses. Using the two models in tandem creates a Decision Support System which Bouhia calls MEIAH after the Arabic word for water. (The acronym MEIAH also stands for Macro-Economic Integrated Analysis of Hydrology.)

In Chapter 5 the wealth of potential applications is demonstrated. Five scenarios were explored:

- the "business-as-usual" scenario which assumed no special measures for environmental protection, no change in cropping pattern policies in agriculture, no change in water systems efficiency, and no change in trade-barriers;

- an "environmentally sustainable" scenario which assumed upper bounds on groundwater development, minimum discharges set for the flow out of the rivers to the oceans to maintain salinity balances, upper limits on the biochemical oxygen demands placed upon the surface waters due to industrial and municipal pollution, in addition to the business-as-usual assumptions;

- a "domestic policy reform" scenario which was the same as the environmentally sustainable scenario except that government's current cropping pattern policy was loosened to allow up to 50% of cropping decisions to be made by formulae in response to market signals;

- a "macroeconomic reform" scenario which was the same as the domestic policy reform scenario except that globalization and essentially free trade could occur;

- a final scenario called "water, trade, and food security" called for environmental sustainability, entirely free cropping patterns, and globalization of trade.

For each of these scenarios full macroeconomic analyses can be made. Examining these results greatly helps in assessing major policy directions for the Moroccan economy. Chapter 5 ends with the question,"how best to invest a million dirham?" Using the MIEAH model for the business-as-usual case, the model suggests whereabouts in the economy the most efficient marginal investments lie.

I believe that this book will be very helpful to water planners in many countries of the world. I can see its usefulness in both developed and developing countries. Even in settings where the necessary data to implement the full model studies are lacking, the conceptual framework should be of great help to motivate the planners toward integrated water resources planning.

January 2001

Peter P. Rogers
Gordon McKay Professor of Environmental Engineering
Division of Engineering and Applied Sciences
Harvard University

List of Abbreviations

A	Leontief Matrix
A*	Closed Matrix to Household
ADO	Amont Dchar EL Oued (PMH)
AET	Actual Evapo-Transpiration
AGU	Applied General Equilibrium
AHA	Amont Hassane 1st (PMH)
–AI	Irrigated Agriculture
ALM	Barrage Al Massira
ALW	Barrage Al Wahda
AMS	Barrage Amesfrane
AOA	Amont EL Abid Ait Ouarda (PMH)
APR	April
ASD	Amont Sidi Driss (PMH)
ASF	Barrage Asfalou
ATD	Barrage Ait Timedrine
ATM	Barrage Ait Messaoud
ATN	Amont Timi Noutine (PMH)
ATO	Barrage Ait Ouarda
ATS	Barrage Ait Sigmine
AUG	August
AYM	Barrage Ait Youb
BAO	Bab Ouandar
BARL	barley
BARLEY-AI	Irrigated Barley
BAS	Bas Sebou (PMH)
BCM	Billion Cubic Meter
BDH	Billion DH (Dirham)
BEEAM	Brookhaven Energy Economic Assessment Model
BEO	Barrage Bin El Ouidane
BHT	Beht (PMH)

BIG	Barrage Bou Inougoudane
BKK	Barrage Boukerkour
BOD	Biochemical Oxygen Demand
BOR	Bas Oum Er Rbia (PMH)
CGE	Computable General Equilibrium
CHA	Chaouia (PMH)
COSP	Spring Corn
COSU	Summer Corn
COTT	Cotton
CROPCAP	Capital for Crops
DBM	Dir Beni Mellal (PMH)
DEC	December
DEO	Barrage Dchar El Oued
DH	Dirham, Moroccan Monetary Currency (US \$1 = 9 DH)
DOU	Doukkala
DRT	Barrage Daourat
DSS	Decision Support System
ELK	El Kansera
ELO	El Oualidia (PMH)
FAC-NTB	Factor for Non-Trade Barriers
FEB	February
FKH	Barrage Foum Khneg
FODD	Fodder
FODDER-AI	Irrigated Fodder
GATT	General Agreement on Tariffs and Trade
GBA	Aquifer Beni Amir
GBE	Aquifer Berechid
GBM	Aquifer Beni Moussa
GCH	Aquifer Chouia
GDB	Aquifer Dir Beni Mellal
GDP	Gross Domestic Product
GDS	Barrage Garde de Sebou
GGH	Aquifer Ghar
GH	Grande Hydraulique—Large Scale Irrigated Area
GHA	Gharb (Large scale irrigated area)
GIS	Geographic Information System
GMA	Aquifer Maamoura
GMF	Aquifer Meknes-Fes

GNP	Gross National Product
GDP	Gross Domestic Product
GOV	Government
GTA	Aquifer Tessaout Aval
GTE	Aquifer Temara
GTU	Aquifer Tironienne
GWS	Groundwater Sequence
GWR	Groundwater Runoff
HAO	Haouz (large scale irrigated area)
HAS	Barrage Hassane 1st
HSG	Haut Sebou Guigou (PMH)
I	Interception
I-O	Input-Output
IDR	Barrage Idriss 1st
IFPRI	International Food Policy Research Institute
IMF	International Monetary Fund
IMZ	Barrage Imezdilfane
INA	Inaouene (PMH)
INDSRV	Industry and Services
IOLP	Input-Output Linear Programming
JAN	January
JUL	July
JUN	June
KWH	KiloWatt Hour
LEB	Lebene (PMH)
LEGU	Legume
LEGUME-AI	Irrigated Legume
LP	Linear Programming
LVST	Livestock
m^3	Cubic Meter
MAIZE-AI	Irrigated Maize
MAR	March
MCH	Barrage Mellah
MCM	Million Cubic Meter
MDZ	Barrage M'Dez
MEH	Barrage Mechra El Hajar
MENA	Middle East and North Africa Region
MEIAH	Macro-Economic Integrated Analysis of Hydrology

MIK	Mikkes (PMH)
MLY	Barrage Moulay Youssef
MOR	Moyen Oum Er Rbia (PMH)
MRJ	Barrage Merija
MSF	Barrage Mechra Sfa
MYS	Moyen Sebou (PMH)
MW	MegaWatt
NFK	Barrage N'fifkh
NGO	Non-Governmental Organization
NOV	November
NTB	Non-Tariff Barriers
OAO	Ouel El Abid Ait Ouarda (PMH)
OBK	Barrage Ouljet Beni Khemis
OCER	Other Cereals
OCT	October
OECD	Organization for Economic Co-Operation and Development
OES	Barrage Ouljet Es Soltane
OINDCRI-AI	Other Irrigated Industrial Crop
ONEP	Office National de l'Eau Potable (Potable Water National Agency)
ORMVA	Office Regional .... et de Valeur Ajoute (Regional Agricultural Office)
OTH	Other PMH
OTHCER-AI	Other Cereals-Irrigated Agriculture
OUG	Ouergha (PMH)
P	Precipitation
PFM	Plateau Fes Meknes (PMH)
PLAN	Plantations
PLANTA-AI	Irrigated Plantations
PMA	Piedmont Moyen Atlas (PMH)
PMH	Petite et Moyenne Hydraulique—Small and Medium Scale Irrigated Area
RAINFED	Rainfed Agriculture
RHA	Barrage Rhafsai
ROW	Rest of the World
SAB	Barrage Sidi Abbou
SAM	Social Accounting Matrix

SAV-INV	Saving and Investments
SDR	Barrage Sidi Driss
SEC	Barrage Sidi Echahed
SEP	September
SGRBT-AI	Irrigated Sugar Beet
SGRCN-AI	Irrigated Sugar Cane
SM	Soil Moisture
SNFLW-AI	Irrigated Sun Flower
S1	Tributary Mellah
S2	Tributary N'fifikh
SB1	Tributary Grou
SB2	Tributary Bou Regrag
SBA	Barrage Si Mohamed Ben Abdellah
SBK	Barrage Bou Khadet
SO1	Tributary Tessaout
SO2	Tributary Lakhdar
SO4	Tributary Ouel El Abid
SO5	Tributary Derna
SO6	Tributary Srou
SO7	Tributary Fellat
SUGB	Sugar Beat
SUGC	Sugar Cane
SS1	Tributary Beht
SS2	Tributary Rdom
SS3	Tributary Mikkes
SS4	Tributary Guigou
SS5	Tributary Inaoun
SS6	Tributary Lebene
SS7	Tributary Ouergha
SS8	Tributary Zloul
SSM	Barrage Sidi Said Maachou
TAD	Tadla (Large scale irrigated area)
TAF	Barrage Tafrant
TAG	Barrage Taghzirt
TAJ	Barrage Tajemout
TAS	Barrage Taskdert
THR	Barrage Touahar
TID	Barrage Tiddas

TMN	Barrage Timi Noutine
TYG	Barrage Tiyoughza
UALJ	Al Jadida
UAZR	Azrou
UBEN	Beni Mellal
UBOU	Boulemane
UCAS	Casablanca
UELH	El Hajeb
UFES	Fes
UIFR	Ifrane
UKEN	Kenitra
UKHA	Khanifra
UKHM	Khemissat
UKHO	Khouribga
UMAR	Marrakech
UMEK	Meknes
UMOH	Mohamedia
UN	United Nations
UNDP	United National Development Program
URAB	Rabat
USAF	Safi
USAID	United States Agency for International Development
USAL	Sale
USEF	Sefrou
USET	Settat
USKA	Sidi Kacem
UTAO	Taounat
UTAZ	Taza
VEGA	Autumn Vegetables
VEGET-AI	Irrigated Vegetables
VEGS	Spring Vegetables
WATTAR	Water Tariffs
WHEA	Wheat
WHT-AI	Wheat—Irrigated Agriculture
WIOP	Water Input-Output Programming

"And from Water have We made every living thing."
The Qur'an, Surat 21, 30

1

Introduction

Throughout human history, water has served as a complex religious symbol. Not surprisingly in light of its strict indispensability for life, water is seen as pointing to the emergence of the cosmos from chaos and of human life from unformed matter. In the world's great religious traditions, water not only nourishes the body, but also purifies the soul. From the sacred waters of the Ganges, to the rebirth of the baptismal font, to the flowing green fields of the Islamic paradise, water plays a central ritual and conceptual role in human religious activity.

Perhaps partly because of its rich symbolic history, until recently water has not been treated as an economic commodity. Water has been used by individuals and countries with a full realization of its importance, but often with little cool-headed measuring and consideration of its economic value. Such traditional approaches to water were acceptable as long as there was enough water to satisfy all demands. However, in recent decades, per capita fresh water availability has dropped precipitously. Conflicting uses and users of water have emerged at both the national and international level, and there is justified concern about meeting the water needs—in terms of both quantity and quality—of rapidly growing populations and economies. Under such pressures, the necessity of moving beyond tradition and achieving planned and rationalized management of water resources has been widely recognized.

Today, water concerns are high on many national and international agendas. However, the link between the management of the water sector and national economic planning remains ambiguous. This ambiguity is often exacerbated by the absence of sufficient dialogue among the different governmental and non-governmental bodies in charge of various aspects of a country's water, a lack of which often leads to fragmented, ad hoc decision-making. The situation can be further complicated by trying to maintain the tradition of providing unlimited water access to all users at a very low price, which in modern circumstances makes water a highly subsidized resource and can place a heavy burden on governmental budgets. For example, in many developing countries up to 90 percent of water is reserved for agriculture. Because of the traditional belief that the farmer should be kept on his farm at any cost, water is allocated to agriculture without consideration of its low productivity in that use. Channeling even a small fraction of this water into industrial and domestic use could bring dramatic economic gains. Although it is currently considered politically difficult, in a water stressed countries, such inter-sectoral water allocation can be essential for sustainable economic development. It is increasingly widely recognized that water resources can no longer be allocated in isolation from broader economic issues, but at the same time, taking an integrated approach to national water planning requires a range of supporting institutional, educational and social adjustments and reforms. Policy makers have been reluctant to embark upon this set of changes because they have not been able to assess accurately and in detail the impacts of changes in water allocation on a society and its economy. By unifying the approaches of engineering and economics in this field, the present study offers an instrument to make just that assessment: to view, and ultimately to allocate, water in relation to economic and social goals that are broader than the water sector alone.

It is a real challenge to bring water into the political arena and to consider it as a resource for the full economy. Water is now undergoing an evolution like that of energy two decades ago. Before the 1970 s, energy was considered cheap and plentiful; only with the impending oil crisis did national planners make energy a central component of economic policy. Similarly, the approach of future water crises is highlighting the need to integrate water into overall national economic planning.

The research presented here is based upon two computerized models: a water resource allocation system and a water input-output table. Together they form an integrated system for policy analysis and decision making. The output of the water resource optimization model is numbers describing sectoral water demands, levels of supply by sources, shadow prices, costs and value added at various stages of water production and distribution, and amounts of effluent discharge, return flows and water losses. These outputs of the first model become data used to modify a traditional social account matrix, converting it to a water input-output table. This second model is denominated in both units of water (cubic meters) and in money, in order to perform macroeconomic analysis. Using this information and the coefficients of the input-output table and the technical coefficient matrix, a linear programming model can be employed to determine the national economic value of water, estimate the scarcity of water, identify strategic macroeconomic sectors affected by water availability and inter-sectoral allocation, and derive an economy-wide demand curve for water.

In addition to clarifying the directions of sustainable water management, the paired modeling system developed in this study can evaluate various macroeconomic reforms, and highlight the water policies needed to advance them. National goals such as a desired level of imports or exports, food self-sufficiency, or an increase in employment can be translated into constraints or objectives in the water resources model, which can then bring out appropriate supporting water policies. The system can flexibly evaluate a spectrum of policy options as a means to targeting priority investments for a strategy that aims at environmental sustainability. Using stochastic simulation, it can assess the effect of precipitation fluctuation on economic growth, and can show the effect of water availability on socio-economic indicators. It is hoped it will foster dialogue among policymakers, economists, financiers, educators, environmentalists and politicians.

This method is applicable worldwide, either at the national level or by international organizations. I have been particularly inspired by the Middle East and North African region (MENA), where the mismanagement of water resources is one of the most immediate—and correctable—impediments to sustainable socio-economic development. While the region's population continues to grow, its per capita water availability continues to shrink. As a result of pollution, overexploitation, expanded irrigation, inefficient usage and especially, institutional fragmentation, the Maghreb will soon be on the brink of a water crisis. Without integrated long-term water strategies, per capita renewable water supplies are expected to fall within two generations to one fifth of what they are today.

The economy of the MENA Region is so tightly intertwined with the use of water, that sustainable economic development is unlikely without integrated and coherent water resources management. With this in mind, I have shaped the combined models, which together make a Decision Support System (DSS) with an emphasis on countries of water scarcity, where the alarm has been raised for long-term policy reform. To name this DSS, an acronym based on the Arabic word for water, *meiah,* has been used: MEIAH—Macro-Economic Integrated Analysis of Hydrology. The Kingdom of Morocco is used as a concrete case for analysis.

To ground the methodology introduced here comprehensively, the book centers on Morocco, where the author grew up—a country which has been transformed in a single lifetime from a water-rich, fertile region into one facing a severe water crisis and a host of attendant ramifications. Morocco's story is a call for an all-embracing national plan that incorporates water resource strategy and treats water as an integral part of the overall economy.

Morocco is blessed with a well-structured water system of dams and canals, a legacy of not only the sophisticated engineering work done during the period of French rule but also a series of proactive post-independence governmental interventions. The original *raison d'être* of the system was a vision of Morocco as an export-oriented breadbasket based on irrigation-fed agriculture. The system was further developed in a large-scale effort to replicate the success of California's agricultural sector, followed a little later by a national goal to bring one million hectares of the country under irrigation. As in many other nations, however, Morocco's water system would be even more useful if it were integrated into in a comprehensive economic national plan.

What complicates the prospect of policy reform is that a substantial part of Morocco's social structure has developed around the current water system. Lifestyles and occupations have come to depend on it. In addition, as part of Morocco's economic backbone, the water system is tightly integrated into international markets and any change in it is likely to induce market responses. While a general program of education and awareness-raising is a vital component of any politically feasible reform, even more important is the prior project of assessing—in a single integrative framework—water's trigger effects in the macroeconomy in a language that policy-makers can absorb and work with.

Today, the expansion of Morocco's large but water-stressed agricultural sector and irrigated areas has created a delicately thorny dilemma: whether to prioritize the farm sector's massive need for water or focus on satisfying the urban sector's water demand. How can we strike the balance between these competing needs? Indeed, how can we even think about them within the same conceptual framework? Population growth, rural-to-urban migration, environmental side-effects, political constraints, and national aspirations for economic development have made it clear that water management can no longer be conducted sector by sector but rather must find a holistic approach that encompasses the entire range of national imperatives, including social stability and economic betterment. That is the challenge taken up by this book.

Chapter 2 provides background for the development of the methodology. It first underscores the importance of considering water as an economic good, not only because of the large investments required by the water sector, but also due to water's pervasive effects throughout the economy as a whole. It also provides an overview of the existing methodologies for economic planning, the emergence and large demand for environmental-economic accounts, and a brief resume of the existing engineering techniques related to water systems.

The MEIAH Decision Support System is outlined in the first part of Chapter 3. The details of the water resource model are provided, highlighting the engineering and hydrological concepts behind it. (The model's formulation is given in Appendix 2.) The second part of Chapter 3 describes in detail the methodology developed in this study, emphasizing the innovation of incorporating the results from a water resource allocation system into an input-output table. After showing the different components of the water budget, the economic value of water—as computed by the water model through shadow prices—is used to determine the flows of water in both physical and monetary units and thereby to capture the trigger effect of hydrology on the economy. The newly defined water-input-output table yields a set of multipliers—output, income, employment and water use—and ratios, which can be manipulated to analyze potential investments and to bring out their policy consequences for evaluation. A macro-economic demand curve is generated using a linear programming approach providing an economy-wide value of water. The last section of this chapter offers a suggestion for using the MEIAH model to assess different policy options, formulate an integrated strategy, and outline a sustainable national plan.

Chapter 4 also gives the necessary background for the practical illustration of this research; the case study is then further developed in that chapter as an application of the methodology to the case of Morocco. After giving an overview of the water situation of Morocco and a description of the studied region of the Oum Er Rbia, Bou Regrag and Sebou (OBS) river basins, the creation of water input-output table is illustrated step by step, showing the water balance at the national level and the incorporation of the water sector into a 1995 Social Accounting Matrix. Like other countries of the MENA region, Morocco suffers from large fluctuations in water availability, which reverberate throughout the economy. Appendix 4 provides MEIAH with ways to take account of flow uncertainty in policy evaluation.

Chapter 5 discusses the policy implications of the MEIAH system for Morocco, through the presentation of different options, which range from sustaining the environment, to implementing agricultural reforms and encouraging international trade. Also, a hypothetical situation with full flexibility in the agriculture sector and a free trade agreement, shifting Morocco from subsistence to food security, is explored. After an exercise determining the most profitable way to allocate one million dirhams among various economic sectors, a set of conclusion and recommendations is presented in Chapter 6.

The system developed here is intended to be user-friendly, and to be available on CD-ROM, and perhaps additionally via the Internet. The reader is encouraged to follow its development, and indeed, operate it directly, using Microsoft Excel.

2

The Water Environment and National Planning

Water in the Economy

Water, a requirement for life, is critical to all production chains of the economy. When it is scarce, we cannot avoid recognizing it as an economic good. Water resource planning and management must then take into consideration both the vertical and horizontal linkages of water to the other sectors and components of the economy.

Priority of the Water Agenda

Agenda 21, negotiated at the 1992 UN Conference on Environment and Development in Rio de Janeiro, spelled out a comprehensive program of action to achieve sustainable development. For the water sector, it stated:

"Effectively integrated management of water resources is important to all socio-economic sectors relying on water. Rational allocation prevents conflict and enhances the social development of local communities, as well as economic planning and productivity. Efficient demand management allows water-using sectors to achieve long-term savings on water costs and stimulates resource-conscious production technologies. Health conditions and environmental quality should also improve, either as a result of integrated development planning or as a beneficial consequence of improved environmental or social conditions."

More definitive statements of good water policies were developed by a preparatory session for the UNCED meeting in Rio, the International Conference on Water and Environment held in Dublin, 1992. Four basic principles were outlined:

■ Fresh water is a finite and vulnerable resource, essential to sustain life, to development and to the environment.

■ Water development and management should be based upon a participatory approach, involving users, planners and policy-makers at all levels.

■ Women play a central role in the provision, management and safeguarding of water.

■ Water has an economic value in all of its competing uses and should be recognised as an economic good.

Agenda 21, as well as the Dublin principles, have been widely accepted by water specialists worldwide. International water organizations, such as the Global Water Partnership and the World Water Council, seek to implement the Dublin principles and spread the concept of water as an economic and social good in the world.

Investments in the Water Sector

In several parts in the developing world, the water sector absorbs a large percentage of the available public investment funds. For example, in Brazil, 30% of the total investments goes to the water sector (Asad et al., 1999). For the most water scarce region of the world, the World Bank reports that in the second half of the 1990s, Algeria, Egypt, Jordan, Lebanon, Morocco, Tunisia and Yemen have invested together about US$ 1.5 Billion annually in water development, of which about US$ 1 Billion originated from official development assistance from other countries. (World Bank, 1995b) This represents on average 1 percent of their combined GDP, but the Bank believes that the dry MENA[1] Region's annual investment in water should increase from about US $ 4.5 to US $ 6 Billion, representing up to 2 percent of the region's GDP. Such investments have large impacts on the national budgets, and clearly must be planned with great care to avoid unnecessary spending and redundancy in the projects undertaken.

In some major sectors of the economy, such as energy, investments have been generally well-linked to national planning. However, the link is not clear and well developed in the water sector. There is a need to move from river basin-by-river basin, or even project-by-project planning, toward broader approaches, much more closely integrated into overall national planning. This is in part because water investments not only must be targeted to yield the greatest returns, but because they depend for their success on coordination with supportive policy reforms. Investments will yield few returns if the right incentives and institutions are not in place. Water resource investments also need to consider such cross-sectoral implications as the problem of displacing people and disturbing ecosystems.

How does the Water Sector Relate to the Economy as a Whole?

Economics has been described as the science of allocating scarce resources among alternative goals. "From the consumers' point of view, their task is to allocate scarce income to purchase competing goods and services to maximize their satisfaction. Businesses employ scarce resources, such as capital, labor and land in alternative productive activities in order to maximize their profit. And finally, societies allocate their resources among a variety of productive activities and distribute the products among consumers in such a manner as to maximize the society's welfare." (Rogers, 1997) For classical economists, the gross domestic product represents a concept of total welfare for a society, and the welfare of a society is maximized when the GDP reaches its maximum value. Traditional macroeconomic analysis does not take into consideration natural resources as one of the components of economic growth. The classical economist and the "ecological" economist are in perpetual conflicts about how to deal with natural resources. For example, for a classical economist a natural resource such as water, although an input to the production chain, is considered to be substitutable by capital and labor, instead of being seen as complementary to those factors of production. But this fails to recognize that water is a primary input to every economic good, directly or indirectly, and that water's available quantity and quality affects output and hence the level of growth. Water is also a source of conflict, and has been seen as a future cause of war in situations of scarcity. An overabundance of water can also have economic and social consequences, for example, in deltaic Bangladesh, which is always threatened with severe flooding.

Water Scarcity: A Major Constraint to Development

In contrast to the diminishing per capita resources available, global demand for water is rising (Postel, 1992). In the developing countries, where water demand is predicted to double by the year 2020, major investment has been undertaken to smooth the imbalance between demand and supply. As mentioned above, in the MENA region water sector investments represent up to 1.5% of national GDP and capture much attention from governments.

A common feature of water allocation in the developing countries is the large proportion of water used by agriculture, nearly 80% on average. This sectoral pattern of water use results from the predominance of traditional rural agrarian structures in society and the economy. But, as time goes on, high population growth, rising urbanization, industrialization and rising household incomes are causing increased industrial and urban household demand, which in most countries has begun to compete with agriculture for limited supplies of locally available freshwater. Water planners often seek non-conventional sources of water to stave off the difficult and politically unpalatable necessity to reallocate agricultural water to higher value uses. Water loss reduction, reuse or recycling of water, use of different qualities of water appropriate to different purposes, inter-basin transfers, desalination of seawater and brackish groundwater, and other options are all being utilized or studied. However, the rapidly increasing supply costs for such "non-conventional water" are accentuating the need to find other policy options.

Allocating water among myriad conflicting potential uses presents a major dilemma to governments, all of which have the primary responsibility for regulating access to water (Rogers, 1992). Governments must achieve a consensus on policy among the multi-sectoral interests represented within them and must maintain that consensus as the effects of their development and management choices emerge in the physical, social and economic dimensions; this requires appropriate incentives and a conducive institutional setting. The MENA Region seems to be the most affected by water scarcity, and its economy is so highly intertwined with the use of water, that sustainable economic development of the region is unlikely if a more sustainable and rational approach to water resources management does not evolve.

Need for a Multi-disciplinary Approach

The prospect of water scarcity and increasing environmental, economic, political, social and financial pressures, calls for coordinated decision-making so that water is allocated to maximize net benefits in a manner which will still be sustainable in the long run. In fact, no country enjoys the luxury that water resources can continue to be considered in sectoral isolation and managed through fragmented institutional control. Today, one can no longer think in terms of an "engineer's view" or an "economist's view" of water. Water must be considered in terms of its interaction with the whole range of traditional concerns, including agriculture, urban demand, economics, finance, infrastructure, environment, public health and national goals.

Horizontal and Vertical Inter-linkages in Water Sector Planning

Water is a primary or a complementary input to the whole range of economic sectors, such as agriculture, energy, industry, and services. These are the horizontal links of the water sector. In order to capture these horizontal relations, it is necessary to have a global, comprehensive and multidisciplinary framework (horizontal linkages are particularly strong with the domains of economic planning and environmental protection). Coordination between these fields should be primarily at the level of policy principles and national planning. The outcomes of such planning will produce boundary conditions and scenario constraints for water planning at a regional or river basin level.

Secondly, water can be a primary determinant of economic growth in a water-stressed region. There has been much ambiguity among economists as to whether to consider water as "a substitute" or as "a complement" in production theory. In many countries where agriculture is an important part of the national economy, and where water is scarce, it is important while examining inter-sectoral linkages, to incorporate social impacts, such as employment, immigration, poverty alleviation, and rural development. These are the water sector's upwards vertical links.

Rogers has outlined the need for comprehensive approaches for water resources management, emphasizing the economic aspects (Rogers, 1992). Munasinghe has presented a conceptual framework for integrated water resources planning and policy analysis (Munasinghe, 1992). Figure 2-1, (adapted from Munasinghe) illustrates the linkages described above. It shows the horizontal dialogue among the different economic sectors (agriculture, energy, transport, industry, etc) as well as the water sub-sectors (potable water, irrigation, hydropower, etc). The downward vertical links are seen to have two levels, first the political stage which is between the macro and the intermediate levels, and then the more technical and sub-sectoral stage, between the intermediate and the micro-level. This figure shows the lower portion of the vertical setting of the system, in terms of the interaction of water with national policies, as well as with water subsectoral planning and management.

Towards Integrated Water Resource Strategies
Formulating an Appropriate Water Strategy

Several countries in the Middle East and North Africa have already developed economic, agricultural or hydrological models to assess project impacts, for example on particular interests within society. However, these are "stand-alone"

FIGURE 2-1
Horizontal and Vertical Water Sector Linkages

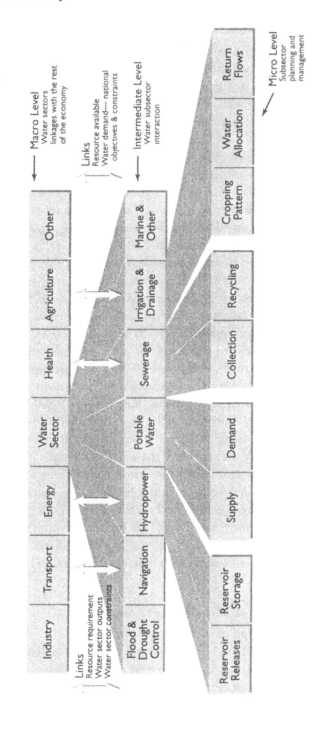

models of limited usefulness in formulating an integrated national or regional strategy. There is a need for a new, broader analytical framework to link river basin and macroeconomic models and to help analyze the effects of policy choices.

An appropriate national water plan has a vital role in economic and social development. It is therefore essential to have a comprehensive and integrated procedure to formulate such a national strategy for sustainable water development and the management of available water resources. A strategy represents a mix of objectives and policies, as well as the short, the medium and long-term action programs to achieve the development goals and to support implementation of the needed policies. A strategy is unique to each nation; there is not a standard formula that can be applied to all countries. Rather it should be tailored to each individual country, reflecting local constraints, resources and objectives. A strategy needs to be tested, refined and periodically updated to adapt to changing circumstances and challenges. Designing and using a strategy is a long-term iterative process that must follow a set of indispensable steps in the formulation stage, and must provide an opportunity to stakeholders to participate in the process.

One of the main complexities of a water strategy is deciding on the appropriate goals. At the outset, they could be found to be multiple, conflicting and difficult to define, but as worked out in the strategy, they must be coherent in relation to non-water sector plans, such as those for food security, trade, rural development, and urban development.

As a first step towards the formulation of a water resources strategy, there is a need for a thorough analysis and assessment of the existing water system. It starts with the collection of information on the existing water sources (rivers, tributaries, lakes, groundwater and precipitation) and water users. A picture of population trends and future water demand is needed. An inventory of relevant existing laws and policies, and scheduled projects will be needed, since they also are "givens" for the future situation to be created, and in programming terms, will probably be translated into scenario limits, or "boundaries."

Use of Analytical Tools for Policy Analysis: Example from the MENA Region

A computer model, such as MEIAH, is a picture of a situation, based on reality but representing that reality, and a range of hypothetical alternative situations, in terms of numbers and rules which can be manipulated by a computer. It is comparable to a painting of a landscape that represents real terrain in terms of colors applied to a canvas; in the process a three-dimensional reality is reduced to two dimensions for easier handling and comprehension, but this process of selection, or abstraction from all the details of the real landscape also makes it possible for the artist to make changes in his picture, and to "try out," for example, how the scene would look in, say, a different season without having to wait six months. Such models and analytical tools have been used extensively by water planners in the assessment of water situations, but few have entered the policy arena. The main role of these computer-based tools is to systematically examine various policy alternatives, to determine the nature, and as far as possible, the magnitude, of the effects of policy steps that are being debated, and thereby to make possible informed and balanced water planning management decisions. At a social level, the problem faced by reformers is often to get a debate started on the relevant issues. Like discussing a province by looking together at a map rather than actually visiting every corner of it, this is another way in which a computerized model, sometimes called a Decision Support System (DSS),[2] can be useful, playing the role of the map or painting representing a physical reality, and thus making discussion possible.

The abstraction, or selection, that goes into a well-designed computer models allows the ordering and manipulating of relevant information in a meaningful manner. Such models are first needed to make predictions of the performance of physical systems under different management strategies, using simulation tools. Typical examples of this category are groundwater flow models, soil moisture and crop yield models and reservoir simulation models (Mass et al., 1962, Major and Lenton, 1979, Loucks et al., 1981, and Goodman, 1984). Second, these models can yield a translation of simulation results into indices in terms of performance evaluation criteria. Examples of this category include financial and economic evaluation models. Third, these analytical tools can be used to structure the decision-making process, using methods based on multi-criteria decision techniques.

Many technical studies have been conducted in the MENA Region dealing with climate, hydrology, agriculture, energy, transport and such. Within the water sector, project- and goal-specific models have been developed for different water subsectors, for example urban water supply networks, cropping patterns for specific irrigated areas and environmental evaluation. Academic modeling efforts are also ongoing, but few of them have been used to weigh strategic, or multi-sectoral, considerations that come before governmental bodies.

The countries of the MENA Region all have water development plans, but they are at different stages of the process of preparing integrated strategic plans. The sector or program oriented models tend to be used only by the small groups of model developers. In some countries, such as Egypt, different types of models have been constructed and are being used by governmental bodies; in that country's agriculture sector, a General Equilibrium Model is used for planning, while another hydrological model for water resource assessment in some urban centers is one of the analytical tools used by the Egyptian department of planning. Also, a research center has developed a water drainage model for the Beheira Region of Egypt's North, which is yet to be approved for use by the government. These activities are very promising and if, in time, they are integrated, they would ensure a coherence among the sectors. Other countries, like Cyprus and Turkey, feel the need for a DSS for the management of their water resource and for the simulation of precipitation uncertainty, as well as for the use of advanced techniques such as Geographical Information Systems (GIS). In terms of integration, Yemen is looking at water as part of the whole economy, and is in the process of developing a national water strategy, with the assistance of international experts and donors, but lacks sophistication in modeling. Morocco is well advanced in using modeling tools for hydraulic planning, and economic and environmental impacts are also viewed through analytical tools. As is also true of Tunisia, it can be expected that output from these instruments is used in national planning, but this has not been announced by the government as of late 1999.

Methodological Overview

Methodologies for Economic Planning

Partial Equilibrium Method

When applied to water resource planning, the partial equilibrium approach is a basic method used to determine the value of water in order to allocate it among competing prospective users. This approach requires the estimation of the "opportunity cost" of using water in a particular sub-sector, which is done by considering the cost to society of depriving other sectors of the use of that water. For example, to determine the value of water to industry, we consider the value of that water if it had been used by domestic households for drinking purposes or in the agriculture sector for irrigation. Similarly, the water's value for domestic use and agriculture can be estimated by reference to its value for alternative use in industry.

General Equilibrium: Input-Output (I-O) Analysis

Wassily Leontief, Nobel laureate in Economics in 1973, approached economics in a structural manner through an input-output model, thus transforming macro-economics to an empirical discipline that could use modern data processing technology. Input-output analysis examines the flow of goods and services and all intermediate transactions among the producing and consuming sectors of a country or a region. This opened up a new window for the study of the complex interdependence within the production system in modern economies.

The ever-increasing importance to the economy of previously unconsidered environmental externalities has stimulated the pursuit of new methods for evaluating sustainable economic development. In the 1960s, Leontief attempted to capture environmental repercussions on economic structure by internalizing pollution in an input/output framework (Leontief, 1986). Isard made the first attempt to establish the link between water and the macro-economy by including a water sector (water quantity) in the then-massive highly-disaggregated input-output table constructed for the city of Philadelphia (Isard, Langford and Romanoff, 1967). Isard also considered environment as an economic sector, and adapted input-output analysis for environmental management. Other researchers incorporated other "externalities" by constructing new regional or national tables incorporating new sectors, depending on the objective of the economic model (e.g. Isard and Romanoff, 1967a included water quality issues in an input-output framework). Often, externalities are computed as proportions of the sectoral economic outputs. The structure of the input-output table generates output of the various economic sectors, and "externalities" refers to issues that are not included as one of the economic sectors, for example, pollution. Pollution is generated by a given economic sector, and can be specified as a proportion of the sector's total output. This way, the pollution level could be aggregated over all the sectors that generate such an externality.

In the late 1970s, a modified input-output model was used to examine economic and ecological consequences of a proposed US Corps of Engineers reservoir project. Dufournaud, Harrington and Rogers (1988), revisited the Leontief incorporation of environment into the macroeconomy using a Computer Generalized Equilibrium (CGE) model approach. Another attempt was made by De Haan and Keuning (1993) to take the environment into account for the national economy of the Netherlands.

Traditionally, economists have rarely seen water resources as an important part of the economy, but many analytical developments are prompted by real-world problems. In arid California, recurring droughts caused much economic hardship, and unsurprisingly the first few attempts to integrate water into macroeconomic systems arose in the dry west of the United States. The concept of integrating water into economy-wide issues was first advanced by S.V. Ciriacy-Wantrup in the early 1950s (Isard and Romanoff, 1967b). In the 1960s, Lofting made the first serious attempt to use regional input-output tables to analyze water resource issues, and later, also in California, economic regional multipliers linked to regional water models were developed (Deichmann, 1989). Other researchers have used techniques other than input-output analysis to link the water sector to the macroeconomy. Rogers, Hurst and Harshadeep (1993) developed a set of optimization models to link the water sector to macroeconomic concerns for Bangladesh, where water plays an important part in the agricultural production that dominates the country's GDP. Many attempts have been made to examine in detail the agricultural sector in I-O tables, and this quickly involves water, depending on the criticality of water use in the farming of a region (Kirsten and Vanzyl, 1990). A complex set of models was developed in France, in which water quality and quantity information for the Seine-Normandy basin interacted with a model based on a regional input-output table (Emsellen and Bordet, 1985). Another approach was developed in the early 1990s in South Africa (Mirrilees, 1991) to determine the economic value of water in different economic sectors by using a linear program based upon an input-output table. The program could evaluate the shadow prices of water for various uses, and choose water resource plans that would not severely impede economic development. This work was based on earlier research done by Henry et al (1981).

Despite these efforts, the integration of water into the macroeconomy has been rather unsatisfactory. Only a segment of the water cycle, rather than the full cycle, from rainfall to final use, evaporation, or flow to the sea, was integrated into these input-output studies. The sectoral or spatial aggregation is usually too broad to be of much practical use in decision-making. Even in the South Africa model, water is often considered a service sector: water supply. The sources of water, return flows and sanitation, and aspects of water quality were not taken up, and the demand for water, notably by households, was not thoroughly analyzed, while the interaction between water resources decision-making and macroeconomic decision-making was not explicitly considered.

This lack of analytical integration between water and the general economy is puzzling, especially since energy has been examined in a linked macroeconomic context, initially as a response to the oil crisis of the 1970s. In the 1980s, the BEEAM (Brookhaven Energy-Economic Assessment Model) attempted to capture the closed cycle of energy from its primary inputs (such as coal) to the final demand, while illustrating the flows linking energy to the other sectors of the economy. In the Netherlands I-O analysis was applied to four material flows (paper, cement and concrete, energy, and iron, steel and zinc) by Konijn et al. in 1994.

There are many parallels between the energy and the water sectors: they both tend to be highly subsidized; they are constrained by existing supply; large important sectors of the economy depend upon them; demands and supplies can vary widely by region and time period; demands are growing rapidly with increasing population pressures; there is scope for conservation and substitution, and proper planning is essential to manage these scarce resources. Of course, there are many significant differences: energy is more readily thought of as a priced resource; water is easier to store but much harder to transport than energy; recycling and return flows must be considered in the case of water; and water quality can vary. However, approaches such as suggested by the BEEAM model could be adapted for use in integrating the water sector into the macroeconomic structure.

Computable General Equilibrium Methods

Computable General Equilibrium models (CGE-models) are constructed in order to understand the chains of reactions within an economy to a change in one of its parts. Within the model itself, such repercussions are seen in the form of changes in relative prices. The formulation of the CGE model is such that both quantities and relative prices are determined endogenously within the model. In fact, CGE models are often called price-endogenous models as all the prices in the model must adjust until the decisions made in the productive sphere of the economy are consistent with the final demand decisions made by households and other autonomous decision makers. The characteristics of non-linear relationships and endogenous prices differentiate CGE models from input-output models.

CGE modeling, also called applied general equilibrium modeling (AGEM), is based on the conversion of the abstract Walrasian general-equilibrium structure to a realistic model of the economy. The CGE model specifies an economy numerically, such that prices and quantities for goods and factors adjust to equate supply and demand based on Walrasian general equilibrium theory (Hall and Taylor, 1986; Dervis et al., 1982; Mankiw, 1998). In the last decades, CGE models have been applied with increasing frequency to problems of structural adjustment, trade strategy, and income distribution, and have become the standard fare of both academic researchers and developing country policy-making units (Devarajan et al., 1994). There is growing interest in efforts to use CGE models to assess the impacts of environmental policies, since some environmental policies, such as reducing pollution emissions, can affect prices, quantities and the structure of the economy.

Environmental Accounts and Engineering Techniques

Although purely economic indicators measure national or regional growth, they do not account for the depletion of natural resources. Several approaches have been undertaken to adjust the system of national accounts to deal with environmental sustainability. (Pearce and Turner, 1990; Rogers et al., 1997) The OECD outlined in 1991 an approach to adjusting the framework and boundaries of national accounts to take the environment into account. (OECD 1994; OECD 1995) This is based on creating natural resource accounts which collect, within a consistent framework, quantitative and qualitative information on the stocks and flows of natural resources, typically expressed in physical units. The OECD has also suggested "satellite" environmental accounts, which complement the economic information in national accounts without modifying the system of national accounts itself.

Types of Environmental Accounts

How the environment is included in an economic analysis differs, depending on who will use the analysis, and their goals. Three levels of aggregation can be distinguished: macro, sectoral and micro.

■ *Macro-level aggregation:* This means alternative national accounts, such as the environmentally adjusted GDP, called "green GDP." These are mainly developed to evaluate the depletion of natural resources and the qualitative degradation of the environment at a broad national level. They capture the consumption of natural capital. Currently, few countries have developed these alternative accounts, and the focus is mainly on air pollution. In this book, the alternative accounts pursued are at the macro-level, and the focus is on water as a natural resource.

■ *Sectoral-level:* These accounts are in physical rather than monetary units, and at a smaller scale than macro accounts. The purposes of sectoral accounts is to link the supply and the demand of a natural resource, and they deal specifically with one resource, such as water, energy, or forest landcover. They are used for planning and management at a regional level. The demand is clearly identified, and could vary depending on the choice of policies. Several countries have developed such accounts, such as the energy accounts in Norway which have well defined roles in energy policy and planning and which are linked to economic models. Forest accounts in Japan are primarily used to trace national and international flows of timber to serve trade and environmental analysis. Sectoral water accounts have been developed for some countries, such as Spain, where they are used to trace the quantity of water flowing in the watershed and give information about the quality of water. In France, water accounts are used to manage river basins.

■ *Micro-economic level:* This refers to accounts at the firm level, which are essentially developed as a reply to green consumerism and can also be a means to reduce costs.

One of the major objective of environmentally adjusted accounts is to provide simultaneously information on the environment and the economy. This combination could be used to analyze various environment/economy issues, including evaluating the physical scarcity of natural resources, generating empirical evidence of over- exploitation of natural resources, valuing environmental degradation and depletion of natural resources, measuring the incidence of environmental regulations and taxes; and measuring the efficiency of natural resource use by the economic sectors.

Systems Analysis and Water Resource Modeling

The field of water resource systems was first significantly developed during the Harvard Water Program in the 1950s and 1960s, the first serious effort to bring together a multi-disciplinary team of engineers, economists and policy makers to establish a systems analysis framework for water resources planning (Maass et al., 1962). Water resource systems analysis has advanced tremendously over the years from a methodological standpoint (Maass, et al, 1962; Loucks, Stedinger and Haith, 1981; Goodman, 1984). One of the first practical applications is described in Major and Lenton (1977). There has been much improvement in the development and application of various kinds of operations research tools (Winston, 1996) to the field of water resources (Loucks et al., 1981).

Stochastic Simulation

Resource models usually fall into one of two categories - simulation and optimization. Each tries to answer a different set of questions. Simulation models focus on the impacts of various "what if" scenarios, whereas optimization models determine what "ought to be" done given a set of objectives and constraints for the decision makers.

In both these kinds of models, simple runs with fixed estimated values can provide initial clues as to the behavior of the water resources system. However, in reality there are usually large uncertainties in the information used in these models. These uncertainties must be taken into account in using the results of a model, but there is a lack of standard frameworks to analyze this uncertainty. This is primarily for three reasons: too many different kinds of uncertainties, too many ways of analyzing them, and too few ways of interpreting the results. Uncertainties can be hydrologic, economic, demand related, concerned with the formulation of goals or objectives, or related to a wide variety of data variability. The problem is complicated by the fact that often very little is known about the uncertainty distribution of the parameters. However, a bigger problem usually confronts water resource modelers: given the wide variety of options to analyze information, which methodologies, tools and techniques should be applied to elicit the economic repercussions of a change in the system. In fact, there are variety of sensitivity, stochastic and other techniques that could be applied in both simulation and optimization models to incorporate the effects of variation in the input parameters or criteria. Appendix 4 presents a set of techniques to handle uncertainty considerations using decision support systems.

Study Focus: Trigger Effects of Water in the Economy

Based on the concept of environmental accounts, our objective is to evaluate the effects on the economy of change in the water sector. The focus will therefore be on water as a natural resource, and we will develop a method of "blue accounting" and generate a kind of "blue GDP." This study seeks to present a first illustration of hydro-economics. Please refer to Figure 2-2, Sectoral Interactions, which illustrates the two-way link between water and the macro-economy.

FIGURE 2-2
Sectoral Interactions

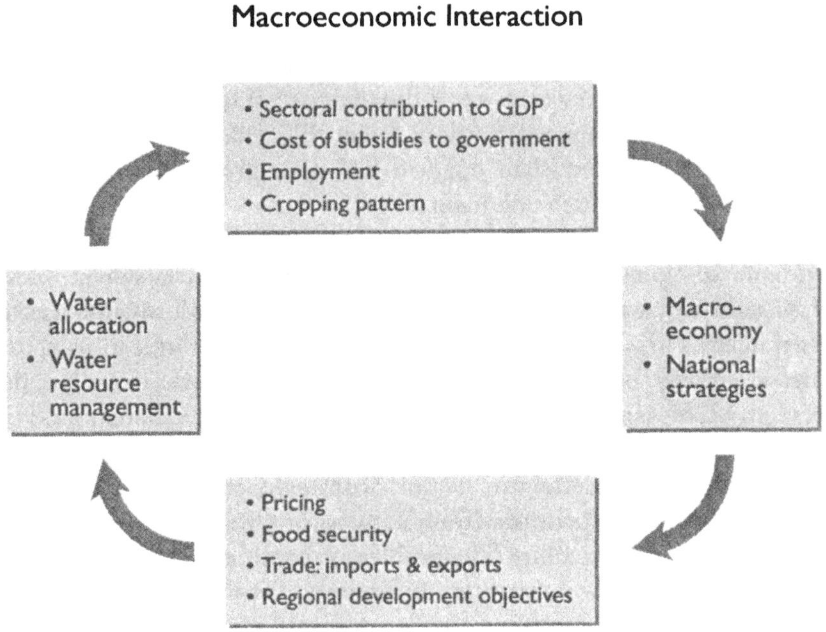

Macroeconomic Interaction

- Sectoral contribution to GDP
- Cost of subsidies to government
- Employment
- Cropping pattern

- Water allocation
- Water resource management

- Macro-economy
- National strategies

- Pricing
- Food security
- Trade: imports & exports
- Regional development objectives

An Empirical Example: Morocco

The methodology developed in this book is illustrated numerically for the case of Morocco. The government and the World Bank have made the data and the parameters necessary to the analysis available to this study (Water Sector Reviews prepared by the World Bank, 1996a and 1998; Royaume du Maroc, 1989a, 1993a to d and 1994a).

Morocco has major water resource management problems due to rising water demands in both agricultural and urban areas and limited supplies of surface and groundwater that face threats of severe pollution. The high variability of Morocco's rainfall leads to large intra- and inter-year fluctuations in flows of runoff. A large number of reservoirs have been constructed that provide storage during low-flows, hydropower, and some flood control, and many more reservoirs are planned in Morocco. Some major conveyance projects are also planned for inter-basin transfer of water (e.g. to supply the city of Casablanca from the relatively water-rich Sebou basin). Major investments are also planned in urban and rural water supply and for agricultural projects. There is a need for coordination of these investments in order to maximize their collective effectiveness.

Water resource problems in Morocco have drawn much attention from the Moroccan government, international lending agencies and water resources experts. Morocco's water models have become excellent prototypes for other countries of the MENA region and the world. Many water management proposals have been implemented and still more are ready for consideration. A primary issue is to create a long-term planning and management tool to rationalize both the future scarce water resource and the use of the scarce funds available for investment in the water sector.

As in most places, a cursory inspection of an aggregated water situation for the whole of Morocco gives a wrong impression of sustainability: out of 30 billion cubic meters (BCM) of water initially and nominally available, only 11 BCM is demanded. However, the temporal and spatial variability of both the supply and the scattered demand points represent the much harsher and more challenging reality. The large annual and seasonal variation of the precipitation leads to wide intra-year and inter-year fluctuations of water availability. Water is supplied from different sources. Groundwater is an important one, but over the extent of the country it varies markedly in geological, hydrodynamic and recharge-rate characteristics. Seventy percent of the renewable groundwater is located in the Atlas and Atlantic hydrogeological regions, which represent only 20% of the national territory. Besides groundwater, precipitation, snow-melt and inter-basin transfers, Morocco has a few non-conventional sources, such as a small desalination plant in the most arid coastal area (which contributed 0.01% of the total potable water) and some recycling plants for agricultural use.

Morocco (Figure 2-3) is a country of 27 million people, with a 2.8% annual growth of its population, which is concentrated in the fertile plains and coastal areas of the northwest of the country, notably around Casablanca and Rabat. Historical water resource development has been designed to support agricultural and urban development, which means that today any changes in the output of agriculture due to weather variations have a pronounced multiplier effect on overall economic activity and serious consequences for employment. Agriculture accounts for 40% of the total employment, but contributes only 14% of the GDP, which in 1995 stood at 10,270 dirhams (DH) per capita, approximately equivalent to US$1,027. Agriculture uses up to 85% of the mobilized water resources, primarily to irrigate 900,000 hectares.

FIGURE   2-3
Map of Morocco

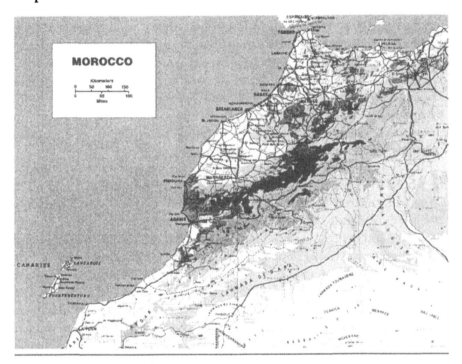

This is commonly divided into large-scale irrigated areas (the acronym GH will be used for the large-scale irrigated areas, referring to the expression in French: Grandes Hydrauliques), totalling 470,000 hectares, administered by a national authority (ORMVA), and small and medium-scale irrigated areas (PMH (Petites et Moyennes Hydrauliques)), which are operated by local communities. Domestic (household) water demands are rapidly increasing and the aim is to supply 98% of the population (currently 76%) through pipelines (the rest by standpipe) by the year 2020. Industrial water demand is rising by 5% per year. Although domestic and industrial uses are a relatively small quantity of water, discharges of used water from cities and factories are large enough to seriously threaten the environment and public health through pollution. Another water-related sector is hydropower, which contributes significantly to meeting the peak electricity demand during the winter time (capacity of 687 MW, representing 30% of the total energy produced).

Morocco's water management focus has been exclusively on the satisfaction of what have been considered pressing and inflexible demands. Environmental and sustainability concerns have not received attention. Both industrial and domestic effluent discharge hurt the quality of water, and saline water intrusion is decreasing the sustainable yield of aquifers. Irrigation-related water logging and salination are also typical environmental problems.

The present stressed water resource situation leads to hasty and unplanned sub-optimal solutions such as high emergency expenditures to overcome drought or flood problems. Over-exploitation of groundwater and heavy chemical and biological pollution jeopardize the quality of water and pose serious health hazards in certain localities. Water losses in the transmission network are costly both in water itself and in revenue. The continuing subsidies to this under-priced resource are starting to weigh heavily on the government. There is little flexibility in the administrative allocation of water among the users.

Coordinated decision-making is needed to allocate water to maximize net benefits under technical, economic, social and policy constraints and still maintain sustainability in the long run. The linkage of water with other sectors will reveal issues at both the macro-level and the micro-level. Micro issues are localized, while macro issues correspond to national interests, such as food security, poverty reduction, the provision of drinking water, economic development and subsidies from the national treasury, as well as equitable inter-sectoral allocation and ensuring an environmentally sustainable development. At either level, policy and institutional regulations and reforms, or technical choices can arise as matters for decision. Options can often be classified as hardware (infrastructure) or software (policy) types, and seen as related to supply-side or demand-side management.

The unprecedented challenges for the future of Moroccan water resources call for rational management tools which will take into account the qualitative as well as the quantitative aspect of water, and be based on a full-cycle river basin approach. They must capture the complexity of the nature of water and take into consideration the participation of the multiple stakeholders. MEIAH, the model or DSS set forth in this study, does not aim to propose solutions nor to play the role of a decision maker. Rather, it hopes to assist decision makers in evaluating various options available to them to maximize the total benefits from water use, while recognizing the various constraints imposed upon the system (Rogers and Bouhia, 1997a).

Notes

1   The Middle East and North Africa (MENA) region refers to the countries and territories of Algeria, Bahrain, Egypt, Iran, Iraq, Israel, Jordan, Kuwait, Lebanon, Libya, Malta, Morocco, Oman, Qatar, Saudi Arabia, Syria, Tunisia, United Arab Emirates, Yemen, and West Bank and Gaza.

2   A DSS is an integrated network of models. Its primary objective is to assist decision-makers with an analysis of the current situation and the consideration of alternative solutions, usually handled in the form of a set of scenarios.

3

The Methodology

This study links together a model of water flows with a model of the economy to form a Decision Support System (DSS), which is a hydro-economic structure. The first model, on water, aims to maximize the social welfare which the use of water can provide. In light of this goal, it can assign an economic valuation, or "shadow price," to each unit of water for the different water-using sectors. This is a first step to capture the links between the two accounts: water, which is originally measured in cubic meters, and the economy, which is denominated in money. The second model is a regional economic model, based on an augmented input-output table. Using the results of the first model, it handles water as an economic good. The two component models, which together form the Decision Support System (jointly called MEIAH, for Macro-Economic Integrated Analysis of Hydrology) will be referred to as MEIAH-1 and MEIAH-2.

To present this methodology, we first take up the computation of account balances within the water system and the determination of the economic value of water in different situations, which are the work of the first part of the MEIAH DSS. Second, we explain the steps to integrate information from that water model into the model of the macroeconomy, which is the second major component of MEIAH. Third, we illustrate how we apply the full DSS to assess the economic consequences and the policy implications of water decisions. We also discuss the algorithms used to make the model reflect the real-world uncertainties of annual rainfall and water availability. The focus is on a country where water shortages raise economic problems, but the approach can also be tailored for countries with an average water endowment or an overabundance of water.

Account Balances

Material Balances

No material is created from nothing, nor is it lost, but everything is transformed.[1] Every material corresponds to a step or a component of a bigger picture, and a link in a longer chain. A material balance can be computed at several levels: micron, micro, macro or global, depending on the objective of a given exercise. Material balance accounts are in physical units, and can be used to analyse the movement of natural resources, such as water, or oxygen, through different locations and states.

The Hydrological Balance

The earth's renewable supply of water follows a hydrological cycle, a system of continuous water circulation, as shown in Figure 3-1. Water supply for human use comes from two sources: surface water is fresh water found in rivers, lakes and reservoirs, collected from snow and precipitation over wider geographies. Groundwater is found in porous layers of underground soil or

---

FIGURE   3 - 1

Hydrological Cycle

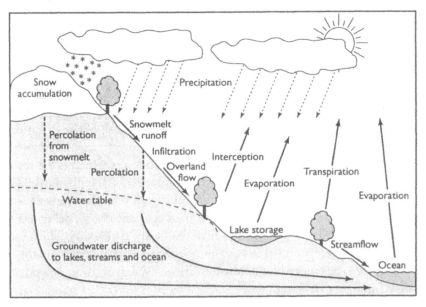

rock, which serve as aquifers; it is renewed through rain and snow melt that infiltrates the soil. A country's available water supply is divided between surface water and groundwater, but these two sources of water are linked.

The Hydrological Cycle

The hydrological cycle describes the way water moves from form to form and around the earth (Dingman, 1996; Freeze and Cherry, 1979; and Viessman et al., 1989). Figure 3-1 shows the endless circulation of water from ocean, to atmosphere, to earth and back to ocean. We will, of course, focus on the fresh water stored at stages of the cycle in streams and lakes, or in the soil as groundwater, which becomes available for human use.

Solar energy evaporates water from the ocean. Water vapor is carried by wind to the continents, and when atmospheric conditions are favorable a portion of this water precipitates as rain or snow. Once the rain or melted snow reaches the soil, a quantity of the liquid is absorbed by the soil, and the rest remains on the surface as "runoff", moving downstream to compose rivers and eventually return to the sea. (A small portion, known as "interception", does not reach the soil, but is evaporated from the surface of plants.) Water absorbed by the soil seeps underground through the process of infiltration, and remains there as soil moisture, held by capillary forces. If the soil moisture is increased, the water in the underground layer becomes part of a pattern of underground movement parallel to the river system, known as sub-surface runoff. When the pores of soil or rock are completely filled with water, a groundwater zone exists. It is possible for groundwater to rise from these zones as springs, streams, swamps or lakes, and thus sub-surface water can become surface runoff, while, of course, it can also be brought to the surface through dug or drilled wells and pumps. Not all rainwater or snow-melt infiltrates into the soil, since some of it goes back to the atmosphere through evaporation from the soil surface, or by transpiration from the leaves of plants as part of the plant's growth process.

The closed cycle of hydrology has been studied by hydrologists for many years, often to analyze how human modification of it can increase the benefits of land and water resources for human beings. The hydrological cycle can be described in terms of a water balance, which shows quantities of water in different forms, stages and locations, and it can also be calculated as a water budget, if the picture includes external human interventions that modify the nature of the hydrological cycle.

Measurements of the Water Balance

The term "water balance" was put forward in 1944 by the meteorologist C. Warren Thornthwaite who studied the balance between the incoming of water from precipitation and snowmelt and the outflow of water by evapo-transpiration, groundwater recharge, and streamflow (Dunne and Leopold, 1978). A water balance can be calculated for a soil profile or for a whole drainage basin. The balance approach has been used extensively for planning purposes, such as working out the seasonal and geographic patterns of irrigation demand, the soil moisture stresses under which crops and natural vegetation can survive, the prediction of streamflow and water-table elevations, the flux of water to lakes, and therefore the lake's variations of water level and salinity. A water balance is also used to predict some of the human impacts on the hydrological cycle, such as the water effects of weather modification or changes of vegetation. Several methods are used to compute a water balance.

The water balance for a small drainage basin takes into account precipitation P, interception I, actual evapo-transpiration AET, overland flow, OF, the change in the soil moisture, dSM, the change in groundwater, $dGWS$, and groundwater runoff, GWR. The different components of the hydrological cycle are represented in Figure 3-2. The relationship among them is:

$$P = I + AET + OF + dSM + dGWS + GWR$$

FIGURE 3 - 2

Components of the Hydrological Cycle

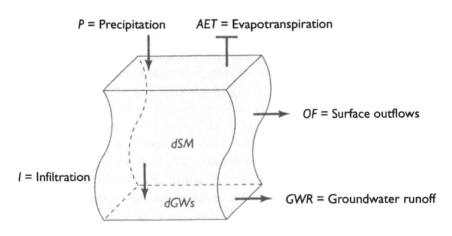

P = Precipitation   AET = Evapotranspiration

OF = Surface outflows

dSM

I = Infiltration

dGWs

GWR = Groundwater runoff

Each term of the water balance equation can be evaluated directly in the field. The water balance will be considered at a regional and a national level, to assess the human impact on the water cycle. For the purpose of this book, we will assume that the effect of change in soil moisture is negligible, and it will not be taken into consideration.

The Water Budget

The water budget is an attempt to capture the effect of human economic water uses on the water balance. It encompasses both the different steps of the water cycle and the economic production chains requiring water as an input. A water budget is computed for a fixed amount of time; we will use one year, to match the cycles of the economic account. As shown in Figure 3-3, the water budget brings out the modifications of a region's hydrological cycle by the changes made by humans in the path of rainwater and snow-melt, as well as groundwater. These are of concern to water planners and economists.

The same water budget is shown in Figure 3-4, illustrating the flows of water from sources to water users and then back to sources. The economic

---

FIGURE 3-3

Conceptual Water Budget

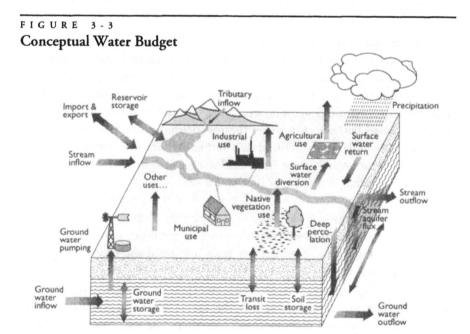

Source: Illustration Courtesy of Colorado Division of Water Resources, Office of the State Engineer

FIGURE   3 - 4
Water Budget

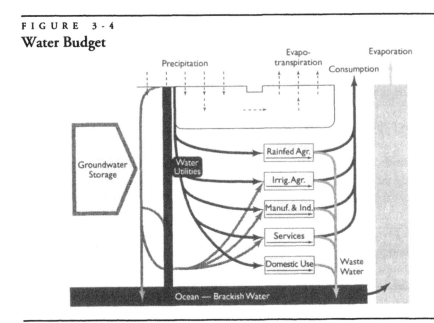

sectors use this water, after it has been handled in some cases by water utilities. Water is consumed by agriculture, both rainfed and irrigated, by manufacturing and industry, by services, and by domestic households. A quite small percentage of the water used is embedded in economic products and leaves the hydrological cycle, which has to be taken into consideration to ensure a closed balance. After use, the rest of the economically-used water follows paths similar to the natural case, either evaporation, infiltration to the ground, or return to a surface stream. However, it is important to note that the quality of water is often modified by its use.

Quantitative balances do not pick up qualitative changes in water in the course of a hydrological cycle which has experienced human economic interventions. Economic processes often impose externalities upon water in the form of releasing it at a lower quality than it entered the process originally. The deteriorated water can be used thereafter only with certain constraints. The effects of qualitative changes, and competition by different economic sectors for one source of water, give the use of water an economic value, which will be discussed in more detail hereafter. The water cycle represents the first half of the hydro-economic system, while the second part is the representation of the full national economy.

Traditional Economic Account

To summarize the flow of goods in an economy, Wassily Leontief developed the input-output table which describes precisely how an industry or activity's output depends on inputs from other industries or activities. An input-output table is divided into four quadrants, as shown in Table 3-1, which summarize information on the flow within the intermediate demand, the primary inputs, and the final demand.

An expanded input-output Table, the Social Account Matrix (SAM) (Baumol and Blinder, 1994; Gillis et al., 1996; and Pyatt and Round, 1985) was developed to account fully for all the economic processes related to the national activities of a country. SAM accounts have been developed for almost all the countries of the world, and are updated regularly to provide an overview of the economy for every year. The layout of a SAM is shown in Table 3-2. Rows represent amounts received by suppliers of goods, services and factors of production; these represent the producers of the inter-industry matrix. The columns represents expenditures, amounts paid out by users of goods and services; these correspond to the users. Each row and column taken together can be seen as an account for each entity, covering receipt and expenditures, so that each row and column must balance. The SAM is a comprehensive account for the entire economy. Each of the national accounting aggregates can be found in it. Gross domestic product at factor cost can be found as the sum of either the rows or the columns of the table.

The SAM serves four main purposes in economic planning. First, it provides a set of comprehensive and consistent frameworks to organize masses of economic data, including the national accounts, balance of payments, household budget surveys, government accounts, tax information, financial mar-

---

TABLE 3-1

Input-Output Table

| | Out | puts | |
Inputs	Intermediate Demand	Final Demand	Total Output
Intermediate Inputs	*(Quadrant I)*	*(Quadrant II)*	
Primary Inputs	*(Quadrant III)*	*(Quadrant IV)*	
Total Outlays			

TABLE 3-2
Simplified Social Account Matrix

Receipts	Expenditures								
	1. Activities	2. Commodities	3. Factors	4. Enterprises	5. Households	6. Government	7. Capital	8. Rest of world	9. Total
1. Activities	domestic sales					export subsidies		exports	total sales
2. Commodities	intermediate demand				household consumption	government consumption	investment		total demand
3. Factors	factor payments								value-added
4. Enterprises			gross profits			transfers			enterprise income
5. Households			wages	distributed profits		transfers		foreign remittances	household income
6. Government	indirect taxes	tariffs	factor taxes	enterprise taxes	direct taxes				government receipts
7. Capital				retained earnings	household savings	government savings		net capital inflow	total saving
8. Rest of world		imports							imports
9. Total	total payments	total absorption	value-added	enterprise expenditure	household expenditure	government expenditure	total investment	foreign exchange	

Source: Robinson, 1989

ket accounts, and others. These data are organized and added up to form the rows and columns of the SAM, which can then be used to analyze the consistency of the internal accounts. Second, this matrix provides a detailed and comprehensive inventory of the economy. Third, it brings out the sectors and areas where data is missing and where more research needs to be undertaken. Finally, this matrix can be used as a base for the development of a dynamic program, offering a potential way to evaluate how different interventions might affect the economy.

Depending on the SAM table's purpose, particular activities and sectors can be disaggregated and looked at in greater detail to highlight their internal flows and composition. In this case, water-intense sectors are particularly dealt with in detail, and irrigated agriculture will be given the most attention. In this book, the SAM will serve as a base for the national economic account, and will be manipulated to incorporate the closed cycle of water. This economic account, which as used here will be called MEIAH-2, represents one of the two major parts of the hydro-economic system to be developed in this book.

This SAM is powerful in its capacity to assist in planning and in offsetting externalities. It provides an ideal tool to capture the flows in the economy. However, its handling of natural resources, particularly water, has not received a great deal of attention from its designers. In contrast to iron, which is seen as a raw material, and then is used to build an automobile, but keeps its characteristics as it passes through the table, water does require special provisions in the model, since it changes form and value as it moves through the economy, for example, from liquid to water vapor, or from a pure to a polluted condition. For this reason, it is necessary to consider the water cycle, water's behavior as it moves through a series of forms, before turning to water's role in the economy.

Water Resource Planning and Management

Especially in a dry country, economic sectors compete to use the limited quantity of water that is available. In a perfect economic world, the allocation of water between sectors would depend on which sector offered the highest economic return from the use of the water, and therefore gave it its highest value. There are several water planning and management systems that, by assessing the economic values of water, permit the detailed evaluation in monetary terms of the economic meaning of the flows of water into and out from various activities, as reflected in the water budget.

The concepts of water resource modeling and a river basin approach are usually followed by water resource planners. In this section, the first model, which we call MEIAH-1, and which represents the first half of the Decision Support System developed in this book is described. This model represents a water allocation system based on operation research tools. Then we outline its main results, which will be used as a link to a description of the second model, MEIAH-2 which forms the second, economic, part of the analytical system. MEIAH-2 consists first of the creation of a water input-output table and the manipulation of its coefficients; its second part is a programming model formulated using the information of the water input-output table.

River Basin Approach

Although water resource projects have been constructed for thousand of years, modern water resources planning has evolved over only about 50 years, and models began to carry the weight of analysis about thirty years ago. Models, which we earlier compared to a painting, or a map, describing real terrain through a reduction to two dimensions and a careful selection of the features to be presented, are abstractions from a reality that needs to be simplified in order to be analyzed and studied. At this point we would like to stress the rules that the model uses to state how significant features of the situation interact. These rules are written in the form of a set of equations that express the relationship between different economic variables and water related components. These equations can be manipulated using computer techniques to provide outcomes which parallel the results of real situations, and thus the model can advance the analysis of either a real situation or a hypothetical one.

A water model should be comprehensive, integrating all users and sources. The approach is appropriately at a river basin scale, where downstream and upstream activities are considered part of the same system (Major and Schwarz, 1990; and Waterbury, 1979). The hydrological situation is simplified and represented in schematic form, to create a hydrological network. Nodes correspond to sources of water, such as aquifers, reservoirs or inflows to a river, and to points of demand for water, such as cities, industries and irrigated areas. Using a watershed as the region of analysis makes it possible to account for both all the water sources and the way the resource is divided among the different users.

Water Allocation System

The MEIAH-1 water allocation model presented here has been developed using an advanced optimization technique from the field of Operations Research (Dorfman et al., 1972 and Hanke, 1978). This optimization model covers several river basins, each one handled as described just above, and with allowance made for transfers between them. The model for the set of basins presents a multi-faceted approach. It involves several sources of water (reservoirs, groundwater), and several points of demand. The optimization draws upon hydrological, physical, social, agricultural, economic, environmental, mathematical and computer tools to model the non-linear relationships among the parameters and the decision variables in the region. We will highlight here some of the important components (input data, objective function, constraints, and decision variables) of this optimization model, but the full formulation of the model is provided in Appendix 2, with the application to the case of Morocco. The optimization model is computed using the Generalized Algebraic Modeling System (GAMS) optimization package (Brooke et al., 1988).

Objective or Goal Function

The optimization model maximizes the aggregated long term net benefit from the use of water to all users existing in the area:

■ *Agricultural Net Benefit:* The model seeks to maximize the total net proceeds from the local sale or export of each crop. The costs which are subtracted to reach this net figure include the cost of labor, the cost of land, the cost of supplying the required water, and other costs to be added later, including conservation measures and water treatment. This net benefit is also reduced by the cost of imports of agricultural production.

■ *Urban Net Benefit:* This is a non-linear term which is the integral giving the area under the demand curve, from which are subtracted the cost of supplying water (including production, treatment, recycling and conveyance costs).

■ *Hydropower Net Benefit:* This is computed using a linear relationship between the benefit of generated hydropower and the price of electric power, which is assumed to be inelastic. However, the hydropower generated is a non-linear term, which is a function of both the head and the discharge rate of water in reservoirs. These factors figure as constraints in the model.

■ *Dam and related infrastructural investment:* The benefits of water control and increased availability which are achieved by building storage dams and transfer facilities are reflected in the above-mentioned benefits accounts of the model. Within the dam-infrastructure operation, they are sought to be maximized, net of the facilities' cost, including capital and operation and maintenance costs, which are divided over the life of an infrastructural project.

Optimization Constraints

Beside the positivity of the variables, the possibilities that the model can reach, in seeking to maximize the benefits, are limited by the way that elements of the problem are defined, by certain rules, and requirements that certain relationships and conditions be respected. Such restrictions on the freedom of decision variables are generally called constraints. In MEIAH-1 they include:

■ *Continuity of the System:* The continuity of the flow should hold in each type of node: from groundwater and starting nodes to reservoir nodes, intermediate nodes, demand nodes and end nodes. This relationship differs for each type of node, responding to the continuity characteristics of each kind of node. For example, losses in the network are dealt with differently, depending on the type of nodes: evaporation losses are seen as a function of storage in reservoirs and conveyance losses are seen as a function of the length of the network.

■ *Balance of Trade:* For agriculture production, this relationship ensures the balance between the local sale, exports and imports of agriculture production.

■ *Definitional Constraints:* This includes the definition of some variables (generally equalities). For example, hydropower generated is expressed as a non-linear function of reservoir head and discharge.

■ *Water demand constraint:* This represents water user constraints in meeting different types of demand. For urban demand, it depends on minimum liters needed per capita per day. For irrigation, it depends on crop water requirements.

■ *Land Constraint:* This limit on irrigated area available could be changed by irrigation expansion policies. Another type of land constraint corresponds to the area under each type of crop, which is a function of the cropping pattern policy. This constraint could be either a minimum irrigated area for a certain crop, a maximum or both.

■ *Environmental constraint:* This includes an upper bound on annual ground-water exploitation, a required minimum discharge from rivers into the sea to avoid saline intrusion at the river's end node, and pollution constraints. The pollution component is the emission of organic wastes (measured as bio-chemical oxygen demand) by industries and cities in the watershed. Other chemicals could also be taken into consideration, depending on data availability.

■ *Other constraints:* lower bound on agriculture production in order to meet a regional or national goal, pollution constraint, hydropower capacity bounds, etc. For the scenarios in the future, there is a budgetary constraint for the construction of new dams. Depending on the scenarios that one would like to consider, other additional constraints can be added.

Decision Variables

This water allocation system yields a range of results, which are very informative to water planners. The primary decision variables, which can be manipulated and grouped in light of the goals being sought,[2] are:

■ water flows in river,
■ groundwater utilization,
■ reservoir releases,
■ sectoral allocation,
■ urban demands,
■ irrigated land for each crop,
■ reservoir storage, and
■ hydropower generated.

Values for this set of decision variables, taken individually, could be considered as primary outputs. Secondary parameters, which are combinations of the primary variables, could be computed to satisfy the interests and the purposes of water resource planners. These include water losses, components of the objective function in terms of the costs and benefits, averages of the various variables and parameters to provide a synoptic view, and others. In addition, by looking at the water demand-supply constraint one can determine a shadow price of water. This reflects the scarcity of water, and will be analyzed in more detail shortly.

This optimization model is for both planning and management purposes. The objective function, which represents the maximum economic welfare achievable in the studied region, is discounted over the period of time considered for long term planning. The structure of this MEIAH-1 water model, which represents one part of the DSS proposed in this book, is also a DSS by itself. It makes it possible to run many water scenarios and to view the results graphically and schematically in an interactive manner. The way this model is formulated gives opportunities for a decision-maker to specify scenarios, or clusters of policy actions, that he or she wishes to investigate. For example, the parameters that could be varied in the scenarios include: year, climate condition, reservoir operation plan, inter-basin and inter-regional transfers, change in price, constraints on agricultural production, environmental constraints, and many others.

Intersectoral Water Allocation

When the specifying data is provided, the MEIAH-1 water optimization model just described can indicate the quantity of water to be allocated to each sector, as well as the source of supplies to be used to attain the stated goals. For agriculture, the model yields details on the type of crop to be produced, the irrigated areas to be used and the water required for such production. For urban uses, both domestic and industrial, the sources of supply and the quantities that should be committed are specified. The model allows evaluation of losses in the supply systems, as well as the quantity of water evaporated from the network.

Intersectoral allocation is tightly dependent on national policies on irrigation and urban water use, as well as environmental considerations. The water model is formulated so that it can accommodate several policy scenarios. For each scenario, the optimization model generates the path of water in the system, from its source (surface and groundwater) to the economic activities that the water serves, taking into consideration water losses, such as evaporation along a stream, as well as the return flows of water from an activity back to the system, such as the portion of irrigation water that is not evaporated through the leaves of the crop, but drains back into the river system or back into the groundwater aquifer. Based on the quantity of water flowing in the system, a detailed water account is developed, highlighting both the demand for water and the quantity of water available to be supplied, and the in and out flows to the different economic activities.

Shadow Price of Water

The generation of "shadow prices" that accompany the optimal solution of a constrained optimization problem is one of the most fundamental results of advanced optimization theory. According to the optimization model, each unit of water generates a certain net benefit, which is a function of the benefit to the sector in which it has been used, reduced by the cost of supplying that unit of water to that sector. The water model operates by allocating water among sectors and regions in order to maximize the overall net benefit received from water. The shadow price evaluates by how much the benefit being maximized would increase if the constraint on water supply were relaxed by one unit. The shadow price of water determined by the model represents the extra unit of benefit resulting from giving an additional unit of water to the considered sector. It is important to note that shadow prices are given by location and by type of node in the network at which they occur. To determine the shadow price for domestic use, for instance, a weighted average of the shadow price to each city in the system is used, where the weight represents the quantity of water allocated to each city divided by the total water supplied for domestic use. The shadow price of water for agriculture, over various localities and crops, is computed the same way.

The concept of shadow price is based on the fact that, when demand for water at a source exceeds what the source can supply, providing a particular user with an additional unit of water will not be without a cost. That unit of water can only be made available to a demander through the deprivation of another demander; the loss of benefits to the unsuccessful demander represents an opportunity loss or cost to which a monetary value can be assigned. This value then becomes the putative value of the water, or shadow price of the water, to the demander who received it.

The economic value of water to each sector is generated by the water allocation system, as just described. Once the water reaches a given sector it has a new economic value. Although the value may change, having a value, or shadow price, remains a characteristic of the flow of water throughout its path in the hydrological cycle, including as evaporated water, or as water embedded in production, or as it returns to the supplying sources through return flows or losses from the system. This value assigned to water means that it is possible to account for the flow of water in the system not only in physical units but also in monetary values. Using the monetary values, or shadow prices, for water, stage by stage, will give an economic interpretation of the change in the quality of water after it has been used, or will give the economic meaning of the losses to the system through leakage, evaporation, or evapo-transpiration. Assigning a shadow "price tag" also helps capture some of the economic externalities of the water sector, which are more difficult to think about and to compare when they are left in physical units, such as a cubic meter of water.

Incorporating Uncertainty into the Process

Water resource planning cannot be undertaken in a deterministic fashion, because real world, year-to-year uncertainty in several parameters can affect the analysis and the results tremendously. For example, the annual availability of surface water or streamflow is the subject of uncertainty. To capture this variability, or stochasticity, in the flows and to assess the response of the different parameters to it, often a set of scenarios are run for different percentiles of past flows. We will see that the effects in the national economy of variations in water parameters, for example between a drought year and one of high rainfall, can be followed using the MEIAH-2 model, which carries the results of the water input-output table as inputs to the national economic accounts. In this way, the final output of the combined models will show the effect of flow variability on a such economic and social indicators as employment, household income, and sectoral output.

Two ways of incorporating uncertainty into such systems are examined. The first involves sensitivity analysis of the optimization model to analyze how decisions would be different under various water flow assumptions. This is equivalent to designing under different reliabilities. It examines the sensitivity or robustness of important design, planning and operational considerations to flow variations, by running the model with a diversity of flows as input conditions. Secondly, an integrated approach has been developed to consider how flow variations may be simulated stochastically to yield responses of various indicative design parameters, such as net benefits, imports, exports, shadow prices, cropping patterns, and amount of water supplied. Finally, we present ways in which a decision-maker can actually use these techniques and their results in decision-making.

Fluctuations in the Flows

Fluctuations in the stage (water height) and discharge of rivers result from variations in precipitation and temperature. These river fluctuations are influenced by the rates of snow melt, the intensity and areal extent of rain, the slope and other geological characteristics of a basin, soil, vegetable cover, stage of groundwater (height of water table), and potentially by climate change.

Streamflow records trace historical fluctuations in flow during an observed period of time, and provide data for statistical analysis to estimate future variations in the flow. There are several methods to generate a set of plausible future flows in a river. Thomas and Fiering (in Maas et al., 1962) developed a mathematical method based on a "lag-1" approach to generate a set of synthetic streamflows, based on the statistical characteristics of the historical flows.

Sensitivity Analysis

Sensitivity analysis tells us to what degree changes in the parameters supplied to the model affect the optimal solution. For water resources, these changes of parameter can consist, for example, in different flows of water in the river basins under consideration. Based on 50 year historical flow data of the tributaries of the river basin of the region, several statistical characteristics of the flow are generated. Also, several percentages of reliability are computed, which represent the share of time during which the water flowing into the river is higher than the mentioned value. Sensitivity analysis over the reliabilities corresponds to running the model for several percentages. Traditionally, the reliabilities considered by water resource planners are: 35%, 50%, 75% and 95%. The water resource allocation system is run for different level of flows and different reliabilities. Also, there are different ways of using flow reliabilities. One can use, for example, a reliability of 75%, meaning the water level in the river which is exceeded 75% of the time.

For each of the scenarios run, a range of results is computed. These are compared among themselves to extract the differences and therefore determine how sensitive the model's output is to changes in input parameters such as the level of streamflow.

Stochastic Simulation

Ultimately, the stochastic simulation input is developed to see the effect of uncertainty in streamflows on the economic parameter of the combined model. This simulation runs for a large number of random variables, which generates a set of synthetic streamflows based on the Thomas-Fiering method. In parallel, the sensitivity functions of some of the determinant decision variables, such as net benefits, shadow prices of water, imports, and exports are seen. For each set of random variables, the various selected model outputs are computed. The process is repeated for all the years in the simulation time horizon, and the distributions of these parameters over the years are derived. Figure 3-5 illustrates a simplified flowchart of the simulation. This is an illustration of how to include the uncertainty of the flows in the system.

Integrating Water into the Macroeconomic System

In this section, we describe how the information yielded by the water model, MEIAH-1 is incorporated into a traditional national economic model. This

---

FIGURE 3-5

Simplified Flowchart of the Simulation

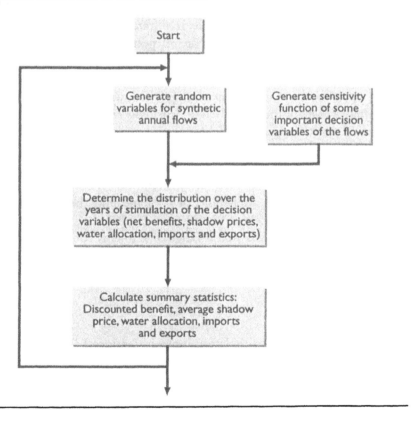

is the step forward developed by the present research. The main objective is to create a link between a country's hydrological cycle and hydraulic management decisions and its economic accounts as they are affected by the water cycle or the water policy choices. The methodology is structured for the national level, but the same approach could be narrowed to the regional level. We create a hydro-economic account table in mixed units, both physical and monetary. To illustrate the methodology, we first consider an economy of four sectors: agriculture (both rainfed and irrigated), industry, services and households.

Initially, we discuss the basic equalities and the table corresponding to the different water balances. Then the water flows are examined at the level of sectors of the economy. Finally, by merging this hydrological account with the traditional national economic input-output table, an augmented water-input-output table is developed and then discussed.

Balancing Water-Related Activities
Primary Inputs
Bulk water—also known as raw water—is the primary input to the system. The two components of it are precipitation (runoff), and groundwater, which is from rainfall in earlier cycles. Bulk water can be used directly by a final demand user, for example, groundwater pumped by a household. More normally, the two forms of bulk water are the main input to the water supply utilities, which then distribute water to users. Some water becomes available for use after already having served another process; this source can be called "return flow."

Water-Related Sectors
Water is a primary input to the economic production chain. In the hydro-economic cycle, a thorough analysis of its path in the economy can be undertaken. If water is consumed in an economic sector, it becomes embedded in the sectoral output, and as part of the sectoral output, it will appear in the traditional national economic account within the monetary value of the output. Thus, there will be a monetary unit assigned to it. The remaining water will stay in the hydrological system. It can either infiltrate into the ground and recharge the groundwater; in which case it will be an addition in physical units to groundwater. Or, the quantity of water that has not been absorbed within the economic production will evaporate and go back to the system from the starting point, i.e., water vapor.

Each water-related activity account should present a certain balance between water inputs and outputs, summarized in an account table, detailing the different sources, types and quantities of water. This is recapitulated in Table 3-3. As part of the water system, wastewater from domestic use is collected, and goes to treatment and recycling. Only a percentage of the used water is reused, for example, for agriculture; the balance is disposed of, and will appear in the accounts as return flows.

After a production process, the remaining quantity of water has an economic value assigned to it. This value corresponds to the shadow price of water for the sector which will next receive it, previously determined in the water optimization model. As mentioned in the previous section, the shadow prices of water are determined by a water allocation system. These outflows from the economic sectors can be summarized as follows:

■ If the wastewater is going to be treated or recycled, then it goes to the Sanitation and Recycling sector. In the industrial sector, 80% of the water used in production processes is typically recycled locally.

■ If the used water infiltrates to the groundwater naturally or through man-made drainage, it will be part of the return flows. The return flows category includes groundwater recharged by either method.

■ If the water evaporates, since it is an addition to water in the atmosphere, it will be counted as a positive change in the Change in Stock column, which is part of the final demand in the table.

An additional category that could be considered separately is Water Losses, but this is counted (as a subtraction) under the heading of primary input, in

---

TABLE 3 - 3

Account for Water Supply

Sources	Uses
Surface Water	Irrigation
Groundwater	Manufacturing and Industry
Return Flows	Services
	Treatment and Recycling
	Domestic Use
	Return Flows

the sense that it represents a reduction in the quantity of water supplied. On average, there is a certain system efficiency that ought to be considered for both the irrigation system and the water supply network in urban areas. For each of the different water related categories, a physical account is determined capturing the input to the system and the output of the system to the different users (agriculture, industry, services, and households). For recycling and sanitation, the sources are the water used in industry, services and households, while for return flows, the sources represent the water used in all the sectors, but mainly in rainfed and irrigated agriculture, from which water infiltrates, naturally or through drainage back into groundwater aquifers.

Water as Part of the Production Process of the Economic Sectors

For each economic sector, the water cycle is closed. The water budget is not only in physical units, but it has some components which are in value terms, as they represent the value of water, embedded in locally-produced economic goods. In fact, for each sector of the economy, the following relationship will account for all input and output to the system:

$$INPUT = OUTPUT$$

in more detail:

INPUT	=	OUTPUT
Primary Input		Water Consumed
+ Water supplied through the Utilities		+ Recycled Water
+ Water for Recycling		+ Return Flows
− Losses		+ Change in the Natural Stock
+ Return Flows		

For each sector of the economy, this relationship illustrates the water cycle in that sector. The outflows are denominated both in physical units and value terms, the latter expressing the sectoral economic value of water multiplied by the quantity of outflows. Also, the percentage allocated is specified for the output side. For each of the economic accounts, a water balance is computed with a similar framework, as in Table 3-4. All the input to these sectors is in physical units while the outputs of each sector are computed in value terms, using the shadow price of water for the sector under consideration. ˙

TABLE   3 - 4

Water Account for the Economic Sectors

Input	Output
Water Supply	Consumed: Embedded the production
Recycled Water	Recycled
Precipitation	Return Flows
Groundwater	Evaporation
Return Flows	

Merging the Two Accounts: Water and the Economy

Traditionally, economic accounts are computed for countries to summarize the flows in the economy, and to determine the different values added by the economic sectors, through employment, investment, cost to the government, and so forth. A table of such accounts is used to evaluate the size of a nation's economy, traditionally denoted by the gross national product (GNP), which is in monetary terms. But the traditional table does not consider the quantity of water that has entered the economy and contributed to the overall output. This is primarily due to the fact that it is difficult to find common units between a physical quantity of water and the monetary values of the economy. Although, as mentioned earlier, some of the water effect could be represented in monetary value (agricultural production for example) the primary input can only be in physical terms as it has not yet affected the economy. Here, we are incorporating the water accounts, in both physical and monetary units, into this table. The flows from the economic sectors to water-related activities enter as part of the economic flows in monetary terms, reflecting the economic value of water in the hydro-economic system. The following paragraph describes the methodology of creating the augmented Water Input-Output Table.

Methodology for Incorporating Water into Input-output Tables

An input-output analysis is an examination of the flow of goods and services and all intermediate transactions among the producing and purchasing sectors of a country or a region. It contains a wealth of information relating to the overall structure of the economy, and it offers a valuable tool for both numerical analysis and descriptive explanations. The input-output table shows not only the details of the income and the product accounts, but also illustrates the transactions among producers and purchasers (Polenske and Fournier,

1993). The input-output method also attempts to capture the impact of exogenous stimuli in one or many sectors of the whole economy.

The hydrological cycle can be mapped to the input-output table by following water from its sources to intermediate and final demands. In order to illustrate these issues, we use an input-output table with the structure shown in Table 3-5.

Water as a whole can be divided into the following components:

■ *Bulk Water:* This represents the production of water from precipitation, groundwater, surface water and seawater. For countries where there is no cross-border river flow into the country or desalinated water, bulk water is represented by precipitation and groundwater.[3]

■ *Water Related Activities:* These are part of the intermediate demand which corresponds to the upper-left quadrant of the I-O table (Table 3-5). They represent all the services related to water and play the role of links from the primary input of water to the different parts of the economy. The water-related activities include water supply (the different water utilities and entities that distribute water to various users) and sanitation services (which collect the water used by the different sectors, treat it, and then can sell it to the water supply to be distributed for re-use). The sanitation service is linked both to intermediate demand (agriculture, manufacturing, services, etc.) and final demand (household, exports, change in natural stock, etc.). This sector could also be divided into different qualities of water to account for the different treatment costs and value added for each sector. However, the sanitation service sector is related only to water supply. The value of the water is increased by the cost of collection, distribution and treatment, as necessary.

TABLE 3-5

Input-Output Structure

	Activities Intermediate Demand	Final Demand	Total Output
Activities Intermediate Inputs	I/O Flows	Sales	
Primary Inputs	Value Added		
Total Outlays			

■ *Return flows:* Water planners distinguish between two types of return flows. The first type represents the water flows that could be captured in the system (a percentage of drainage or infiltration) and supplied at later period of time or reduced by undertaking efficient water use techniques. This type of return will be considered part of the water related activities in the first quadrant of the table. The second type of return flow corresponds to the water that goes back to nature through evaporation or evapo-transpiration (also the rest of drainage and infiltration water that does not go back to the primary input within a short term period). This second type will yield a change in the natural stock of water in the final demand quadrant. Water recycling is also counted as part of return flows. For example in industry, up to 80% of the water used is typically recycled within the production cycle, which will show as part of the return flows.

■ *Change in the overall water stock:* This is part of the final demand, and captures the negative change in the total availability of water that happens within the considered year (percentage of drainage and infiltration).

■ *Evaporation:* This is considered separately, as part of the final demand. It includes both evaporation from the system and evapo-transpiration from plants.

To see schematically the different type of flows, Figure 3-6 highlights the linkages and the type of flows, meaning monetary or physical units. If we follow the path of water from its primary stage to its last use, we can cover all the flows of water in the economy. Note that as part of the primary inputs there is an entry for losses, which is a negative value that balances the water flows in the table. For the water supply activity, besides bulk water input, other inputs are labor, capital, and government (subsidies). The water supply sector is also an input to the other sectors; water will be sold as an intermediate input to the different economic sectors and to satisfy the final demand (household).

Used water is collected by the sanitation service and, after treatment, may be redistributed. Some of the water used in agriculture infiltrates into the ground or leaves the sector through surface drainage; evaporation also accounts for a large amount. Infiltration or drainage to the aquifer can reappear as return flows, while evaporation appears as a negative change in the water stock. One of the contributions of this figure is that flows from the economic sectors to water-related activities are in terms of value. The quantity of water that returns from the economic sectors to the water system is multiplied by

FIGURE 3-6
Flows of the Water-Related Sectors

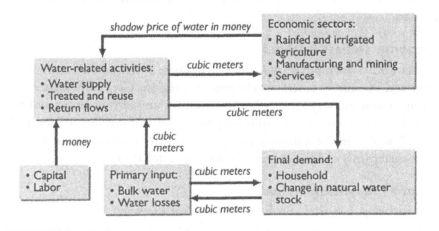

the shadow price of water for the considered economic sector. Table 3-6 illustrates the I-O table adjusted to incorporate the previously discussed water components.

This new structure accounts for both the water and the economic activities, and represents the account table for the hydro-economic system. The use of the input-output structure makes it possible to capture the linkages among not only the economic activities but also among the water related activities. Therefore, this represents a newly defined water input-output table, which

TABLE 3-6
Structure of the Water Input-Output Table

	Activities Intermediate Demand	Final Demand	Change in Natural Stock of Water	Total Output
Economic Activities	I/O Flows	Sales		
Water Related Activities	I/O Flows	Sales		
Water Input				
Primary Inputs	Value Added			
Total Outlays				

illustrates the flows of water within the economic sectors, and which high-lights the linkages that exist between the water sector, both as a primary input and an intermediate activity, and intermediate economic activities and final demand.

Economic Impact Analysis

Impact studies use input-output tables to evaluate effects on output, employment and income of economic changes in a region. Generally, the model's output results are very sensitive to variations in any of the elements of the final demand, causing the input-output model to be called a "demand-driven" model. In the following paragraph, the physical unit of water is the cubic meter (m^3) and the monetary value is the dollar ($).

Leontief's Input-Output Analysis

As a first step, Leontief's analysis requires that the water I-O table that we have just defined be transformed to a coefficient matrix, which represents the inputs to any sector as a portion of the output of that sector. All the coefficients of the rows corresponding to the economic sectors are in monetary terms, as are the flows from the economic sectors to the water-related activities, while the coefficients of the row corresponding to the water-related activities are in physical units. The sums of the coefficients of these two types of rows are homogeneous and represent the total output of each sector in value terms for the economic sectors and in physical terms for water-related activities. Therefore, the coefficient matrix is defined by dividing all entries in each sector by the total outlays of that sector.

The first quadrant of this newly defined coefficient table corresponds to the well known Leontief A^4 matrix (Leontief, 1986), inter-relating the components of the intermediate demand, where the coefficients are called "technical coefficients " [aij]: "i" is the input sector (row) and "j" the destination sector (column). Each coefficient of the table [aij] refers to the amounts of input "i" required by the sector "j" for each unit of output. As represented in Table 3-7, matrix A has 4 distinct quadrants, if we consider the value unit to be the dollar ($) and the physical unit of water, a cubic meter (m^3):

$/$ corresponds to the input from the economic sector per unit of output of one of the economic sectors

$/m^3$ corresponds to the input from the economic sectors to the water related sector per unit output of the water related sectors

TABLE 3 - 7

Structure of the Coefficient Matrix A

	Economic Sectors	Water Related Activities
Economic Sectors	$/$	$/m^3$
Water Related Increment	m^3/$	m^3/m^3

$m^3/\$$ corresponds to the input from the water related activities to the economic sectors per unit of output of these economic sectors

m^3/m^3 corresponds to the input from the water related activities to themselves per unit of output of these sectors.

These coefficients represent the direct, or first round effects of the economy. Some assumptions regarding the linearity and constancy of the coefficients have to be made: one has to keep in mind that any application that uses these coefficients assumes their stability and that each economic sector keeps the same pattern of goods purchased. The quantity and prices can still be changed.

For the purpose of this research, the focus is mainly on the water sector, although any change in the water allocated among sectors and the price used could be implemented by insuring a permanent balance through a change in the natural stock of water. (However, the linearity assumption of sectoral output and water supply would still hold.)

Using the A matrix and applying the Leontief inverse mathematical model, the link between the final demand, the output of each sector and the matrix itself can be expressed using an algebraic relationship, which models the complicated economic relations. This relation can be represented as follows:

$$AX + Y = X \qquad (1)$$

where: A = [aij] is the matrix of technical coefficients,
                  X is the column vector of sectoral output, and
                  Y is the column vector of the total final demand.

Both vectors X and Y have two types of coefficients: in value terms for the coefficients corresponding to the economic sectors and physical unit terms (cubic meters) for water-related activities. The matrix algebra preserves the characteristics of the four quadrants through the tools of matrix transformation.

Equation (1) represents a system of simultaneous equations which can be solved if one of the two vectors X or Y is known. If the input-output table exists, and we are interested in forecasting the output level for a given change in the final demand Y, solving this system of equations yields the corresponding output. As stated by Leontief, this could be shown in a more simplified way by expressing the equation (1) as follows:

$$X = (I - A)^{-1} Y \qquad (2)$$

The matrix $(I - A)^{-1}$ represents the Leontief inverse matrix also used to determine the input-output multipliers. The inverse[5] has the same characteristics in terms of unit as the matrix A (Table 3-7). The earlier defined matrix A is open to all the final demand sectors, as it considers the final demand exogenous to the economy. Analysts get around this problem by constructing a new matrix A^* closed to one of the sectors of the final demand. A commonly computed matrix is the one closed in terms of households. A new column corresponding to household consumption and a new row corresponding to household income (labor) are added to the A matrix. The closed inverse is also computed in order to determine the consumption-induced direct and indirect effects. These indicators are larger than the one determined from the first matrix A, as they include household consumption. The closed matrix A^* has the same characteristics as the matrix A in terms of units, and is used hereafter to determine the consumption-induced effects on the economy.

Multipliers and Ratios

Parameters that depend on the final I-O table coefficients, such as employment, pollution, etc., can be computed from a table of multipliers for the sectoral outputs to attempt to address direct and indirect effects. They give empirical measures of the relationships among the component sectors of the economy. The multipliers take account of the fact that the total effect on output depends on the sectors that are affected by the initial changes in the final demand. In addition to the multipliers most frequently used to estimate the economic changes (Miller and Blair, 1985), the following are used here:

■ *Output Multipliers:* outputs of the sectors in the economy. This multiplier represents the ratio of the direct effect (from matrix A) and the indirect effect (from the Leontief inverse matrix).

■ *Income Multipliers:* change in income earned by households (as a result of the change in output). These multipliers are determined from the coefficients of the Leontief inverse matrix, which translate the direct and indirect effects into terms of the value of household income using household coefficients.

■ *Employment Multipliers:* employment in physical terms (to be generated as a result of the change in outputs). By determining the relationship between the value of the output in a given sector (such as agriculture) and the total employment (a physical term), we can determine the effect of the change in output on the level of employment, using the same method as the income multipliers. For example, this would help us determine the effect of water or macroeconomic policies on agricultural employment.

To these, we have added:

■ *Water Use Multipliers:* represent an indicator of the effect of water on the output of each sector, by looking at the total quantity of the different water qualities that are needed, and at both primary inputs (bulk water) and intermediate inputs (water supply) of water in value terms as part of the total output of a given sectors. Using the employment multipliers, the impact of water availability on employment can be evaluated through employment and water use multipliers.

This set of multipliers represents a tool for deciding upon the level of investment in the different economic sectors, as well as the level of water to be supplied. These multipliers give also a hint regarding strategic sectors of the economy. Depending on the objectives and constraints, in terms of meeting a national goal, such as an increase in the GDP or creation of new opportunities for employment, the alternatives and options can be evaluated using these multipliers. Also, in order to highlight the relationship between the initial effect (own sector income effect) and the total effect (including the consumption induced effect), input-output analysts commonly compute two type of ratios, Type I and Type II. These two ratios are defined as follows:

Type I = (Direct and Indirect Effect) / Initial Effect

Type II = Total Effect / Initial Effect

where: Total Effect = Direct, Indirect and Consumption Induced Effect

The structure of the table is such that the coefficients are not homogeneous and cannot be summed together. In this book, in order to overcome these characteristics for the multipliers, we distinguish between the total effect due to the economic sector expressed in value terms, and the total effect due to the water-related activities in physical units. Using the shadow price of water for each economic sector, the effect from the water-related sectors to the considered economic sector can be evaluated in value terms and therefore summed with the previous effect, generated by the economic sectors.

Economy-Wide Value of Water
A Programming Approach

A central goal of this methodology is to estimate the economic value of water to various sectors of the economy, individually and collectively. Such knowledge is a foundation stone of water resource planning to support sustainable economic development. We presume a national goal to maximize the net benefit from all sectors that use water, taking into consideration the scarcity of the resource and the implementation of a water strategy which will merit investment and subsidies from the government. The I-O table illustrates the inter-linkages among sectors and the Linear Program yields the shadow prices of water. Integrating these two approaches provides a tool for estimating the value of water across the entire economy, and for pointing out the strategic sectors mostly affected by water shortage. The output of each economic-and water-related sector represents the decision variables of the model, which appear in mixed units, either money ($), or m^3 of water.

The value added to the different sectors represents the following components: household income (labor), land (mainly for agriculture), capital, payment to government (negative for water subsidies), imports and gross operating surplus. The objective can be expressed as follows:

$$Z = V_a.X \qquad (3)$$

where: V_a = row vector representing the total value added to each sector per unit of output.
This is given for the economic sectors in $/$ and for the water related activities in $/m^3.

X = column vector representing the total output of each sector (in $ for economic sectors and m^3 for water related sectors).

In order to determine the macro-economic value of water, which is the change in the objective due to a unit increase in water availability, there is a need for a constraint on water availability. Sectors will then compete for the available water supply, but each sector is dependent on the output of other sectors, and this is expressed using the A matrix defined above. The final demand has both an upper and a lower bound. The lower bound Y_{min} represents the maintenance of a minimum level of activity below which the sector will cease to be viable. Those Y_{min} values corresponding to economic sectors are in $ terms, while the coefficients for water related sectors are in m³.

$$(I - A)^{-1}.X \geq Y_{min} \tag{4}$$

The upper bound of the final demand Y_{max} (same characteristics as Y_{min}) represents the limit to the sector's capacity to develop and is represented by the constraint 5:

$$(I - A)^{-1}.X \leq Y_{max} \tag{5}$$

For the constraint on water requirement per sector for an economy of n sectors (equation 6), the coefficient w_i corresponding to each output i represents the quantity of water used per unit value of output in m³ per dollars. These coefficients can be determined through an optimization model for water resource planning and management:

$$\sum_{i=1}^{n} w_i X_i + W_{\text{``household''}} \leq W_{max} \tag{6}$$

The water requirement for household $W_{\text{``household''}}$ should be added to the water used for the other economic sectors, as the total water available W_{max} is for all the users. If we consider an economy of seven sectors (rainfed agriculture (*rfag*), irrigated agriculture (*irag*), water supply (*ws*), sanitation (*s*), return flows (*rf*), manufacture and mining (*m*) and services (*srv*)) the equation 6 could be written as follows:

$$
\begin{aligned}
w_{rfag} X_{rfag} + w_{irag} X_{irag} + w_{ws} X_{ws} + w_s X_s + w_{rf} X_{rf} \\
+ w_m X_m + w_{srv} X_{srv} + W_{\text{``household''}} \leq W_{max}
\end{aligned} \tag{7}
$$

In an agriculturally-oriented country, employment is heavily dependent on water through agriculture. A constraint on labor availability (equation 8), as well as the minimum employment offered by agriculture (equation 9), could be added to the set of constraints of this optimization in order to highlight the effect on employment of any change in water use. These constraints are expressed using the employment multipliers for each sector, $i\, l_i$, where L_{max} refers to the labor availability and L_{agrlo} is the minimum employment to be offered by agricultural sector:

$$\sum_{i=1}^{n} l_i X_i \leq L_{max} \tag{8}$$

$$l_{agr} X_{agr} \geq L_{agrlo} \tag{9}$$

The last equation of this optimization corresponds to the non-negativity of the decision variable which is the output:

$$X \geq 0 \tag{10}$$

Results and Post-processing

The Water Input-Output Programming (WIOP) model estimates the output of each economic sector, focusing on the effect in each sector of the availability of water. Across all the sectors, water's contribution to the GDP can be seen through the value of the objective function, which decreases as the economy is threatened by water scarcity. However, the most important result is the economy-wide shadow price of water, which corresponds to the change in the objective function (value added) due to a unit change in the availability of water. This shadow price is a good indicator of the scarcity of water.

One of our purposes is to test the behavior of the economy given any change in water availability. By varying the availability of water from a very low quantity (the linear programming becomes infeasible at a certain point, due to the lower bound on final demand), to a high quantity, we can observe that change in the shadow price of water is disproportionate to change in water availability. At each quantity of water, the infeasibility of the model is due to a different sector where the final demand cannot be met. This brings out which sector is the strategic one for each level of water availability, which also corresponds to a specific economic value of water.

An economy-wide demand curve for water can be derived by noting the shadow price of water corresponding to different constraints on water availability, as shown in Figure 3-7. One should note that this aggregated demand

FIGURE 3-7

Macroeconomic Water Demand Curve

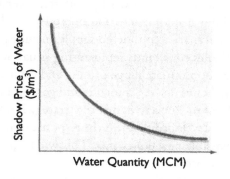

curve is valuable for the short and medium term only, due to the fact that the I-O table assumes a static situation. For long term analysis, the A matrix should be modified to incorporate technical changes in the economic sectors, changes in water allocation and changes in the sectoral output.

The ability to construct demand curves for various supply scenarios brings out the marginal net benefits of water use from an inter-sectoral point of view, rather than a limited sectoral one. This may also yield useful clues for decision-makers seeking to determine optimal water pricing systems for water use in various sectors.

From a policy-oriented point of view, this type of model can generate a structure as a support for decision-makers and policy-analysts, in order to target appropriate investments and evaluate the prospective projects. Using the WIOP model (which correspond to the second part of the MEIAH-2), proposed investments in water treatment can be represented by an increase in the availability of a higher quality water, which will generate a new set of shadow prices. Similarly, the implementation of water loss prevention measures will increase water availability and relax the water constraints in the model. The implementation of water efficiency techniques will result not only in a change in the water availability constraint, but also a change in the coefficient corresponding to water losses in the value added (objective function) of the WIOP. A comparison of the change in the economic value of water (which measures the benefit of a potential investment) with the capital proposed to be invested in treatment, or conservation or other measures provides a guide for water sector investment decisions.

Framework for an Integrated Water Resource Strategy
Scenarios for Selected Water Policy Options

Policy choices are evaluated by considering different scenarios using the developed model, looking at both macro and micro level policies, as well as their combination. The scenarios considered should include parameter variations and decision variables constraints representing situations that could be implemented within an appropriate range of time and capital.

Scenario analysis facilitates debate, tradeoffs and compromises among the policy analysts. In light of the objectives that the strategy is working towards, a set of scenarios will be developed to assess the response of the economy and the water sector to a possible new policy mix. This will help target appropriate options and policy reforms.

Water policy can be categorized in many ways, but we adopt the approach of Schaible et al. (1995), dividing policies into regulatory and incentive-based (Figure 3-8). The former impose restrictions on water use for surface water or groundwater for specific users, through reductions in flow, diversion, or a lowering of permitted groundwater extraction rates. Incentive policies use price changes and conservation measures to encourage resource efficiency in both urban and agricultural use. Conservation policies can include institutional reform, the creation of alternative water market structures, redefinition of conserved water property rights, and other measures.

Each national goal which has been decided appears as a constraint or a boundary in the system, which affects the parameters and the decision variables. Food security objectives and trade agreements will largely determine cropping patterns and the quantity of water needed for irrigation. Environmental standards will affect industrial effluent, either by giving incentives to consume a lesser quantity of freshwater or by charging fees for the chemicals discharged. The need for energy (hydropower) production will affect levels of reservoir storage. Each country has its particular national economic and social development objectives. The scenarios considered should therefore include parameter variations and decision variable constraints which are able to express these development objectives, but be realistic and implementable, as noted above, within an appropriate range of time and capital.

The MEIAH modelling system, as described above, provides an interlinked two-stage analytical framework. MEIAH's flexibility permits estimation of the impact of a set of decision variables on the water sector, the economy and the environment. The water input-output table yields additional socio-economic indicators, including employment, income and others. MEIAH-1

FIGURE 3-8

Macro- and Micro-Level Water Policy Options

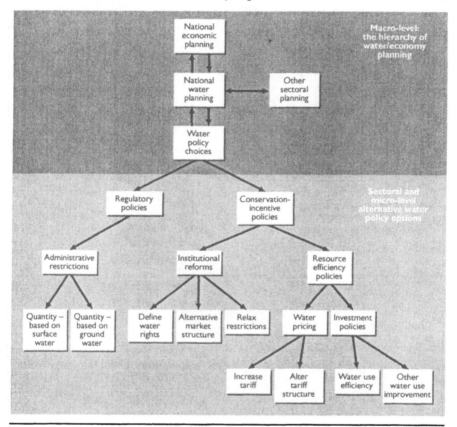

covers a more horizontal setting and evaluates water use scenarios in the light of conflicting users. This feeds into MEIAH-2 to provide economy-wide indicators, in order to evaluate the socio-economic impact of the considered scenarios, through a set of multipliers. The linkage in the other direction, (macroeconomic to water resource policies) is also very important. Macroeconomic policies could have such targets as as a desired level of imports or exports, food self-sufficiency, a given employment level, a particular sectoral contribution to the GDP, or a sectoral growth rate. These can be combined with the input-output table information to specify a modification of constraints or objectives in the water resources model, which in turn determines a new set of water policies to best reflect the macroeconomic goals (Figure 3-9).

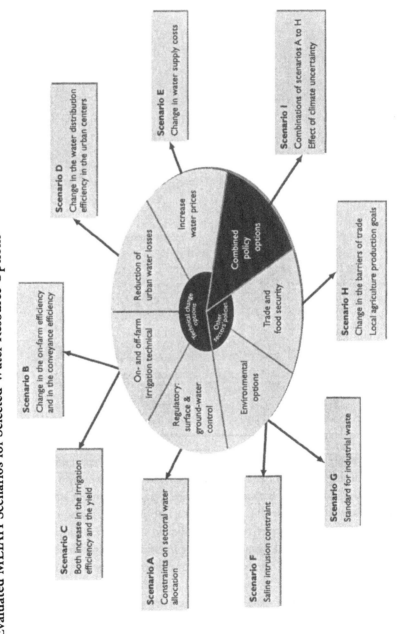

FIGURE 3-9
Evaluated MEIAH Scenarios for Selected Water Resource Options

Towards an Action Plan

To implement a strategy, an action plan will be necessary, reflecting national priorities and the urgency of the situation. An action plan is a comprehensive package of technical, economic, financial and institutional measures to accomplish broad water management objectives in service of national economic goals. It will reflect the necessary trade-offs and compromises.

We are moving from sectoral objectives towards a broader economic and social picture. An action plan will have different dimensions: social as it needs education and incentives, as well as it targets employment goals; economic, in terms of agricultural production and the balance of trade; institutional, as a succession of officials and participants may take charge of it over time; and financial, in terms of new infrastructural investment.

There are several domains that must be considered in forming a country-wide action plan. Eight are suggested here:

- *Property rights, water user associations,*

- *Poverty, population and rural development:* distributional implications of large scale irrigation systems vs small-scale irrigation, efficiency versus equity, assistance for groundwater development,

- *Externalities:* effects of irrigation project coverage, flooding, waterlogging, environmental and ecological consequences, or effects of groundwater exploitation on the lowering of the water table,

- *Pricing and taxation:* water pricing, land taxes, taxes on polluting inputs or outputs, subsidies on taxes and technologies,

- *Privatization and public enterprise:* irrigation system maintenance and management, land consolidation, groundwater development, industrial waste, sewage treatment,

- *Macropolicies:* interest rates, exchange rates, trade taxes and wage rates,

- *Legislation:* improvement and conservation of national environmental quality, environmental quality legislation, fisheries and navigation legislation,

- *Administration:* including the different national bodies dealing with water or water related components.

Conclusion

The water input-output structure, as a DSS, can assist policy-makers in targeting the appropriate choice of investments in the water sector and in evaluating their attractiveness to the overall economy. Once the data have been developed for the Social Accounting Matrix (I/O table) the same data base can be used to estimate the coefficients for a Computable General Equilibrium (CGE) model. Dufournaud, Harrington, and Rogers (1988) give an example of how this may be implemented and how it may be compared to the more traditional Leontief analysis pursued here.

The approach used here takes a step toward closing the gap that currently exists between the evaluation of water resources and macroeconomic decision-making. It should act as a catalyst for policy debate, assist fruitful cooperation, and help in formulating an integrated national water strategy, facilitating the implementation of a sustainable national plan.

Notes

1   Translated from the 17th century French scientist Lavoisier: "Rien ne se crée, rien ne se perd, mais tout se transforme."

2   The model can be run using a laptop computer, through the use of a file of multiple spreadsheets on Microsoft Excel for Windows. In MEIAH.I.xls, the different decision variables that are considered in the model are described. When one clicks with the mouse on MODEL, from DEFINE SCENARIO, the different set of constraints are provided to choose from, and to change the upper or lower bound when applicable. Once the scenario has been defined, the model can be run and the decision variables that have been generated from the run of the programming model should completely describe the decision to be made.

3   In order to close the cycle of water, another row could be added corresponding to the water used by households, which represents an intermediate stage, to return the water used by household to the collection unit, which is also the water utility.

4   The A matrix coefficients are also called technical coefficients or input-output coefficients.

5   The Leontief inverse matrix can be expressed as:

$$(I - A)^{-1} = I + A + A_2 + A_3 + \ldots$$

The matrix I is the initial effect, the matrix A represents the direct effect and the rest $(A_2 + A_3 + \ldots)$ represent the indirect effect.

4

Application: Case Study of Morocco

The methodology presented in Chapter 3 aims to help any country where water scarcity or over-abundance constrains sustainable national socio-economic development. This chapter provides an application of that methodology to the existing situation in Morocco, and further discussion of the method's structure and operation. As a part of the Middle East and North Africa (MENA), a region on the brink of a crisis of water insufficiency, Morocco offers for analysis a water-scarce country where the macro-economy is highly intertwined with the water sector and year-to-year climatic fluctuations reverberate throughout the economy.

In this chapter, first, background is provided on Morocco and an overview of the country's water sector is presented. First, MEIAH-1,the water resources component of the model generates a set of results based on the three major Moroccan river basins of Oum Er Rbia, Bou Regrag and Sebou. A selection of these results is then extrapolated to provide indices for the national level. Thereafter, as the first component of MEIAH-2, a water input-output table (WIOP) is developed for Morocco, and its output is made part of the Social Account Matrix, which gives an overall macroeconomic picture of the country. The following section describes the national economic consequences and the policy implications of water management decisions. The model can bring out these consequences by taking into consideration such factors as the goal of environmental sustainability, trade agreements, and existing and potential domestic policies, like cropping patterns. Finally, the multipliers yielded by the water input-output model are used to link up with the overall national economy, in order to target strategic investments and priority sectors. For this initial application of the MEIAH methodology to Morocco, the existing status quo, or "business as usual" provides the specifications of the scenario which will later be called the "base case," or Scenario A. The data have been taken from 1997, and the year 2000 has been chosen as the year of forecast, although with updated data, the model can also forecast for other years.

Morocco

The Kingdom of Morocco is the westernmost of the three North African countries known to the Arabs as Jezirat al Maghreb or "Island of the West." It has an extensive coastline on both the Atlantic Ocean and the Mediterranean Sea. Owing to its position and the interposed mountain ranges, it long remained relatively isolated from the rest of the Maghreb and historically served as a refuge for descendants of the native Berber-speaking inhabitants of northwest Africa. Morocco, where the author grew up, is a country which has been transformed in a single lifetime from a water-rich, fertile nation into one facing a severe water crisis and a host of attendant ramifications. It is blessed with a well-structured water system of dams and canals, a legacy of not only the sophisticated engineering work done during the period of French rule but also a series of proactive post-independence governmental interventions.

In 1912, Morocco became a French protectorate, and early efforts began to exploit its water resources (Swearingen, 1987; and Europa, 1994). A rainfed wheat policy, designed to convert Morocco into a breadbasket for France, monopolized development efforts during the first two decades of the protectorate period, but without great success. In the 1930s, it was replaced by a new approach which aimed to replicate the success of irrigated agriculture in the similar climate of California. The new "California Image" played a major role in reorienting Morocco's export agriculture towards its present form of fruit and vegetables. Fruit and vegetable production by irrigated means accounted for over four-fifths of Morocco's agricultural exports in 1986, and Morocco today is the world's second largest exporter of oranges. A highly ambitious irrigation plan was developed in Morocco for the development of one million hectares by the year 2000. Since independence in 1956, nearly twenty new dams have been constructed, and the modern irrigated areas have grown from 65,000 hectares to 900,000 hectares at present. Unfortunately, this has not brought with it the necessary broad economic development: although agricultural exports doubled, imports increased eightfold between 1969 and 1982, and foreign debt increased due to the money borrowed for dam building and irrigation projects. Spain's entry into the European Community and its transformation into a "winter garden" has led to the gradual closing of European markets to Moroccan citrus and market garden exports. After struggling mightily through droughts, and spending tremendous capital on dams and irrigation systems in the drive to irrigate a million hectares, Morocco has difficulty finding markets for its agricultural production, and is strongly aware that many of its economic issues have roots in the colonial period.

The Moroccan Economy

Morocco is a lower middle-income country with a per capita income of about US $1,100 in 1995. Its economy is well diversified with a large and varied natural resource base. Its population of 27 million, growing at 2.8% per annum is concentrated in the fertile plains and coastal areas of the northwest, where water-resource development has made agricultural and urban development possible. The most important natural resource is rock phosphate, of which Morocco has about 75% of the world's reserves, and which it processes domestically into phosphoric acid and fertilizers for export. The nonchemical industrial sector produce a wide range of goods: leather, mechanical and electrical products. The agriculture sector employs 44% of the labor force and is predominantly rainfed and oriented towards food production—cereals, edible oil seeds, potatoes, and pulses—and livestock—sheep, poultry and beef. Irrigated agriculture covers 10% of the land, but contributes to more than half of farming's value added, mainly in citrus, vegetables and sugar. It also generates two-thirds of farm exports. Along the extended Moroccan coast, the fishing sector is of growing importance, producing canned sardines, and fresh and frozen white fish. Tourism is also a leading contributor to the economy, as are remittances from the many Moroccans working abroad.

The composition of the GDP has gone through several variations, with the share of agriculture fluctuating due to droughts. Overall, GDP growth has been irregular and on occasion less than population growth itself, which is close to 3% per year. Agriculture represents 18% of the GDP, while industry covers 31% (energy 3.6%, mining 3.4%, manufacturing 18.5% and construction 5.6%), and services represent 44.4% (among which, transportation 20.1% and commerce 12%). Import taxes correspond to 6% of the GDP.

Today, Morocco faces unprecedented challenges on both the external and domestic fronts. Externally, it is losing much of its long-time preferential access to the European market, at a time when the global market had became extremely competitive. Domestically, high urban unemployment, extensive rural poverty, and a fragile economy hold socio-political stability hostage. In the mid-1980s, structural adjustment measures enabled a regain of balance and a refuelling of growth, but in the 1990s Morocco lost some ground, due to macro-economic imbalances and social tensions. The economy remains highly protected and distorted, to a greater extent than most developing countries, and poverty is widespread in the rural areas. Although irrigated farmers are subsidized through low water charges, they are discriminated against by an export bias. Low water charges contribute to extensive inefficiency in water use, even as competing demands rise for an increasingly scarce resource.

According to World Bank studies on Morocco's economy, integration into the international market will not only promote rural well being, but also will provide important opportunities to raise incomes and welfare. But such an integration will require extensive reforms at trade, macro and sectoral levels. The overall dilemma is between promoting efficient production in the long term and losing employment among the poor in the short term.

Overview of the Water Sector in Morocco

Water-resource problems in Morocco receive considerable attention from the Moroccan government, international lending agencies and water-resources experts. Many plans have been implemented (and even more proposed) for the development and management of water resources. The focus has been on satisfying what have been considered inflexible needs for water. Environmental issues have generally been neglected, even though they may threaten the sustainability of the water resource. For example, both industrial and domestic effluent discharges continue to damage the quality of water, and saline water intrusion is decreasing the usable yield of aquifers. Waterlogging and soil salination from irrigation are also typical environmental problems with very concrete impacts which need attention in national water analysis, as do the linkages between the water sector and the macro-economy.

Water-Stress Situation

Situated on the northwest tip of Africa, Morocco is subject to the influence of highly diverse climatic conditions. Any changes in the output of agriculture due to weather variations have a pronounced multiplier effect on overall economic activities and serious consequences for employment. The north of the country is characterized by Mediterranean influences, the south is part of the arid Sahara, the west is subject to Atlantic influences and in the east the High Atlas mountain range has its own microclimates. Average annual precipitation varies from 750 mm per year in the Mediterranean region of the

Loukkos to under 100 mm in the Sahara regions of Ouarzazat and Tafilalt. Total precipitation for Morocco averages 150 billion cubic meters (BCM) per year, 30 BCM of which replenishes surface and groundwater flow, the remainder being lost to evaporation. The challenges associated with the uneven geographical distribution of Morocco's water resources are compounded by the uneven and erratic nature of rainfall; most of the precipitation occurs between October and April. The country is highly susceptible to long droughts, which can continue up to six years. This creates highly variable surface flows and threatens water supplies to households and farmers alike. Per capita renewable water resources are estimated at 800 m^3. Morocco is hence, according to international categorizations, defined as "water stressed." By 2020, per capita water resources are expected to fall to 400 m^3, which will bring Morocco to a "chronically water stressed level" (The World Bank, 1995b).

Up to 85% of Morocco's mobilized water resources are used in agriculture, irrigating 900,000 hectares. Priority has traditionally been attached to securing potable water supplies, and at present, household water demands are rapidly increasing. Currently 76% of the urban population is supplied with water, and the aim is to supply 98% of the national population through pipelines (the rest by standpipe) by the year 2020. Industrial water demands are rising by 5% per year. Hydropower (687 MW of capacity, supplying 30% of the total electricity produced) contributes particularly to meeting peak power demand during the winter. Environmental concerns, particularly in the Sebou basin, need to be incorporated into strategic water approaches, but bringing the whole system into a sustainable balance is impeded by the variability of water supplies, including the high frequency of drought.

Today the total mobilized water faces a demand of 10.9 billion cubic meters (BCM) per year for the three sectors. This demand can be met in a year with a normal precipitation, considering that 11 BCM can in principle be mobilized and supplied in that circumstance, but the tight balance between supply and demand is highly vulnerable to the variability in precipitation. Although the mobilized water resource is planned to be developed to 16.8 BCM by the year 2020, the pace at which the demand increases is much higher, and will lead to a water demand of 17.6 BCM at that time, a clear deficit position.

Total yearly water supply and demand balances for Morocco are constructed on a basin-by-basin basis, usefully emphasizing regional deficits and surpluses. Figures 4-1 and 4-2 illustrate the water balance for the eight regions of Morocco for 1990 and 2020 (The World Bank, 1996a). Bearing in mind that all regions are subject to tremendous uncertainty due to annual

FIGURE   4-1
Regional Water Balance—1990

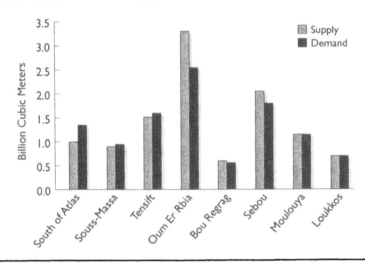

rainfall fluctuations, we see that almost 50% of Morocco's total water resources, and 93% of current regional surpluses, are concentrated in the
Sebou and Oum Er Rbia basins. The Casablanca and Rabat-Salé metropoli-
tan areas, which accounted for 25% of all residential and industrial
water demand in 1990, are supplied with potable water from the Sebou,
Oum Er Rbia and Bou Regrag basins. As discussed below, these three basins
are the area of empirical study for this book.

Recent droughts have highlighted Morocco's dependence on water and the
economy's vulnerability to the climate. The principal challenges of a drought
include the decline in per capita water supplies and the exhaustion of available water resources in a number of key basins, the rapidly rising marginal
cost of water and sharp increases in water mobilization investment costs,
which are not matched by cost recovery. There is an expected 30% decline by
2020 in water available per hectare (World Bank, 1996a), which, together
with higher water prices and lower output prices, requires sharp improve-
ments in farm productivity and water efficiency.

Oum Er Rbia, Bou Regrag and Sebou River Basins
A major region in Morocco is the Oum Er Rbia, Bou Regrag and Sebou River
Basins area. Its 700 km opening on the Atlantic coast runs from the City of

FIGURE 4-2

Regional Water Balance—2020

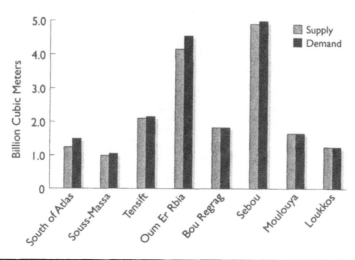

Kenitra to the south of Casablanca, and the region also includes two coastal rivers: Mellah and N'fifikh (Figure 4-3). The hydrological schematic of this region is represented in Figure 4-4, and a detailed description is provided in Appendix 1. This area encompasses more than half of the national population, and the three largest provinces in Morocco: Casablanca, Rabat, and Fez. 80% of Morocco's industrial capacity is located in the watershed of the Sebou River and the coastal areas from Mohammedia to Casablanca. Agriculture is scattered throughout the whole region, with both large-scale, and small- and medium-scale irrigated areas (GH and PMHs). Rainfed agriculture is important as well.

This three-basin area represents the backbone of the Moroccan economy. It contributes 68% of the national production in cereals, 87% in legumes and 90% of the industrialized production. The large water consumers in the industrial sector are sugar processing (10 out of the 12 national sugar refineries are in the region), paper manufacturing (at Gharb and Kenitra), thermal electricity production (at Kenitra, Mohammedia and Casablanca) and petroleum refining. Table 4-1 summarizes the water demand in the three-basin region, differentiating the household, industrial and agricultural sectors.

These river basins have a Mediterranean (wet winter, dry summer) climate, with an oceanic influence, manifested in the rainy winds from the west

FIGURE 4-3
Oum Er Rbia, Bou Regrag and Sebou River Basins

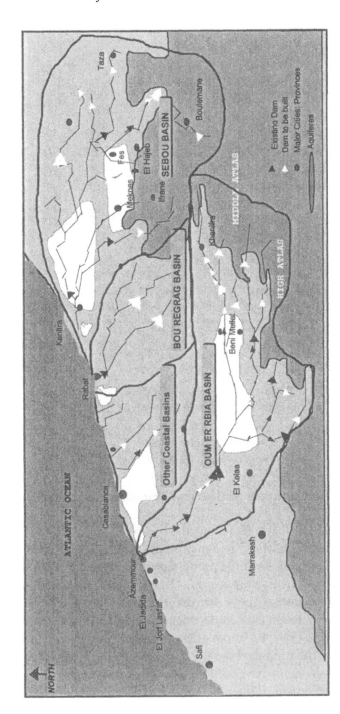

FIGURE 4-4
Schematic of the Region Showing the Different Nodes of the System

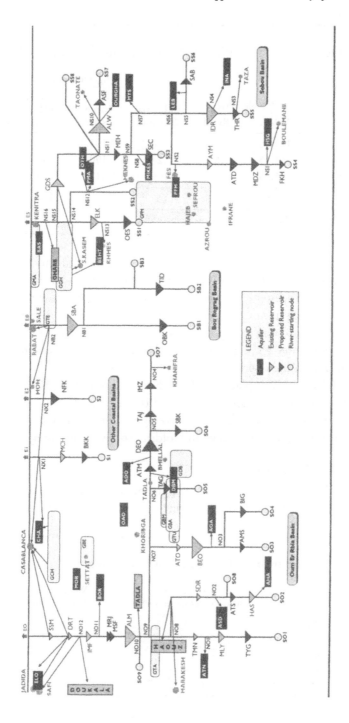

TABLE 4 - 1

Water Demand in the Region in MCM for the Base Year 1995

| | Potable Water | | Industrial | Irrigated Agriculture | | Total |
	Urban	Rural	Demand	Large Scale	Small & Medium Scale	Demand
Sebou	194.35	33.8	30.7	1,193.3	682.5	2134.8
Bou Regrag	361.35	18.8	27.6	190.5	145.4	743.65
Oum Er Rbia	75.25	23.2	106.1	1,411.9	283.1	1,899.55
Total	630.95	75.8	164.4	2795.7	1111.0	4,778.0

Source: Plan Directeur Integre—Royaume du Maroc, 1992

and a level of precipitation that decreases with distance from the sea. Differing situations of altitude, latitude, and ocean exposure create local microclimates, where winter cold, snow, and rain often contrast with the heat and the storms of the summer season. Precipitation in the basins has two distinct seasons, dry from May to September and rainy from October to April, as well as very strong inter-annual variation. Table 4-2 shows the seasonal division of precipitation in the region.

Snowfalls can take place in the Sebou and Oum Er Rbia basins from November to March at an altitude of 800 meters and above. In the Middle Atlas mountains, snow falls for an average of more than 20 days per year, contributing to the water flows and adding to reservoir storage.

Institutional Framework

Present Moroccan water-resource management has several unresolved issues. Large hasty and unplanned emergency expenditures to overcome drought or

TABLE 4 - 2

Seasonal Distribution of Precipitation in the Region

Basin	Dry Season May to September (%)	Wet Season October to April (%)
Sebou	11	89
Oum Er Rbia	15	85
Bou Regrag	8	92

Source: Plan Directeur Integre—Royaume du Maroc, 1992

flood problems are sub-optimal. Over-exploitation of groundwater and the use of heavy chemical and biological pollutants jeopardize the quality of water and pose serious health hazards. Subsidies of the under-priced water resource are starting to weigh heavily on the government, and there is little flexibility in the administrative allocation of water among users.

Several ministries and governmental bodies deal with different aspects of Morocco's water sector. The Ministry of Agriculture is in charge of water for irrigation, while the urban water supply is managed by the National Organization for Potable Water (ONEP). The Ministry of Public Works manages the water production system and the infrastructure, the Ministry of Environment deals with the environmental and health aspects of Water Resources, and the Ministry of Finance oversees investments in the water sector. This diversity makes it clear that water must be considered in terms of its interaction with a broad range of considerations, including agriculture, urban demand, economics, finance, infrastructure, environment, public health and national goals. Water's links with multiple other sectors means there must be a choice of policy and technical options at both the macro- and micro-levels. The "macro" policy arena handles national goals, such as food security, poverty reduction, drinking water supply, economic development, suitable intersectoral allocation, and environmentally sustainable development. The "micro" level includes policy and institutional regulations and reforms, or technical choices; within it, options can be classified as hardware (infrastructure) or software (policy) types, after having been categorized as seeking their effects through either supply-side or demand-side management.

The Social Account Matrix for Morocco

Several international institutions such as the Organisation for Economic Co-operation and Development (OECD), United Nation Agencies, the United States Agency for International Development (USAID), the World Bank, and the International Monetary Fund (IMF) have extensively analyzed the overall economic situation of Morocco. As part of ongoing research on sustainable development, the Development Center of the OECD collaborates with the Moroccan Ministry of External Affairs and the World Bank to evaluate the economy-wide implications of trade and resource policies for the country. The result of this collaborative research is a Computable General Equilibrium model (CGE) of the Moroccan economy, which forms the basis of empirical policy studies. The first phase of this model development program was database construction, and the development, from official information and various other sources, of a detailed 1990 input-output table for Morocco, which served as the central component of a social accounting matrix (SAM) for the country. In 1995, this SAM was used for a rural development analysis by the International Food Policy Research Institute (IFPRI) (Lofgren et al., 1997). The coefficients of the original 1990 SAM were updated to produce a 1995 SAM, which distinguishes between irrigated and rainfed sectors in agriculture, and between urban and rural households and labor. This 1995 SAM forms the backbone of the input-output model in this study.

As described in detail in Appendix 3, the 1995 SAM is aggregated to generate a 15-sector input-output table. As shown in Table 4-3, it considers twelve irrigated agriculture production activities. In the 1995 table, rainfed agriculture, livestock, industry and services are all treated as separate economic activities. The thirteen primary inputs to each sector are: capital, land, water, labor income, government, rest of the world, invested savings, water tariffs, direct taxes, indirect taxes, subsidies, tariffs, and non-tariff barriers (NTBs). This 15-sector input-output table will be manipulated to integrate water into the economic sectors, and thereby, into national economic planning. A static input-output table cannot be used for long-term planning, since it assumes there is no technical change, but it can be used for short- to medium-term planning. A five year period is within the short to medium category, and therefore we can use the 15-sector input-output table for 1995 to model water sector behavior for the year 2000.

Macro-Economic Integrated Analysis of Hydrology Model (MEIAH)

The application of a Decision Support System (DSS) to Morocco requires a tremendous amount of data and information. Based on data from studies conducted or supervised by the World Bank, as well as data collected by the Moroccan authorities, two interlinked MEIAH models have been developed for this study, as discussed in the previous chapter. The first (MEIAH-1) is based on the large Oum Er Rbia, Bou Regrag and Sebou River basins area. The information drawn from this model is carefully extrapolated to cover the whole country, and then used as an input for the second model (MEIAH-2), which is a national-level macroeconomic input-output table. Our usual direction of analysis is from the water sector to the overall economy, but intrinsically and mathematically, the order of using the models does not matter.

Modeling Approach

MEIAH-1 is an optimization model, a multi-faceted approach. The river basins studied involve multiple supplies (surface, groundwater, storage) and several demands, which are integrated through a variety of dimensions: hydrological, physical, social, agricultural, economic, environmental, and mathematical. Computer tools and concepts are used to model the nonlinear relationships among the parameters and the decision-variables in the region. The model maximizes the aggregated net benefits, discounted over 25 years, to all users in the area (agriculture, urban, hydropower), constrained by the continuity of the system, water demand, land availability, and environmental, financial, macroeconomic and other considerations. It does so by determining optimal values of various decision variables including water flows, groundwater utilization, reservoir storage and releases, sectoral allocation, urban demands, cropping patterns, and generated hydropower. Shadow prices are determined to assess the scarcity of water, and to permit the representation of water in either monetary (dirham (DH)) terms or in material terms (cubic meters (m³)).

The second component model, MEIAH-2, modifies the traditional input-output economic accounting framework to incorporate the closed cycle of water and the shadow prices of water for each sector of the economy. This model uses information from the water model about water allocation and the value added by various sectors, and generates information on the sectoral impacts and associated multipliers (such as employment, output, income, water, etc.). It also yields shadow price information to help identify sectors of strategic importance and to develop an economy-wide demand curve. The combination of the two models is the specific contribution of the present study.

A User-Friendly Framework

A DSS can be used by a broad range of policy makers; this is one of its greatest advantages. This model is formulated to provide opportunities for specifying scenarios a decision-maker might wish to investigate. For example, the parameters that can be varied in the scenarios include:

■ *The year:* 1995 to 2020,

■ *Climate conditions:* wet, normal, dry, very dry, corresponding to different levels of flow,

TABLE   4-3

Aggregated 1995 Social Accounting Matrix for Morocco

		1 WHT-AI	2 BARLEY-AI	3 MAIZE-AI	4 OTHCER-AI	5 LEGUME-AI	6 FODDER-AI	7 SGRBT-AI
1	WHT-AI	1.052	—	—	—	—	—	—
2	BARLEY-AI	—	0.341	—	—	—	—	—
3	MAIZE-AI	—	—	0.169	—	—	—	—
4	OTHCER-AI	—	—	—	0.051	—	—	—
5	LEGUME-AI	—	—	—	—	0.079	—	—
6	FODDER-AI	—	—	—	—	—	0.420	—
7	SGRBT-AI	—	—	—	—	—	—	0.382
8	SGRCN-AI	—	—	—	—	—	—	—
9	SNFLW-AI	—	—	—	—	—	—	—
10	OINDCRI-AI	—	—	—	—	—	—	—
11	VEGET-AI	—	—	—	—	—	—	—
12	PLANT-AI	—	—	—	—	—	—	—
13	RAINFED	6.411	4.544	0.873	0.207	1.069	0.217	0.115
14	LVST	—	—	—	—	—	—	—
15	INDSRV	0.093	—	0.003	—	—	—	—
16	CROPCAP	0.392	0.100	0.026	0.010	0.011	0.030	0.043
17	LAND	0.661	0.265	0.104	0.019	0.058	0.264	0.136
18	WATER	0.329	0.154	0.092	0.041	0.018	0.232	0.080
19	LABOR+INCOME	0.169	0.088	0.083	0.012	0.044	0.229	0.174
20	FAC-NTB	—	—	—	—	—	—	—
21	GOV	—	—	—	—	—	—	—
22	ROW	1.029	0.131	0.007	—	0.006	—	—
23	SAV-INV	—	—	—	—	—	—	—
24	WATTAR	—	0.024	—	—	—	—	—
25	DIRTAX	—	—	0.003	—	—	—	—
26	INDTAX	—	—	—	0.007	—	—	—
27	SUBSIDY	—	—	—	—	0.011	—	—
28	TARIFF	—	—	—	—	—	0.005	—
29	NTB	—	—	—	—	—	—	0.033
30	TOTAL	2.287	0.740	0.355	0.107	0.174	0.839	0.808

WHT-AI = Irrigated Wheat; BARLEY-AI = Irrigated Barley; MAIE-AI = Irrigated Maize; OTHCER-AI = Irrigated Cereals; LEGUME-AI = Irrigated Legume; FODDER-AI = Irrigated Fodder; SGRBT-AI = Irrigated Sugar Beet; SGRCN-AI = Irrigated Sugar Cane; SNFLW-AI = Irrigated Sun Flower; OINDCRI-AI = Irrigated Industrial Agriculture Production; VEGET-AI = Irrigated Vegeables; PLANTA-AI = Irrigated Plantations; RAINFED = Rainfed Agriculture; LVST = Livestock; INDSRV = Industry and Services; CROPCAP = Capital; FAC-NTB = Factor for Non-trade Barriers; GOV = Government; ROW = Rest of the World; SAV-INV = Saving and Investments; WATTAR = Water Tariffs; DIRTAX = Direct Tax; INDTAX = Indirect Tax; NTB = Non-Trade Barriers

Source: Computed from the 104-sector SAM matrix of 1995 developed by IFPRI (Lofgren et al , 1997)

8 SGRCN-AI	9 SNFLW-AI	10 OINDCRI-AI	11 VEGET-AI	12 PLANT-AI	13 RAINFED	14 LVST	15 IND-SRV	
—	—	—	—	—	1.052	0.054	0.929	1
—	—	—	—	—	0.341	0.050	0.161	2
—	—	—	—	—	0.169	0.053	0.139	3
—	—	—	—	—	0.051	0.098	—	4
—	—	—	—	—	0.079	—	0.027	5
—	—	—	—	—	0.420	0.817	—	6
—	—	—	—	—	0.382	—	0.728	7
0.146	—	—	—	—	0.146	—	0.283	8
—	0.019	—	—	—	0.019	—	0.021	9
—	—	0.222	—	—	0.222	—	0.918	10
—	—	—	2.471	—	2.471	—	0.337	11
—	—	—	—	2.867	—	—	1.690	12
—	0.292	0.195	0.921	2.066	14.843	2.090	10.349	13
—	—	—	—	—	—	—	24.717	14
—	—	—	—	—	0.771	11.960	909.101	15
0.005	0.004	0.015	0.104	0.152	2.543	4.671	72.418	16
0.059	0.012	0.082	0.481	0.831	16.329	1.676	—	17
0.114	0.014	0.086	0.300	1.511	—	—	—	18
0.065	0.005	0.068	1.100	1.362	5.690	2.635	119.265	19
—	—	—	—	—	—	—	—	20
—	—	—	—	—	—	—	—	21
—	0.059	0.764	0.224	0.031	2.221	—	71.610	22
—	—	—	—	—	—	—	—	23
—	—	—	—	—	—	—	—	24
—	—	—	—	—	0.027	—	—	25
—	—	—	—	—	0.012	0.615	22.255	26
—	—	—	—	—	0.142	—	—	27
—	—	—	—	—	0.029	—	18.350	28
—	—	—	—	—	0.015	—	6.322	29
0.292	0.039	0.464	5.029	5.733	14.056	24.717	569.920	30

continued

T A B L E   4 - 3

Aggregated 1995 Social Accounting Matrix for Morocco *(continued)*

		16	17	18	19	20	21	22
		CROPLAND	LAND	WATER	HOUSEHOLD	FAC-NTB	GOV	ROW
1	WHT-AI	—	—	—	1.623	—	—	0.019
2	BARLEY-AI	—	—	—	0.430	—	—	0.066
3	MAIZE-AI	—	—	—	0.144	—	—	—
4	OTHCER-AI	—	—	—	—	—	—	—
5	LEGUME-AI	—	—	—	0.110	—	—	0.012
6	FODDER-AI	—	—	—	—	—	—	—
7	SGRBT-AI	—	—	—	—	—	—	—
8	SGRCN-AI	—	—	—	—	—	—	—
9	SNFLW-AI	—	—	—	0.027	—	—	0.005
10	OINDCRI-AI	—	—	—	0.536	—	—	0.103
11	VEGET-AI	—	—	—	2.177	—	—	2.279
12	PLANT-AI	—	—	—	2.965	—	—	0.934
13	RAINFED	—	—	—	19.542	—	—	2.170
14	LVST	—	—	—	—	—	—	—
15	INDSRV	—	—	—	171.602	—	40.781	54.394
16	CROPCAP	—	—	—	—	—	—	—
17	LAND	—	—	—	—	—	—	—
18	WATER	—	—	—	—	—	—	—
19	LABOR+INCOME	74.585	19.300	2.971	—	9.593	7.501	21.396
20	FAC-NTB	—	—	—	—	—	—	—
21	GOV	5.938	—	—	1.871	—	—	—
22	ROW	—	—	—	4.674	—	7.947	—
23	SAV-INV	—	—	—	44.959	—	7.772	6.684
24	WATTAR	—	—	—	—	—	—	—
25	DIRTAX	—	—	—	15.214	—	—	—
26	INDTAX	—	—	—	—	—	—	—
27	SUBSIDY	—	—	—	—	—	3.195	—
28	TARIFF	—	—	—	—	—	—	—
29	NTB	—	—	—	—	—	—	—
30	TOTAL	80.556	18.004	2.971	416.270	9.593	67.196	88.735

WHT-AI = Irrigated Wheat; BARLEY-AI = Irrigated Barley; MAIE-AI = Irrigated Maize; OTHCER-AI = Irrigated Cereals;
LEGUME-AI = Irrigated Legume; FODDER-AI = Irrigated Fodder; SGRBT-AI = Irrigated Sugar Beet; SGRCN-AI = Irrigated Sugar
Cane; SNFLW-AI = Irrigated Sun Flower; OINDCRI-AI = Irrigated Industrial Agriculture Production; VEGET-AI = Irrigated Vegeables;
PLANTA-AI = Irrigated Plantations; RAINFED = Rainfed Agriculture; LVST = Livestock; INDSRV = Industry and Services;
CROPCAP = Capital; FAC-NTB = Factor for Non-trade Barriers; GOV = Government; ROW = Rest of the World;
SAV-INV = Saving and Investments; WATTAR = Water Tariffs; DIRTAX = Direct Tax; INDTAX = Indirect Tax; NTB = Non-Trade
Barriers

Source: Computed from the 104-sector SAM matrix of 1995 developed by IFPRI (Lofgren et al., 1997)

23 SAV-INV	24 WATTAR	25 DIRTAX	26 INDTAX	27 SUBSIDY	28 TARIFF	29 NTB	30 TOTAL	
—	—	—	—	0.267	—	—	3.014	1
—	—	—	—	—	—	—	0.707	2
—	—	—	—	—	—	—	0.341	3
—	—	—	—	—	—	—	0.102	4
—	—	—	—	—	—	—	0.160	5
—	—	—	—	—	—	—	0.839	6
—	—	—	—	—	—	—	0.764	7
—	—	—	—	—	—	—	0.292	8
—	—	—	—	0.003	—	—	0.058	9
—	—	—	—	—	—	—	1.592	10
—	—	—	—	—	—	—	5.285	11
—	—	—	—	—	—	—	5.785	12
—	—	—	—	1.678	—	—	18.367	13
—	—	—	—	—	—	—	24.717	14
59.415	—	—	—	1.247	—	—	1,263.930	15
—	—	—	—	—	—	—	80.523	16
—	—	—	—	—	—	—	20.975	17
—	—	—	—	—	—	—	2.971	18
—	—	—	—	—	—	—	416.303	19
—	—	—	—	—	—	9.593	9.593	20
—	0.196	15.214	23.528	—	20.449	—	67.196	21
—	—	—	—	—	—	—	88.735	22
—	—	—	—	—	—	—	59.415	23
—	—	—	—	—	—	—	0.196	24
—	—	—	—	—	—	—	15.214	25
—	—	—	—	—	—	—	23.528	26
—	—	—	—	—	—	—	3.195	27
—	—	—	—	—	—	—	20.449	28
—	—	—	—	—	—	—	9.593	29
59.415	0.196	15.214	23.528	3.195	20.449	9.593	2,220.010	30

■ *Linkages within the water system:* intrabasin or out-basin water transfers,

■ *Changes in the price of water by sector:* industrial, irrigation or domestic,

■ *Food security goals:* national production or trade, and

■ *Pollution standards.*

The optimization model seeks to maximize the aggregated net benefit gained by different water users. It is also possible to examine the effect of each objective in isolation by regions, users, or goals. Weighting the objectives also allows the model to be a good tool for analyzing investment priorities.

In addition to making it possible to run different scenarios, the MEIAH DSS allows analysts to view results graphically and schematically in an interactive manner. Both the input and output data are displayed in a user-friendly manner as a simplified Geographic Information System, in order to highlight the spatial and temporal distribution of results with respect to water supply and demands.

The Moroccan Base Scenario

Although in the following chapter alternatives and variants will be considered, in this chapter, we apply and discuss the Moroccan "base scenario," or presently existing situation as represented in MEIAH. It provides a starting point, which reflects "business-as-usual" in the year 1997, from which the data are drawn. The year chosen for analysis is 2000, which is far enough away from the date of the data to provide a certain planning vision, yet close enough so we can reasonably assume there will not be any tremendous policy change which will significantly affect the national economy. Reflecting existing reality, the base case disregards environmental considerations, such as sustainability, managing water pollution, and saline intrusion into coastal aquifers. Existing GATT/WTO restraints on trade, aiming to preserve the domestic agricultural market as it is today, and to regulate agricultural imports and exports, are present as constraints in the base model. Domestic policy on cropping patterns is implemented through a system of subsidies, and is motivated in part by a desire for national food self-sufficiency. It is very strict for both small and large scale irrigated areas, and is held in its present configuration in the base scenario. Current planned extension of irrigated areas and planned dam construction are reflected in the base scenario. For hydropower generation, maintaining a sufficient reservoir to supply a generating capacity of 20 megawatts (mw) or above, is assumed. Hydropower demand is assumed to be inelastic, and priced as fixed by the Moroccan Ministry of Energy at 0.6 dirham (DH) per kilowatt hour (kWh).

In the base scenario, water can be transferred from one region to another when there is an existing physical connection. Urban demand is based on the authoritative demand forcast of the Moroccan National Water Planning Unit. It is determined by a water demand curve, based on an elasticity of −0.25. Water prices used are the prices currently charged for the different cities, as described in more detail in Appendix 2. For agriculture, the monthly water requirement per crop is specific to each type of irrigated area (small and medium-scale (PMH) or large-scale (GH)), as well as its location. Domestic production is linked to the level of trade, through the relative prices of exports and imports internationally, as specified by IMF—International Monetary Fund—international statistics.

Regarding the inflows to the system, for the year 2000, that year is assumed to be an average year for precipitation as a starting point, where the level of precipitation represents the 50th percentile of the historical flow data at the starting nodes of the tributaries. Rainfed agriculture production is therefore assumed to be similar to the normal year of 1994. The effect of uncertainty in the hydrology is analyzed in detail in Appendix 4, on stochasticity.

Base Scenario Results and Economic Framework

Understanding that MEIAH-1 takes statistics from the Oum-Er-Rbia, Bou Regrag and Sebou region which are reported on a monthly basis and uses them after they have been extrapolated to represent the entire country, we first look at the results from MEIAH-1, highlighting those relevant to the economic analysis. (For additional results, see Appendix 2.) After generating the water balance for Morocco, the water accounts are determined for each economic sector and then the water input-output table is computed. This will be the base of the socio-economic impact study described below.

Analysis of the River Basin Approach

A river basin optimization model yields a wide range of results relevant to water planners. Information is produced on a monthly basis for each specific node, corresponding to cities, irrigated areas, continuity in the flows, reservoirs, inflows, and end nodes. The main decision variables of the model are:

■ water flow in the system in MCM per month,

■ groundwater extraction in MCM per month,

■ cropping pattern, in terms of the area prescribed for each type of crop for each irrigated node and for domestic agriculture production,

■ reservoirs' storage,

■ hydropower generation, and

■ agricultural imports and exports.

These decision variables can be manipulated to evaluate different hydrologic and economic indicators relevant to the analysis. Also, each constraint generates a marginal value that expresses the change in the value of the objective function as the result of a unit increase in the right hand side of the constraints. This is especially valuable for the inequality relationship between the demand and supply of water for domestic, industrial, and urban use. Relaxing the constraints represents an increase in the quantity of water supplied. Therefore, change in the aggregated net benefit is equivalent to the economic value of the extra unit of water used to relax the supply-demand inequality constraints. In this section, we emphasize the valuational result, which is used in the water input-output model.

We will now comment in greater detail on what is found under the headings of Table 4-4.

Economic Benefits

Although the structure of the objective, or goal, function is over a long-term period of 25 years, for the numerical analysis only the component in the objective function corresponding to the year 2000 will be considered.

The objective, or goal, function of an optimization model represents the social welfare of the studied region. Thus, it corresponds to the aggregate net benefit for the year 2000 from agricultural production and trade, domestic and industrial water use, and also from selling hydropower. For the year 2000, the base scenario generates an aggregated net benefit of 26,090 million DH. The urban sector contributes 17% of the economic net benefit with 4,400 million DH. This represents the area under the urban demand curve, reduced by the cost of supplying the water. Taking into consideration the barriers to trade existing currently in Morocco, which are reflected in the base scenario, the level of agricultural imports is equal to 14,209 Million DH, while agricultural exports represent only 8,700 Million DH. Taking into account the cropping pattern policy, the area under the demand curve for domestic agriculture production, reduced by the cost of water production, is

TABLE 4-4

Summary of the Categories of Base Scenario Results

Economic Net Benefit	Agriculture Net Benefit (local production, exports and imports)
	Domestic and Industrial Net Benefit
	Benefit from Hydropower Generation
	Cost of Water Supply: production and conveyance of both surface and ground water
Water Supply	Groundwater Extraction for Each Aquifer
	Water Flow in the River at Different Points of the River Basin
	Monthly Reservoir Storage
	Monthly Reservoir Release
	Water Flowing to the Ocean at the End Nodes of the Rivers
Water Demand	Domestic and Industrial Water Demand
	Each Irrigated Area (*PMH* and *GH*)
	Each Type of Irrigated Crop
Agriculture Production and Trade	Cropping Pattern Policy (area under each type of production)
	Level of Domestic Production both Irrigated and Rainfed
	Imports and Exports of Agriculture Production
Economic Value of Water	Urban Shadow Prices of Water
	Agricultural Shadow Prices of Water
Hydropower	Hydropower Generation (from each reservoir with an installed capacity)
Water Efficiency	Water Losses in the Urban Agglomerations
	Water Losses in the Irrigated Areas (system and on-farm)
	Water Losses in the System of Conveyance
Environmental Consideration	Groundwater Over-Extraction
	Biochemical Oxygen Demand (BOD) Concentration in the River (Sebou)
	Water Flowing to the Ocean at the End Nodes of the Rivers

almost twice that for imports, and is equal to 25,509 Million DH. It is important to note that this value represents the total social welfare produced by the agricultural sector; it does not simply evaluate the marginal return of water used for irrigation. The benefit from the sale of hydropower in the studied region is 27.42 Million DH.

The cost of water production is mainly from groundwater pumping, totaling 1,183 million DH. Because of the unconstrained extraction rate, the model picks groundwater pumping as its optimal solution rather than costly inter-basin transfers.

Water-Supply Management and Quality Control

The year from which the base scenario is drawn, 1997, was a year of average rainfall, and in the base scenario, the total water inflow to the three-basin region from the tributaries of the rivers is 8.3 billion cubic meters (BCM). This quantity is distributed throughout the basins among the competing users, and reaches the urban or agricultural demand node after being reduced by a percentage of losses or evaporation. A total of 153 million cubic meters (MCM) returns to the system through infiltration and drainage.

3.2 BCM is pumped from the eleven aquifers of the region in the base scenario year. This is 1.67 times more than the yearly sustainable extraction rate of 1.9 BCM per year, except for three aquifers, as shown in Figure 4-5. In this figure, RQG represents the quantity of water extracted while Sustainable Yield gives that value for each aquifer. The three aquifers which are not overpumped (Turonienne, Dir Beni Mellal, and Beni Moussa) are located in the same area in the Oum Er Rbia river basin, and are supplying the same demand node as Beni Amir, which, it will be noted, is selected by the model as the exclusive supplier.

FIGURE 4-5

Groundwater Extraction in MCM per Year

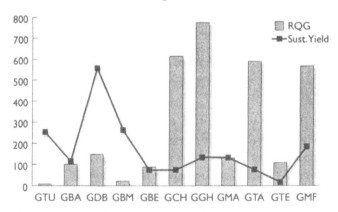

Source: MEIAH-1 output—Base Scenario "business-as-usual"

Water losses are high in both the irrigation network and the urban water supply system. Up to 55% of the water supplied to agriculture, amounting to 1.7 BCM, is lost, and 30% of that for urban areas is lost, equivalent to 30 MCM. Also, evaporation is taken into account in this analysis, mainly during the months with high temperatures; for example, 848 MCM evaporates from the total reservoir storage throughout the year, a figure substantially larger than urban demand in the region.

Urban Demand: Domestic and Industry

Because water allocated to urban concentrations has the highest value return, the model gives priority to the cities. Most cities in the region under consideration are surrounded by industrial establishments. For the year 2000, MEIAH allocates 353.42 MCM to domestic urban use and 69.12 MCM to industries. Water devoted to urban use represents 16% of the total water supply in the region.

For the three-basin region, we have used its geopolitical division into twelve provinces, following the practice of the national Ministry of Statistics. Figure 4-6 illustrates the quantity of water allocated to these provinces for both urban domestic and industrial use, as well as its source (reservoirs,

---

FIGURE 4 - 6

Urban Water Allocation for the Main Provinces

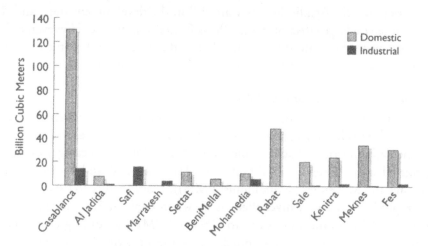

Source: MEIAH-1 output—Base Scenario "business-as-usual"

---

groundwater). In Casablanca and its vicinity, where the population is expected to increase to 8 million, representing 26% of the total population of Morocco, the demand for water is the largest: 144 MCM for household and industrial use. Casablanca's water is mainly supplied by the coastal aquifer of Chaouia.

In the base case the water used in urban areas comes mainly from unconstrained groundwater pumping; the surface river water is used for agriculture. The total cost of production for surface water—including both conveyance and treatment—ranges from 3 to 4.5 DH/m^3, while groundwater has an average cost of 1.14 DH/m^3. Clearly an optimal solution seeks the most cost-effective source of water. In fact, 85.5% of the water demand is provided by groundwater, while only 14.5% comes from surface water. This explains the over-extraction of the Meknes-Fez aquifer, which supplies the city water systems of Fez, Meknes, and some small towns nearby.

For urban use, the model tells us that 137 MCM of surface water, without accounting for water losses, would result in a treatment cost of 411 Million DH or 3 DH/m^3, while 520 MCM of groundwater requires only 593 Million DH, or 0.9 DH/m^3 for extracting and chlorinating the water to a potable level.

Coastal cities discharge effluent to the ocean, causing high levels of coastal pollution. The first sanitation project for coastal protection is now being implemented for the city of Casablanca. In southern Morocco, where water is very scarce, some pilot projects have been designed to recycle water and use it in agriculture for Agadir, but they are still in the development stage and do not yet have a large effect on return flows from domestic use. However, cities in river watersheds are discharging their effluent and wastewater into the rivers, jeopardizing the water quality by increasing pollution.

Agricultural Production and Trade

In Morocco, a system of agricultural subsidies gives government policy-setters effectively complete control over farm cropping choices and patterns, particularly in irrigated areas, which are organized into two categories (large irrigated areas (Grandes Hydrauliques-GH) and small and medium ones (Petites and Moyennes Hydrauliques-PMH)). From locality to locality, however, production is very diversified, as shown in Figure 4-7. Water allocation is handled by committing water to GHs and PMHs according to an agronomic determination of how much water the prescribed crop consumes. Unless there is a change of cropping decisions at the policy level, the cropping

FIGURE 4-7
Cropping Pattern—Base Scenario—1995

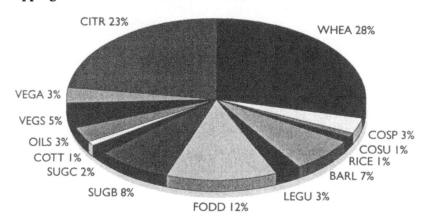

CITR 23%
WHEA 28%
VEGA 3%
VEGS 5%
OILS 3%
COTT 1%
SUGC 2%
SUGB 8%
FODD 12%
LEGU 3%
BARL 7%
RICE 1%
COSU 1%
COSP 3%

Source: MEIAH-1 output—Base Scenario "business-as-usual"

pattern that existed in 1997 in principle will continue and still be applicable in the year 2000. In this system, production depends on the yield of each type of crop and area. As shown in Figure 4-8, citrus plantations consume a large quantity of water, 719 MCM per year, followed by barley, at 394 MCM, and wheat at 259 MCM. These high water-consuming crops cover 59% of the irrigated areas.

Water Allocation to Agriculture

The agricultural sector in the three-basin area consumes 84% of the total water supplied to the economy, a net quantity of 2.3 BCM. Water is allocated among the crops, as shown in the pie chart of Figure 4-7, according to agricultural policy set by the government, as mentioned just above. Ground-water aquifers provide 39% of the total water demand, and the remaining 61% is diverted from rivers. Losses are high in the irrigation system. For large-scale irrigation areas (GH), the distribution irrigation efficiency is 86%; and it is 69% at the on-farm level. For small and medium-scale areas (PMH), although the on-farm efficiency is a higher 75%, the distribution system has higher water loss and waste, giving a much lower distribution efficiency of 53%. Table 4-5 summarizes the quantity and sources of water supplied to each type of irrigated area.

FIGURE   4 - 8

Water Allocation in Irrigated Agriculture—1995

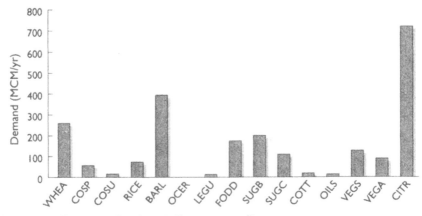

Source: MEIAH-1 output—Base Scenario "business-as-usual"

International Trade

Morocco both exports and imports agricultural goods, and it is generally clear that trade considerations, including trade barriers erected by countries importing from Morocco, constrain the nation's agricultural sector. In fact, domestic production is very much guided by export agreements as well as domestic consumption needs. For instance, for wheat, Table 4-6 shows that 1.814 million tons are exported to the international market, mostly from rainfed production. Barley is also split between irrigated and rainfed production. For another cereal, corn, although 30,000 tons are produced by irrigated areas and 132,000 tons by rainfed ones, the far larger quantity of 1.5 million tons is imported from outside Morocco. The local sugar industries along the Sebou river demand a large quantity of sugar beet and sugar cane; the former is locally produced (2.035 million tons) while 75% of the latter is imported, in order to meet the demand for 2.89 million tons of cane sugar. A large quantity of vegetables is exported: 2.76 million tons of spring vegetables and 125,000 tons of autumn vegetables. Figure 4-9 summarizes agricultural domestic production and trade.

Economic Value of Water

The shadow price of water represents the economic value of water, and is computed in MEIAH using the marginal value of the constraints on water

TABLE 4-5

Sources and Quantity of Water Allocated to the PMH and GH

Sources (MCM)	Type of Irrigated Areas		
	GH	PMH	Total
Groundwater	1,200	1,400	2,600
Surface Water	810	3,500	4,310
Total Supply	2,010	4,900	6,910

Source: MEIAH-1 output—Base Scenario "business-as-usual"

TABLE 4-6

Agriculture Production and Trade

	Production for Local Use in '000 Tons	Imports in '000 Tons	Exports in '000 Tons
Wheat	432.1	0	1814.5
Corn Spring	22.6	641.7	0
Corn-Summer	7.4	857.3	0
Rice	32.3	540.1	0
Barley	46.8	0	1000
Other Cereals	0	1269.7	0
Legumes	19.3	0	100
Fodder	2765.5	0	3188.8
Sugar Beet	2035.5	0	300
Sugar Cane	736.4	2163	0
Cotton	4.4	150	0
Oil Seeds	21.2	0	0
Vegetables-Spring	388	0	2760.8
Vegetables-Autumn	230.7	0	125.6
Citrus Plantations	768.4	0	1500

Source: MEIAH-1 output—Base Scenario "business-as-usual"

availability for both urban and agricultural areas. For both areas, this is first calculated by sub-localities, such as a city, and an average value, weighted by the quantity of water allocated to each sub-unit, is carried forward.

Urban Shadow Prices

We thus generate shadow water prices of the studied region for the farm and city sectors. The economic value of water for the urban area is equal to 1.78

FIGURE 4-9

Agriculture Production and Trade

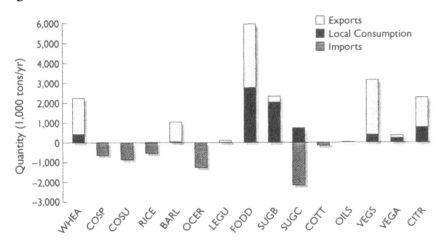

Source: MEIAH-1 output—Base Scenario "business-as-usual"

DH/m³, while an extra unit of water supplied to the agricultural sector generates only 0.36 DH/m³. However, for each individual demand node, the shadow price varies depending on the location, source of water and number of users competing for the same supply. For example, for Casablanca, the shadow price is 1.61 DH/m³, because all the water is supplied from the aquifer of Chaouia, with, in the base case, no environmental restrictions on pumping. The situation is similar for the twin cities of Rabat and Salé, which are located on the Temara aquifer and have a shadow price of about 1.45 DH/m³. In a city like Beni Mellal, supplied from reservoirs and groundwater, and surrounded by both small/medium and large irrigated farming operations (PMH and GH), water has an economic value of 1.59 DH/m³. Some cities are supplied exclusively by quantitatively limited surface water from a river, which makes the shadow price quite high. Taza, supplied from the Sebou river, has a very high shadow price of 4.02 DH/m³.

Taza represents the high economic return that can be expected from the use of an additional unit of surface water, reflecting the fact that at present there are limits in the quantity that can be supplied; this is different from the cases of Casablanca, Rabat and Salé which all use more abundant groundwater. The shadow prices for a number of cities are summarized in Table 4-7.

TABLE 4-7

Shadow Prices of Urban Water Use

	Shadow Price in DH per m³	Shadow Price in $ per m³
Mohamedia	4.07	0.45
Taza	4.02	0.45
Marrakesh	4.01	0.44
Al Jadida	3.68	0.41
Khmissat	3.65	0.41
Casablanca	1.61	0.18
Beni Mellal	1.59	0.18
Meknes	1.58	0.18
Settat	1.52	0.17
Rabat	1.46	0.16
Sale	1.43	0.16

Source: MEIAH-1 output—Base Scenario "business-as-usual"

Agricultural Shadow Prices

For the agricultural sector, the lower value of water, 0.36 DH/m³, suggests lower returns from agriculture than from the urban sector per unit of water. Indeed, the agricultural return is about a fifth of the urban return. This value also differs from one location to another, depending on the source of water, crop, production yields, and water use efficiency. Large cultivations (GHs) have a higher weighted average shadow price than small and medium ones (PMHs). But the economic value can be as high as 0.97 DH/m³ for some small-scale irrigated areas, such as Moyen Oum Er Rbia and Plateau Fez-Meknes. These are areas where the use of advanced techniques means greater efficiency in irrigation and high productivity. An example of a low shadow price, 0.02 DH/m³, is the large irrigated area (GH) at Doukkala. Doukkala, it may be noted, competes for the same water as Casablanca, with a far higher shadow price, located downstream on the Oum Er Rbia River.

These shadow prices have a close inverse relationship to the level of precipitation. During a drought period, the shadow prices are much higher than in wet seasons, because water supply is lower than water demand. Also, groundwater availability, as long as it is unconstrained by any restrictions on overpumping, amounts to an infinite availability of groundwater for any single year. This will therefore result in constant marginal cost of any extra unit of water supplied from the region's aquifers. Thus, the low value of the shadow price in the base scenario reflects the large groundwater availability for the demand nodes connected to the groundwater wells.

Reservoirs: Storage and Hydropower Generation

In the three-basin area (Oum Er Rbia, Bou Regrag and Sebou rivers), there are seventeen reservoirs that regulate the rivers and store the quantities of water not released to satisfy the surrounding demand nodes. Figure 4-10 illustrates the total monthly storage of these reservoirs; the majority of which generate hydropower. We have considered in the base case reservoirs with a generating capacity greater than 20 MW. However, because of high temperatures mainly in the months of July and August, up to 30% of reservoir water evaporates, amounting to a loss of 848 MCM. When this happens the reservoir shows the effects for the following 3–4 months until the rains start to fill it again. Because the irrigation season starts in the month of April, there is a noticeable drop in reservoir storage between March and April.

The type of optimization offered by the MEIAH DSS can help water planners to determine rules and schedules for the release of water from reservoirs, including for hydropower generation, which is an active sphere in the operation of the national water infrastructure. The reservoir Al Wahda, the largest in Morocco with a physical storage capacity of 3.73 BCM, is a good example. A flow of water, totaling 5.35 BCM, is largely stored up during the rainy months from December to March and then released in the month of April for both agricultural and urban use. The total hydropower

---

FIGURE 4-10

Total Monthly Reservoir Storage

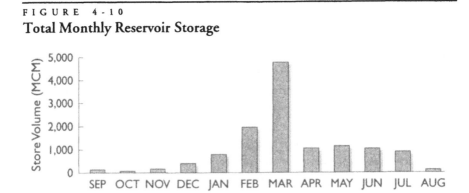

Source: MEIAH-1 output—Base Scenario "business-as-usual"

generated by Al Wahda, which is the highest dam in Morocco, will be 45.7 Million kWh for the year 2000, representing 50% of the total electricity generated by the six largest dams in Morocco. Figure 4-11 shows the monthly generation of hydropower by the six largest dams in the studied region.

Environmental Considerations

As noted earlier in presenting the "business-as-usual" character of the base case, the protection of the environment is not now considered a priority in Morocco. Thus, there is no monitoring of the over-exploitation of ground-water nor of the quantity of pollution put into a river from industrial and domestic waste, nor are saline-intrusion problems take into consideration in regulating the rivers.

Several environmental concerns need attention, and they can be intercon-nected in complex ways. Saline intrusion, for example, is an important form of damage, mainly to coastal aquifers. One might expect that ending all flow of water to the sea would represent a complete-use, zero-waste goal for Morocco. However, that is not the case, since without a positive discharge from the land to the sea, sea water will infiltrate coastal aquifers and largely destroy their usefulness through salt contamination. At present, despite the lack of any environmental constraints to preserve the saline/freshwater inter-faces of the aquifers, a quantity of 13.4 BCM flows to the ocean from Morocco, mainly from the Sebou river, which represents 96.8% of Morocco's

---

FIGURE 4-11

Monthly Hydropower Generation from the Six Largest Reservoirs

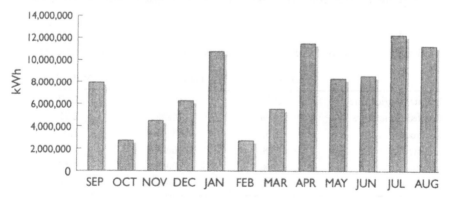

Source: MEIAH-1 output—Base Scenario "business-as-usual"

total discharge to the sea. This large quantity of flow at the end node of the Sebou, which it would be a mistake to look upon as lost water, is essentially due to heavy use of groundwater, instead of river water, along the Sebou. It could be advisable to adjust the balance of groundwater and river water use in this important basin, but it must be remembered that the quality of a river's water varies substantially with the volume of its flow. In the case of the Sebou, the large quantity of water retained along the river's course to the downstream end node is very important to keeping the river clean. With its large flow, the Sebou has a Biological Oxygen Demand (BOD) level of 1.9 milligram per liter (mg/l), which is acceptable from a health standard point of view (Kiely, 1997).

Water Accounts for the Base Scenario—Adjustment of Three-Basin Data to National Level

The results generated by applying the water-resource model to the three-basin area cover almost two-thirds of Morocco, both economically and hydrologically. For the purposes of this study, through careful use of a set of muliplication factors as discussed in the following paragraph, the situation in in the Oum Er Rbia, Bou Regrag, and Sebou Region has been extrapolated and generalized, in terms of both economic and water-related activities, to the entire country.

As summarized in Table 4-8, the water-related parameters are multiplied by different parameters depending on the particular economic sector. For the agricultural sector, the 577,017 hectares (ha) of irrigated area cover 60% of the entire irrigated land; thus, the multiplier is 1.67, while for rainfed agriculture, the multiplier is 2.22. In both cases, the agricultural areas outside the

TABLE 4-8

Multipliers to Adjust the Three Basin Region to the National Level

	Regional Level	National Level	Multiplier
Irrigated Agriculture	60%	100%	1.67
Rainfed Agriculture	45%	100%	2.22
Livestock	55%	100%	1.82
Industry	75%	100%	1.33
Services	70%	100%	1.43
Household	50%	100%	2.00

Source: MEIAH-1 output—Base Scenario "business-as-usual"

three-basin region are reckoned to have the same characteristics as those within it in terms of soil, water requirements, production yield, and climatic conditions, which at a level of practical approximation is the case. Half of urban household demand is located in the three-basin region; multiplying by a factor of two will enable the analysis to cover all the Moroccan households, while a factor of 1.33 suffices for industry, because 80% of the country's industrial establishments are in the studied three-basin region.

Primary Sources of Water

The information extracted from the regional optimization model and the multipliers provided to adjust it to cover the national scale are now used to determine the national hydrological cycle of water as well as the water accounts for each sector of the national economy.

Using output of the MEIAH-1 model, the Moroccan water cycle for the year 2000 is depicted in Figure 4-12 (also using the Moroccan water cycle of 1992 for comparison, shown in Figure 4-13), and the balancing of the overall water account is provided in Table 4-9. Morocco's annual rainfall is approximately 144 BCM. Evaporation accounts for a loss of about 127 BCM. In Figure 4-12, evaporation is equal to 133 BCM, which incorporates additionally the quantity of water evaporated and transpired from rainfed agriculture. Roughly 16 BCM enters the water cycle in the year 2000, with 3.2 BCM infiltrating aquifers and 2.6 BCM contributing to surface water, while 10 BCM is available for the rainfed agriculture of the country. The total water processed by the water utility totals 5.4 BCM, of which 1.6 BCM is pumped from groundwater and 3.7 BCM diverted from river streams. The rest of the mobilized groundwater resource is pumped directly from the sector itself: 27 MCM to industry and services, 1.5 BCM to irrigated agriculture and 145 MCM to livestock.

We divide the water universe into five economic sectors: rainfed agriculture, livestock, irrigated agriculture, industry and services, and domestic households. Each demands different quantities of water from different sources. After being allocated to the different sectors, 4.4 BCM re-infiltrates the groundwater, of which 404 MCM is reused in irrigated agriculture. Each of the five sectors has its own water account, described in the following sections.

Return Flows

The water used by the five different economic sectors can be consumed, evaporated or returned to the system, if it is not treated and reused within an

FIGURE 4-12
Water Budget for Morocco in MCM—Base Scenario

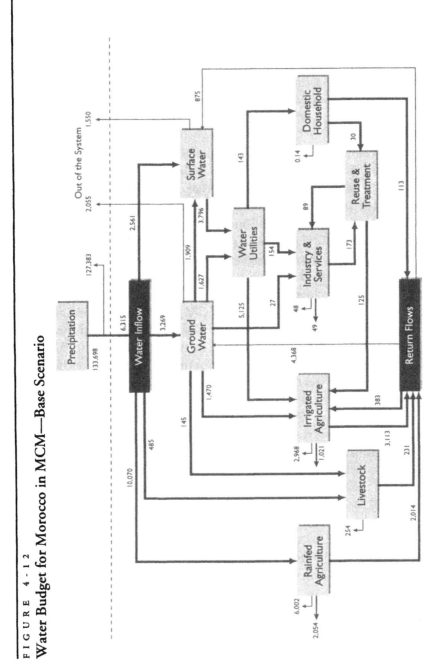

Source: MEIAH-1 output—Base Scenario "business-as-usual"

FIGURE 4-13

Water Cycle for Morocco in Billion m³ for 1995, Based on the World Bank Report, 1996a

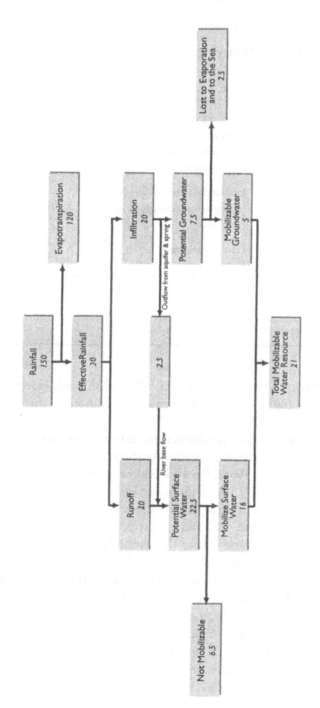

Source: MEIAH-1 output—Base Scenario "business-as-usual"

TABLE   4-9

Balancing the Overall Water Account

		in MCM
Evaporation	Non-beneficial evapotranspiration	127,383
	Beneficial evapotranspiration	6,002
	From irrigated agriculture	2,968
	From industry and services	48
	From domestic use	0.14
Consumption induced in the products	In rainfed agriculture production	2,054
	In irrigated agriculture production	1,043
	In industry	49
Out of the System	From groundwater	2,550
	From surface	1,550
Total		143,647
Precipitation		143,700

Source: MEIAH-1 output—Base Scenario business-as-usual

economic activity. The return flows are collected through either infiltration to groundwater (80%, 4.4 BCM), or through drainage to the surface water (875 MCM, equivalent to 16%).

There is an outflow from the aquifers to surface water that should be taken into consideration in the water cycle. As shown in Figure 4-13, the water cycle as analyzed by the World Bank for Morocco for the average rainfall year of 1995, estimates that 25% of the water infiltrated into the groundwater returns to surface water. This represents a quantity of 1.9 BCM, as shown in Figure 4-12. Also, Figure 4-12 shows that 33% of remaining groundwater flows to the ocean or evaporates to the atmosphere. This represents a non-mobilizable quantity of water equal to 2 BCM, of which it is assumed that only 205 MCM is evaporated and the rest flows to the ocean underground. The water stored in aquifers comes from infiltration from precipitation, as well as from return flows from the economic users through infiltration. This quantity is then allocated to different users, as shown in Figure 4-12.

Surface water represents the quantity of water in rivers and tributaries, which originates from precipitation (2.6 BCM), outflows from aquifers (1.9 BCM), and the 20% of the total return flows (875 MCM). This quantity is allocated among the different economic users, through the water utilities, after being reduced by the quantity that flows to the ocean. According to Figure 4-13, 29% of the surface water flows annually to the ocean, a quantity of 1.6 BCM.

Sectoral Water Accounts

If we disregard weather variability, the sectors of the economy can be considered to compete for a fixed annual quantity of surface water, but because extraction of groundwater is unrestricted in reality and therefore unconstrained in the base scenario model, the competition is less intense for groundwater. From MEIAH-1, the water optimization model, the quantity to be allocated among the different sectors is determined by the model's optimal overall solution. We can therefore generate a water account for each of the five sectors in an "average" year.

Industry and Services. This include all the industrial establishments around the cities, which require 91.68 MCM, as well as the services, e.g., tourism, water, and electricity services, administration, and other activities, which demand up to 42.9 MCM. It also includes water for hydropower generation, which returns fully to the cycle and is not consumed. Table 4-10 illustrates the water account for industry and services in MCM. Once water has been used by the Industry and Services sector, there is an economic value to it, which is represented by the shadow price of water to the next sector to use that water. In this case for the most part, the quantity of water labeled "Out" from the Industry and Services sector is multiplied by 1.784 DH/m^3, which is the shadow price of water for urban use. This economic value is used to develop the water input-output table described later on.

We have assumed that 80% of the water used in industry and services is internally recycled for an additional passage, or several, through the produc-

T A B L E   4 - 1 0

Water Account for Industry and Services, 1995

In	MCM	Out	MCM	Million DH
Precipitation	108	Embedded in Production	49	87
Groundwater	27	Recycling	173	309
Recycling	89	Losses	48	85

Source: Model output—Water Budget for Morocco for the Base Scenario

tion process for industries as well as for some services, such as hotels. This represents 173.43 MCM, or 308.72 Million DH.

Rainfed Agriculture: The water used in rainfed agriculture is directly retrieved from precipitation, and for a normal year, represents 10 BCM. 20% of this water infiltrates and drains into the ground, while 6 BCM evaporates; the rest is embedded in agricultural production. The latter mainly consists of cereals, fodder, and vegetables, as represented in Figure 4-14. The water account for rainfed agriculture is represented in Table 4-11.

Livestock: Morocco has a large and diversified reserve of livestock, representing approximately 22 million head, mainly raised for consumption within the country. Livestock, owned by farmers in both irrigated areas and rainfed areas, demands 630 MCM of water annually, of which 60% is from surface water and 40% from groundwater (Table 4-12)

Irrigated Agriculture: 85% of the water produced in Morocco is used for irrigation. This means 5.1 BCM diverted from rivers, 1.5 BCM pumped from groundwater, and 404 MCM re-used through return flows. Around

---

FIGURE 4-14

Rainfed Agriculture Production in '000 Tons for year 1995

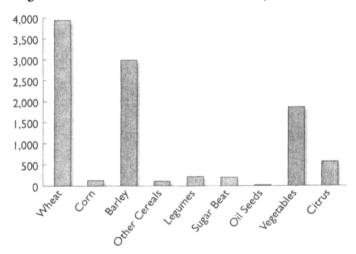

Source: Figure based on Nedeco study from 1994 (Royaume du Maroc, 1994)

20% of the water used in irrigation infiltrates through the ground or drains back to the main river. The accounting of water for the overall irrigation sector is represented in Table 4-13. For the economic value of water, the average shadow price used for irrigated agriculture is 0.36 DH/m³, but the input-output table used provides detailed information on the different irrigated crops. Using the output of the three-basin water model and the 1.67 multiplier to extend it to the national level, a water balance could be developed for irrigated agriculture. Table 4-14 summarizes the information for different forms of agricultural production.

TABLE 4-11

Water Account for Rainfed Agriculture, 1995

In	MCM	Out	MCM	Million DH
Precipitation	10,070	Embedded in Production	2,054	1,007
		Return Flows	2,014	987
		Evaporation	6,002	2,941

Source: Model output—Water Budget for Morocco for the Base Scenario

TABLE 4-12

Water Account for Livestock, 1995

In	MCM	Out	MCM	Million DH
Precipitation	485	Embedded in Production	109	53
Groundwater	145	Return Flows	376	184

Source: Model output—Water Budget for Morocco for the Base Scenario

TABLE 4-13

Water Account for Irrigated Agriculture, 1995

In	MCM	Out	MCM	Million DH
Surface Water	5,125	Embedded in Production	1,043	511
Groundwater	1,470	Return Flows	3,113	1,525
Return Flows	404	Evaporation	2,968	1,454
Recycling	125			

Source: Model output—Water Budget for Morocco for the Base Scenario

TABLE 4-14
Water Use in Irrigated Agriculture, 1995

| | In—Sources (MCM) | | | | Out (MCM) | | |
	Groundwater	Water Utility	Return Flows	Recycling	Embedded in Production	Evaporation	Return Flows
Wheat	168.48	587.52	46.35	14.28	119.59	340.20	356.83
Barley	255.50	890.99	70.29	21.65	181.37	515.92	541.15
Maize	47.59	165.95	13.09	4.03	33.78	96.09	100.79
Other Cereals	47.87	166.95	13.17	4.06	33.98	96.67	101.40
Legume	9.06	31.58	2.49	0.77	6.43	18.29	19.18
Fodder	113.61	396.19	31.25	9.63	80.65	229.41	240.63
Sugar Beat	129.62	452.00	35.66	10.98	92.01	261.73	274.52
Sugar Cane	70.63	246.30	19.43	5.99	50.14	142.62	149.59
SunFlower	8.97	31.29	2.47	0.76	6.37	18.12	19.00
Industrial Crop	12.57	43.84	3.46	1.07	8.92	25.39	26.63
Vegetables	139.41	486.16	38.35	11.81	98.96	281.51	295.27
Citrus	466.44	1626.57	128.31	39.53	331.10	941.86	987.90

Source: Model output—Water Budget for Morocco for the Base Scenario

According to the water-resource model, the cropping pattern in 60% of the irrigated areas of the country is determined by the optimal solution of the base scenario, described above. Only 2% of the 12.1 BCM of water for irrigation is embedded in production. The rest of the water returns to the system through return flows or evaporation and results in a change in the natural stock of water by the year 2000. For each type of crop, water is supplied from both surface and groundwater, and comes back to the system, through either evaporation or infiltration and drainage, if it is not consumed by the crop (Table 4-14).

Household Use: Morocco's population by the year 2000 will demand 143 MCM for household use, which returns fully to the system; only in southern Morocco, are there some projects for recycling this water for use in irrigation. The shadow price of water to households is 1.78 DH/m³, which gives some clue about the price level for water to households (Table 4-15).

Water Balance

The total water balance summarizes each water account for each particular economic sector. The water balance also has a detailed hydrological component, as shown earlier in Figure 4-12. The graph represents the path of water from each source to its use.

Water Input-Output Table for Morocco

To create the water input-output table for Morocco based on the methodology described in Chapter 3, we first use the aggregate input-output table from the 1995 Social Accounting Matrix (SAM), described above, and in

---

TABLE 4-15
Water Account for Households, 1995

In	MCM	Out	MCM	Million DH
Water Supply	143	Embedded in the Production	—	—
		Return Flows	113	201
		Recycling	30	54
		Evaporation	0.143	0.255

Source: Model output—Water Budget for Morocco for the Base Scenario

more detail in Appendix 3. The water balance extracted for the considered base scenario is then used to incorporate water into this traditional economic input-output table. Water is presented in billion cubic meters (BCM) in order to remain consistent with the SAM matrix which is in billion dirhams (BDH).

There are two "primary inputs," i.e., primary sources of water: groundwater and precipitation. As part of the economic sector, water-related activities represent water supply, recycling and sanitation, and return flows, which provide water to the fifteen economic sectors. The quantity allocated is shown in the previously defined sectoral water accounts. The final demand encompasses two columns that will close the water cycle. First, there is a large quantity of water that evaporates to the atmosphere and cannot be directly used within the year of study. Second, the quantity of water embedded in production is a drawdown from the natural stock of available water.

Taking into consideration the shadow prices of water for each of the economic sectors, return flows are evaluated in DH in order to capture both the quantity of water as well as the economic returns associated with it. Table 4-16 shows the newly defined water input-output table.

It is important in the input-output table to distinguish between transactions that are end results of economic activity and those that are intermediate in economic activity, or that represent inputs absorbed by other sectors in the production process. It is conventional to divide the table into four quadrants: intermediate demand, final demand, primary input, and primary input to final demand. The water input-output table that we have developed is divided accordingly.

Intermediate Demand

The intermediate demand quadrant (Quadrant I) refers to the flows within the sectors themselves, which correspond to the intermediate demand of each sector. For example, if we look at the column of vegetables (Column 11), the intermediate input to this irrigated production includes 5.313 billion dirham (BDH) from irrigated vegetables, 1.842 BDH from rainfed agriculture, and 2.609 BDH from industrial output. Also, this sector necessitates water input from water-related activities; 0.0358 BCM is provided from the irrigation supply systems, and 0.038 BCM from return flows, which represent groundwater pumping of the water that has re-infiltrated into the ground after a use, in addition to an original groundwater supply of 0.139 BCM. Column 11, requires besides these components, some primary inputs which are located in the second quadrant, and will be explained below. The row corresponding to irrigated vegetables captures the output of the sector.

From the table, we can see that vegetables provide an input of 5.313 BDH to the sector itself, 0.304 BDH to rainfed agriculture, and 0.550 BDH to the industrial sector. Also, 20% of the water used in the production of vegetables reappears in the table as return flows; this quantity is equal to 0.402 BCM. However, this quantity of water has an economic value to it, which is the shadow price of water of 0.36 DH/m^3. This quantity enters the input-output table in value terms and is equal to the total of 0.145 BDH in the table. This is similar for the economic sectors; the only difference for water-related activities is that the output flows are in physical units. Water-related activities comprise the water utilities from which the water flows to all the intermediate sectors, and the return flows, which also flow to the intermediate sectors in BCM. Recycled and reused water, with a quantity of 0.089 BCM, flows only to industries and services, as none of the other sectors uses recycled water for production processes in Morocco's "business-as-usual" base case.

Final Demand

The final demand quadrant (Quadrant II) captures the flows of output from both the economic sectors and the water-related activities to destinations other than inputs to other sectors in the economy, or in other words, to the final use of goods and services as far as the economy is concerned. The final demand represents the expenditure side of the national account. For the purpose of simplicity, we have chosen 14 final demand sectors. Twelve of these sectors were provided from the aggregation of the SAM, while the two last sectors, referring to evaporation of water and the change in the natural stock of water, correspond to change in the water cycle which does not reappear as an input within the one-year period of the cycle; this quantity is not lost, but leads to a change in the natural stock.

The column "evaporation" refers to water that has evaporated from the economic sectors; the elements of this column are in value terms, determined by multiplying the physical quantity of water evaporated by the shadow price. For instance, for the rain-fed agriculture, a value of 24.025 BDH is evaporated, which represents 8.169 BCM multiplied by 2.941 DH/m^3. Change in stock also refers to water that is embedded in final products. In the industry and services sectors, 0.047 BCM is the quantity that gets transformed during the production chain, which represents 0.085 BDH, as shown in the table. For water-related activities, the only entry to "change in the natural

TABLE 4-16

Water Input-Output Table (in Billion DH and Billion m³)

		1	2	3	4	5	6	7	8
		WHEAT	BARLEY	MAIZE	OTHCER	LEGUME	FODDER	SGRBT	SGRCN
1	WHEAT	2.198		0.003					
2	BARLEY		0.705						
3	MAIZE			0.340					
4	OTHCER				0.109				
5	LEGUME					0.169			
6	FODDER						0.845		
7	SGRBT							0.798	
8	SGRCN								0.300
9	SNFLW								
10	OINDCRI								
11	VEGET								
12	CITR								
13	AGR-RAIN	12.823	9.088	1.746	0.415	2.138	0.434	0.230	0.000
14	LVSTK								
15	INDUSTRY	0.591	0.089	0.032	0.013	0.030	0.055	0.291	0.015
16	WATER NETWORK	0.433	0.656	0.122	0.123	0.023	0.292	0.333	0.181
17	SANITATION & REUSE								
18	RETURN FLOWS	0 046	0.070	0.013	0.013	0.002	0.031	0.036	0.019
19	PRECIPITATION	0.000	0.000	0.000	0.000	0.000	0.000	0.000	0.000
20	GROUNDWATER	0.168	0.256	0.048	0.048	0.009	0.114	0.130	0.071
21	WATER-HH								
22	HOUSEHOLD	0.169	0.088	0.083	0.012	0.044	0.229	0.174	0.065
23	CAPITAL	0.392	0.100	0.026	0.010	0.011	0.030	0.043	0.005
24	LAND-R	0 661	0.265	0.104	0.019	0.058	0.264	0.136	0.059
25	FAC-NTB								
26	GOV								
27	ROW	2.058	0.263	0.014		0.013			
28	SAV-INV								
29	DIRTAX								
30	INDTAX	0.030	0.010	0.005	0.002	0.001	0.009	0.044	0.018
31	SUBSIDY								
32	TARIFF	1.126	0.108	0.006					
33	NTB	3.271							
34	TOTAL	23.67	10.88	2.46	0.62	2.48	2.11	1.80	0.58

WHEAT= Irrigated Wheat; BARLEY= Irrigated Barley; MAIZE= Irrigated Maize; OTHCER= Irrigated Cereals; LEGUME= Irrigated Legumes; FODDER= Irrigated Fodder; SGRBT= Irrigated Sugar Beet; SGRCN= Irrigated Sugar Cane; SNFLW = Irrigated Sun Flower ;
OINDCRI = Irrigated Industrial Agriculture Production ; VEGET =Irrigated Vegeables ; CITR = Irrigated Citrus ; RAINFED = rainfed agriculture ; LVST= Livestock ; INDUSTRY = Industry and Services; WATER- HH =Household water; HOUSEHOLD = Income to households;
LAND R = Land Rents; FAC-NTB = Factor for Non-trade Barriers; GOV =Government; ROW=Rest of the World; SAV-INV=Saving and Investments; DIRTAX= Direct Tax; INDTAX= Indirect Tax; TARIFF = Water Charges; NTB=Non-Trade Barriers

Source: Water related activities have been added to Table 4-3

9 SNFLW	10 OINDCRI	11 VEGET	12 CITR	13 AGR-RAIN	14 LVSTK	15 WATER INDUSTRY	16 SANIT-NETWORKS	17 RETURN REUSE	18 FLOWS	
				0.771	0.385	6.774			0.175	1
					0.715	2.361			0.265	2
				0.027	0.326	0.874			0.049	3
				0.012	0.497	0.006			0.050	4
				0.142		0.401			0.009	5
				0.029	1.239	0.000			0.118	6
				0.015		0.990			0.135	7
						0.283			0.073	8
0.039				0.005		0.340			0.009	9
0.001	0.468			0.040		1.742			0.013	10
0.583		5.313		0.304		0.550			0.145	11
			5.961	0.110		2.908			0.484	12
0.583	0.389	1.842	4.133			2.661			0.987	13
						24.717			0.184	14
0.003	0.178	2.609	1.505	10.019	11.960	909.101		0.309		15
0.023	0.032	0.358	1.198		0.218	0.154				16
						0.089				17
0.002	0.003	0.038	0.128			0.000				18
0.000	0.000	0.000	0.000	10.070	0	0.000				19
0.009	0.013	0.139	0.466		0.145	0.027				20
							0.223			21
0.005	0.068	1.100	1.362	5.690	2.635	119.265	10.900	0.050		22
0.004	0.015	0.104	0.152	2.543	4.671	72.418				23
0.012	0.082	0.481	0.831	16.329	1.676					24
										25
										26
0.118	1.528	0.448	0.062			71.610				27
										28
										29
	0.004	0.041	0.050	0.444	0.615	22.255				30
										31
0.182	0.627	0.023	0.027			18.350				32
						6.322				33
0.96	3.45	12.28	15.69	36.48	24.72	78.65				34

continued

TABLE 4-16

Water Input-Output Table (in Billion DH and Billion m³) *(continued)*

		19	20	21	22	23	24	25
		HOUSEHOLD	CAPITAL	LAND-R	FAC-NTB	GOV	ROW	SAV-INV
1	WHEAT	11.511					0.133	1.000
2	BARLEY	6.159					0.940	
3	MAIZE	0.891						
4	OTHCER	0.000						
5	LEGUME	1.597					0.174	
6	FODDER	0.000						
7	SGRBT	0.000						
8	SGRCN	0.000						
9	SNFLW	0.438					0.085	
10	OINDCRI	1.005					0.194	
11	VEGET	2.988					3.128	
12	CITR	5.102	0.000	0.000	0.000	0.000	1.607	0.000
13	AGR-RAIN	33.818						
14	LVSTK	14.607					0.461	
15	INDUSTRY	171.602				40.781	54.4	59.415
16	WATER NETWORK	0.143						
17	SANITATION & REUSE							
18	RETURN FLOWS							
19	PRECIPITATION							
20	GROUNDWATER	0.080						
21	WATER-HH							
22	HOUSEHOLD	147.803	74.585	20.975	9.593	7.501	21.396	0.000
23	CAPITAL	0.000						
24	LAND-R	0.000	0.000	0.000	0.000	0.000	0.000	0.000
25	FAC-NTB	0.000						
26	GOV	1.871	5.938					
27	ROW	4.674				7.947		
28	SAV-INV	44.959				7.772	6.684	
29	DIRTAX	15.214						
30	INDTAX	0.000						
31	SUBSIDY	0.000				3.195		
32	TARIFF	0.000						
33	NTB	0.000						
34	TOTAL	415.814	80.52	20.975	9.59	67.20	88.73	59.42

For label meanings, please refer to legend on previous page

Source: Water related activities have been added to Table 4-3

26 DIRTAX	27 INDTAX	28 SUBSIDY	29 TARIFF	30 NTB	31 EVAPORATION	32 CHANGE NAT. STOCK	33 TOTAL	
		1.893			0.167	0.059	25.1	1
					0.253	0.089	11.5	2
					0.047	0.017	2.6	3
					0.047	0.017	0.7	4
					0.009	0 003	2.5	5
					0.112	0.040	2.4	6
					0.128	0.045	2.1	7
					0.070	0.025	0.8	8
		0.055			0.009	0.003	1.0	9
					0.012	0.004	3.5	10
					0.138	0.048	12.6	11
0.000	0.000	0.000	0.000	0.000	0.462	0.162	16.8	12
					2.941	1.007	75.2	13
					0.053	0.000	40.0	14
		1.247			0.085	0.024	1,264.3	15
							4.3	16
						0.223	0.312	17
							0.4043	18
							11.0	19
							1.72	20
							0.22	21
0.000	0.000	0.000	0.000	0.000			423.8	22
							80.5	23
0.000	0.000	0.000	0.000	0.000			21.0	24
				9.593			9.6	25
15.214	23.528		20.449				67.0	26
							88.7	27
							59.4	28
							15.2	29
							23.5	30
							3.2	31
		0.000					20.4	32
							9.6	33
15.21	23.53	3.20	20.45	9.59			2,292	34

stock" is from recycling and water reuse, as a large quantity of this category is injected into the ocean, or is dumped in a source that is unused within the one-year period of the analysis. The cell corresponding to input from the recycling and reuse of water is in physical units, equal to 0.223 BCM.

Of the 12 components in the final-demand category, household consumption refers to goods, services, and water resources purchased for consumption by households. Reading down column 19, households purchase 11.511 BDH of wheat, 6.159 BDH of barley, and other irrigated products, 33.818 BDH of rainfed agriculture production, and 171.602 BDH of services and industrial production. Also, households consume 0.143 BCM of water, supplied by the water utilities. These entries together with those in quadrant IV represent the regional consumption function. Column 19 represents a source of detailed information on regional household consumption patterns for both economic goods and water resources. Column 24 records exports to the "rest of the world." This column allows the analyst to identify the significant exporting sectors in the economy. It seems that the largest export of irrigated agriculture is vegetables, worth 3.128 BDH, and plantation products (citrus), worth 1.607 BDH. Also, up to 54.4 BDH of industry and services are oriented towards the international market.

Primary Inputs

The primary input quadrant (Quadrant III) lists inputs into each intermediate sector which originate outside the production system. This quadrant is traditionally divided into a number of rows that represent the income-earned side of the national accounts. The role of the primary inputs quadrant is twofold. It first illustrates the source of primary input by sector, and for each row, the income earned by each primary factor of production from each production sector. Table 4-16 shows the elements of the primary input, which are: salaries and wages of households, capital, land, government, imports from the rest of the world, savings, direct and indirect taxes, and tariffs. By incorporating water into the system, we have added the primary inputs of water in its two forms: precipitation and groundwater. Row 21 refers to water used by households, of which only a part, 0.223 BCM, flows into the water utilities. This happens when there is a recycling of sewage water for use in the garden, for example, but it is entered as a change in the natural stock of the one-year cycle. Another primary input to the water-related activities is the salary and wages of the labor working in the water utilities and involved in water collection and supply. The governmental subsidies allocated to each of the sectors of the economy enter as a cost to the government, which is then allocated through governmental costs, capital, or other type of primary input. Other categories of the primary input do not enter the water-related columns, but are inputs to the other sectors of the economy, such as land, imports, and taxes.

Primary Inputs to the Final Demand

The primary-input-to-final-demand quadrant (Quadrant IV) illustrates the transactions that directly link the primary inputs and final demand quadrant, without transmission through the production system or the intermediate quadrant. It records for example, the extraction of groundwater by households through private wells, which reaches 0.080 BCM. Households also purchase 4.674 BDH of imported consumer goods, and total household income through wages, for instance, is 147.803 BDH.

Hydro-Economic National Output

The way water enters in different forms in the four quadrants distinguishes the different functions and inputs of the sector. As in the first economic transactions, there is an important distinction between four types of hydrologic transactions: the first type represents quantities that are determined exogenously by economic or natural forces external to the economy and the water sector represented by the table in the final-demand quadrant; the second type shows the linkages and captures the inter-sectoral flows of both water and the economy, which is represented by the intermediate quadrant; the third type shows the usage of inputs that are of primary need to the national economy, which comprises the water resources as well, and this is the primary input quadrant; and the fourth type corresponds to primary inputs, which are not directly linked to the regional production system. The last column of the table records the total output of each sector. Rows 1 through 15 are in value terms, referring to the economic sectors, while rows 16 through 21 are in material units and represent the total quantity of water produced from the different sources.

It is important to note that the sum of the total output of both the economic sectors is slightly greater than the gross national output. It is equal to 2,291 BDH, as we are considering a system that includes both economic and hydrological accounts. This system merges both the economic system and the hydrological balance. By adding to it the water-related activity, multiplied by the shadow prices defined earlier for the different sources of water, we obtain a new indicator that evaluates in economic units what we have previously called the hydro-economic system. This gross output assesses both economic growth and water availability and allocation, and it can be used as an indicator of hydro-economic development.

Water Input-Output Table

The transactions shown in Table 4-16 represent an accounting statement for the Moroccan economy and its water resources for the year 2000. This section deals with the first step in the transition from the transactions table, which is of limited analytical application, to the structure of an input-output model. Such a transition involves the calculation basis of some technical coefficients as an analytical and algebraic manipulation of the input-output table for the input-output analysis. The previously described water input-output table is organized in such a way that its total output is homogeneous for the different sectors. Using this table, we can determine the Leontief coefficient matrix, and undertake an impact-assessment analysis, through the generation of a set of multipliers and ratios. Also, we generate an economic demand curve through the Linear Program model described earlier in Chapter 3.

Technology Coefficient Matrix

The last column of Table 4-16 represents the total output of each sector and will be used to construct the Leontief matrix by dividing each cell of a given row by the total output of this row. We obtain a new input-output table, shown in Table 4-17. For example for the column of livestock, all the cells of column 14 are divided by the total output, 40 BDH, which represents the sum of row 14 of livestock. Similarly for the water utility, all the cells in column 16 are divided by the total output of the water utility computed for row 16, which is 4.3 BCM.

In each column of the coefficient matrix, the coefficients represent the amount of input required by each sector shown at the left of the table, for each DH of output. For example, each DH of output from livestock requires:

        0.010 DH in inputs from irrigated wheat

        0.018 DH in inputs from irrigated barley

        0.008 DH in inputs from irrigated maize

        0.012 DH in inputs from other cereals

        0.031 DH in inputs from fodder

        0.299 DH in input from industrial production and services

        0.005 m^3 in input from the water system.

And in addition:

0.00363 m³ of groundwater

0.066 DH in salaries and wages

0.117 DH in capital

0.042 DH in land

0.015 DH in indirect taxes.

These figures represent the direct purchases of inputs, and they do not include indirect effects. Each column of the matrix relating the production sectors (column 1 through 18) represents a pattern of input purchases; this corresponds to the amount purchased from each sector, including households, land, taxes, water, etc.

Column 19, corresponding to households, in Table 4-17, shows the national consumption function, which represents each DH of household consumption spent locally on the products of each sector, as well as on water consumption, and the amount spent on imported products. Similarly, column 24, Rest of the World, provides the national export function by defining the proportion of exports from each source. As there are no cross-border water resources, there are no international transactions involving water-related activities. However, if the table were at the regional level, for instance if we had looked at the Sebou river basin, a quantity of water would have been exported from the Sebou region to the Oum Er Rbia river basin.

Looking at the first quadrant of Table 4-17, as represented in Table 4-18, we see that this could also be divided into four parts referring to different combinations of the economic sectors and the water-related activities. We therefore distinguish among the following:

■ Inputs from a given economic sector per unit of output from the economic sectors, which are in DH of input per DH of output. For example, in the industry and service sectors, this refers to all the DH input from the sectors of row 1 through row 15.

■ Input from the economic sectors per unit of output from the water-related activities; this is in DH of input per m³ of output of water from the water utilities, recycling and reuse and return flows. In the table, this corresponds to rows 1 through 15 and columns 16 through 18.

■ Input from water-related sectors per unit of output from economic sectors; this is in m³ of input per DH of output, i.e., the quantity of water required per DH of output. For example for 1 DH of sugar beet output,

TABLE 4-17

Direct Input Coefficient Matrix

		1 WHEAT	2 BARLEY	3 MAIZE	4 OTHCER	5 LEGUME	6 FODDER	7 SGRBT	8 SGRCN
1	WHEAT	0.088	0.000	0.001	0.000	0.000	0.000	0.000	0.000
2	BARLEY	0.000	0.061	0.000	0.000	0.000	0.000	0.000	0.000
3	MAIZE	0.000	0.000	0.132	0.000	0.000	0.000	0.000	0.000
4	OTHCER	0.000	0.000	0.000	0.147	0.000	0.000	0.000	0.000
5	LEGUME	0.000	0.000	0.000	0.000	0.068	0.000	0.000	0.000
6	FODDER	0.000	0.000	0.000	0.000	0.000	0.355	0.000	0.000
7	SGRBT	0.000	0.000	0.000	0.000	0.000	0.000	0.378	0.000
8	SGRCN	0.000	0.000	0.000	0.000	0.000	0.000	0.000	0.400
9	SNFLW	0.000	0.000	0.000	0.000	0.000	0.000	0.000	0.000
10	OINDCRI	0.000	0.000	0.000	0.000	0.000	0.000	0.000	0.000
11	VEGET	0.000	0.000	0.000	0.000	0.000	0.000	0.000	0.000
12	CITR	0.000	0.000	0.000	0.000	0.000	0.000	0.000	0.000
13	AGR-RAIN	0.512	0.791	0.679	0.562	0.853	0.182	0.109	0.000
14	LVSTK	0.000	0.000	0.000	0.000	0.000	0 000	0.000	0.000
15	INDUSTRY	0.024	0.008	0.013	0.018	0.012	0.023	0.138	0.020
16	WATER NETWORK	0.017	0.057	0.048	0.167	0.009	0.123	0.158	0.241
17	SANITATION & REUSE	0.000	0.000	0.000	0.000	0 000	0.000	0.000	0.000
18	RETURN FLOWS	0.002	0.006	0.005	0.018	0 001	0.013	0.017	0.026
19	PRECIPITATION	0.000	0.000	0.000	0.000	0.000	0.000	0.000	0.000
20	GROUNDWATER	0.007	0.022	0.019	0.065	0.004	0.048	0.061	0.094
21	WATER-HH	0.000	0.000	0.000	0.000	0.000	0.000	0.000	0.000
22	HOUSEHOLD	0.007	0.008	0.032	0.016	0.018	0.096	0.083	0.087
23	CAPITAL	0.016	0.009	0.010	0.013	0.004	0.013	0.020	0.007
24	LAND-R	0.026	0.023	0.041	0.026	0.023	0.111	0.065	0.079
25	FAC-NTB	0.000	0.000	0.000	0.000	0.000	0.000	0.000	0.000
26	GOV	0.000	0.000	0.000	0.000	0.000	0.000	0.000	0.000
27	ROW	0.082	0.023	0.006	0.000	0.005	0.000	0.000	0.000
28	SAV-INV	0.000	0.000	0.000	0.000	0.000	0.000	0.000	0.000
29	DIRTAX	0.000	0.000	0.000	0.000	0.000	0.000	0.000	0.000
30	INDTAX	0.001	0.001	0.002	0.002	0.000	0.004	0.021	0.023
31	SUBSIDY	0.000	0.000	0.000	0.000	0.000	0.000	0.000	0.000
32	TARIFF	0.045	0.009	0.002	0.000	0.000	0.000	0.000	0.000
33	NTB	0.130	0.000	0.000	0.000	0.000	0.000	0.000	0.000
34	TOTAL	0.944	0.947	0.956	0.846	0.991	0.887	0.854	0.777

For label meanings, please refer to legend in Table 4-16

Source: Computed from Table 4-16, by dividing each cell of a given row by the total output of this row

9 SNFLW	10 OINDCRI	11 VEGET	12 CITR	13 AGR-RAIN	14 LVSTK	15 INDUSTRY	16 WATER NETWORKS	17 SANIT- REUSE	18 RETURN FLOWS	
0.000	0.000	0.000	0.000	0.010	0.010	0.005	0.000	0.000	0.432	1
0.000	0.000	0.000	0.000	0.000	0.018	0.002	0.000	0.000	0.656	2
0.000	0.000	0.000	0.000	0.000	0.008	0.001	0.000	0.000	0.122	3
0.000	0.000	0.000	0.000	0.000	0.012	0.000	0.000	0.000	0.123	4
0.000	0.000	0.000	0.000	0.002	0.000	0.000	0.000	0.000	0.023	5
0.000	0.000	0.000	0.000	0.000	0.031	0.000	0.000	0.000	0.292	6
0.000	0.000	0.000	0.000	0.000	0.000	0.001	0.000	0.000	0.333	7
0.000	0.000	0.000	0.000	0.000	0.000	0.0002	0.000	0.000	0.181	8
0.040	0.000	0.000	0.000	0.000	0.000	0.000	0.000	0.000	0.023	9
0.001	0.135	0.000	0.000	0.001	0.000	0.001	0.000	0.000	0.032	10
0.000	0.000	0.421	0.000	0.004	0.000	0.000	0.000	0.000	0.358	11
0.000	0.000	0.000	0.355	0.001	0.000	0.002	0.000	0.000	1.197	12
0.593	0.112	0.146	0.246	0.000	0.000	0.002	0.000	0.000	2.441	13
0.000	0.000	0.000	0.000	0.000	0.000	0.020	0.000	0.000	0.455	14
0.004	0.051	0.207	0.090	0.133	0.299	0.719	0.000	0.989	0.000	15
0.023	0.009	0.028	0.071	0.000	0.005	0.000	0.000	0.000	0.000	16
0.000	0.000	0.000	0.000	0.000	0.000	0.000	0.000	0.000	0.000	17
0.003	0.001	0.003	0.008	0.000	0.000	0.000	0.000	0.000	0.000	18
0.000	0.000	0.000	0.000	0.000	0.000	0.000	0.0	0.000	0.000	19
0.009	0.004	0.011	0.028	0.000	0.004	0.000	0.000	0.000	0.000	20
0.000	0.000	0.000	0.000	0.000	0.000	0.000	0.052	0.000	0.000	21
0.005	0.020	0.087	0.081	0.076	0.066	0.094	2.540	0.160	0.000	22
0.004	0.004	0.008	0.009	0.034	0.117	0.057	0.000	0.000	0.000	23
0.012	0.023	0.038	0.049	0.217	0.042	0.000	0.000	0.000	0.000	24
0.000	0.000	0.000	0.000	0.000	0.000	0.000	0.000	0.000	0.000	25
0.000	0.000	0.000	0.000	0.000	0.000	0.000	0.000	0.000	0.000	26
0.120	0.439	0.036	0.004	0.000	0.000	0.057	0.000	0.000	0.000	27
0.000	0.000	0.000	0.000	0.000	0.000	0.000	0.000	0.000	0.000	28
0.000	0.000	0.000	0.000	0.000	0.000	0.000	0.000	0.000	0.000	29
0.000	0.001	0.003	0.003	0.006	0.015	0.018	0.000	0.000	0.000	30
0.000	0.000	0.000	0.000	0.000	0.000	0.000	0.000	0.000	0.000	31
0.186	0.180	0.002	0.002	0.000	0.000	0.015	0.000	0.000	0.000	32
0.000	0.000	0 000	0.000	0.000	0.000	0.005	0.000	0.000	0.000	33
0.978	0.991	0.974	0.934	0.485	0.618	0.062	0.000	0.000	0.000	34

continued

TABLE 4-17

Direct Input Coefficient Matrix *(continued)*

		19	20	21	22	23	24	25
		HOUSEHOLD	CAPITAL	LAND-R	FAC-NTB	GOV	ROW	SAV-INV
1	WHEAT	0.027	0.000	0.000	0.000	0.000	0.001	0.017
2	BARLEY	0.015	0.000	0.000	0.000	0.000	0.011	0.000
3	MAIZE	0.002	0.000	0.000	0.000	0.000	0.000	0.000
4	OTHCER	0.000	0.000	0.000	0.000	0.000	0.000	0.000
5	LEGUME	0.004	0.000	0.000	0.000	0.000	0.002	0.000
6	FODDER	0.000	0.000	0.000	0.000	0.000	0.000	0.000
7	SGRBT	0.000	0.000	0.000	0.000	0.000	0.000	0.000
8	SGRCN	0.000	0.000	0.000	0.000	0.000	0.000	0.000
9	SNFLW	0.001	0.000	0.000	0.000	0.000	0.001	0.000
10	OINDCRI	0.002	0.000	0.000	0.000	0.000	0.002	0.000
11	VEGET	0.007	0.000	0.000	0.000	0.000	0.035	0.000
12	CITR	0.012	0.000	0.000	0.000	0.000	0.018	0.000
13	AGR-RAIN	0.080	0.000	0.000	0.000	0.000	0.000	0.000
14	LVSTK	0.034	0.000	0.000	0.000	0.000	0.000	0.000
15	INDUSTRY	0.405	0.000	0.000	0.000	0.609	0.613	1.000
16	WATER NETWORK	0.000	0.000	0.000	0.000	0.000	0.000	0.000
17	SANITATION & REUSE	0.000	0.000	0.000	0.000	0.000	0.000	0.000
18	RETURN FLOWS	0.000	0.000	0.000	0.000	0.000	0.000	0.000
19	PRECIPITATION	0.000	0.000	0.000	0.000	0.000	0.000	0.000
20	GROUNDWATER	0.000	0.000	0.000	0.000	0.000	0.000	0.000
21	WATER-HH	0.000	0.000	0.000	0.000	0.000	0.000	0.000
22	HOUSEHOLD	0.349	0.926	1.000	1.000	0.112	0.241	0.000
23	CAPITAL	0.000	0.000	0.000	0.000	0.000	0.000	0.000
24	LAND-R	0.000	0.000	0.000	0.000	0.000	0.000	0.000
25	FAC-NTB	0.000	0.000	0.000	0.000	0.000	0.000	0.000
26	GOV	0.004	0.074	0.000	0.000	0.000	0.000	0.000
27	ROW	0.011	0.000	0.000	0.000	0.119	0.000	0.000
28	SAV-INV	0.106	0.000	0.000	0.000	0.116	0.075	0.000
29	DIRTAX	0.036	0.000	0.000	0.000	0.000	0.000	0.000
30	INDTAX	0.000	0.000	0.000	0.000	0.000	0.000	0.000
31	SUBSIDY	0.000	0.000	0.000	0.000	0.048	0.000	0.000
32	TARIFF	0.000	0.000	0.000	0.000	0.000	0.000	0.000
33	NTB	0.000	0.000	0.000	0.000	0.000	0.000	0.000
34	TOTAL	0.981	1.000	1.000	1.000	1.003	1.000	1.000

For label meanings, please refer to legend in Table 4-16

Source: Computed from Table 4-16, by dividing each cell of a given row by the total output of this row

26	27	28	29	30	31	32 CHGE NAT.	33	
DIRTAX	INDTAX	SUBSIDY	TARIFF	NTB	EVAPORATION	STOCK	TOTAL	
0.000	0.000	0.592	0.000	0.000	0.000	0.000	2.184	1
0.000	0.000	0.000	0.000	0.000	0.000	0.000	2.762	2
0.000	0.000	0.000	0.000	0.000	0.000	0.000	3.266	3
0.000	0.000	0.000	0.000	0.000	0.000	0.000	4.283	4
0.000	0.000	0.000	0.000	0.000	0.000	0.000	5.099	5
0.000	0.000	0.000	0.000	0.000	0.000	0.000	6.678	6
0.000	0.000	0.000	0.000	0.000	0.000	0.000	7.712	7
0.000	0.000	0.000	0.000	0.000	0.000	0.000	8.581	8
0.000	0.000	0.017	0.000	0.000	0.000	0.000	9.082	9
0.000	0.000	0.000	0.000	0.000	0.000	0.000	10.174	10
0.000	0.000	0.000	0.000	0.000	0 000	0.000	11.826	11
0.000	0.000	0.000	0.000	0.000	0.000	0.000	13.586	12
0.000	0.000	0.000	0.000	0.000	0.000	0.000	20.309	13
0.000	0.000	0.144	0.000	0.000	0.000	0.000	14.654	14
0.000	0.000	0.390	0.000	0.000	0.000	0.000	20.762	15
0.000	0.000	0.000	0.000	0.000	0.000	0.000	16.958	16
0.000	0.000	0.000	0.000	0.000	0.000	0.000	17.000	17
0.000	0.000	0.000	0.000	0.000	0.000	0 000	18.102	18
0.000	0.000	0.000	0.000	0.000	0.000	0.000	19.146	19
0.000	0.000	0.000	0.000	0.000	0.000	0.000	20.375	20
0.000	0.000	0.000	0.000	0.000	0.000	0.000	21.052	21
0.000	0.000	0.000	0.000	0.000	0.000	0.000	29.103	22
0.000	0.000	0.000	0.000	0.000	0.000	0.000	23.324	23
0.000	0.000	0.000	0.000	0.000	0.000	0.000	24.775	24
0.000	0.000	0.000	0.000	1.000	0.000	0.000	26.000	25
1.000	1.000	0.000	1.000	0.000	0.000	0.000	29.078	26
0.000	0.000	0.000	0.000	0.000	0.000	0.000	27.900	27
0.000	0.000	0.000	0.000	0.000	0.000	0.000	28.297	28
0.000	0.000	0.000	0.000	0.000	0.000	0.000	29.036	29
0.000	0.000	0.000	0.000	0.000	0.000	0.000	30.101	30
0.000	0.000	0.000	0.000	0.000	0.000	0.000	31.048	31
0.000	0.000	0.000	0.000	0.000	0.000	0.000	32.440	32
0.000	0.000	0.000	0.000	0.000	0.000	0.000	33.135	33
1.000	1.000	1.000	1.000	1.000	0.000	0.000	58.229	34

TABLE 4 - 1 8
Upper Quadrant of the Direct Input Coefficient Matrix

	WHEAT	BARLEY	MAIZE	OTHCER	LEGUME	FODDER	SGRBT	SGRCN
WHEAT	0.088	—	0.001	—	—	—	—	—
BARLEY	—	0.061	—	—	—	—	—	—
MAIZE	—	—	0.132	—	—	—	—	—
OTHCER	—	—	—	0.147	—	—	—	—
LEGUME	—	—	—	—	0.068	—	—	—
FODDER	—	—	—	—	—	0.355	—	—
SGRBT	—	—	—	—	—	—	0.378	—
SGRCN	—	—	—	—	—	—	—	0.400
SNFLW	—	—	—	—	—	—	—	—
OINDCRI	—	—	—	—	—	—	—	—
VEGET	—	—	—	—	—	—	—	—
CITR	—	—	—	—	—	—	—	—
AGR-RAIN	0.512	0.791	0.679	0.562	0.853	0.182	0.109	—
LVSTK	—	—	—	—	—	—	—	—
INDUSTRY	0.024	0.008	0.013	0.018	0.012	0.023	0.138	0.020
WATER NETWORK	0.017	0.057	0.048	0.167	0.009	0.123	0.158	0.241
SANITATION & REUSE	—	—	—	—	—	—	—	—
RETURN FLOWS	0.002	0.006	0.005	0.018	0.001	0.013	0.017	0.026

Quadrant III—m³/DH

For label meanings, please refer to legend in Table 4-16
Source: Represents the left-upper quadrant of Table 4-17

Quadrant I—DH/DH

Quadrant II—DH/m³

	SNFLW	OINDCRI	VEGET	CITR	AGR-RAIN	LVSTK	INDUSTRY	WATER NETWORKS	SANIT-REUSE	RETURN FLOWS
	—	—	—	—	0.010	0.010	0.005	—	—	0.432
	—	—	—	—	—	0.018	0.002	—	—	0.656
	—	—	—	—	0.000	0.008	0.001	—	—	0.122
	—	—	—	—	0.000	0.012	0.000	—	—	0.123
	—	—	—	—	0.002	—	0.000	—	—	0.023
	—	—	—	—	0.000	0.031	—	—	—	0.292
	—	—	—	—	0.000	—	0.001	—	—	0.333
	—	—	—	—	—	—	0.00022	—	—	0.181
	0.040	—	—	—	0.000	—	0.000	—	—	0.023
	0.001	0.135	—	—	0.001	—	0.001	—	—	0.032
	—	—	0.421	—	0.004	—	0.000	—	—	0.358
	—	—	—	0.355	0.001	—	0.002	—	—	1.197
	0.593	0.112	0.146	0.246	—	—	0.002	—	—	2.441
	—	—	—	—	—	—	0.020	—	—	0.455
	0.004	0.051	0.207	0.090	0.133	0.299	0.719	—	0.989	—
	0.023	0.009	0.028	0.071	—	0.005	0.000	—	—	—
	—	—	—	—	—	—	0.000	—	—	—
	0.003	0.001	0.003	0.008	—	—	—	—	—	—

Quadrant IV—m³/m³

0.158 m³ of water resources are needed from the irrigation system and 0.017 m³ from return flows through groundwater extraction; also, 0.061 is pumped from groundwater (shown in Table 4-17). Therefore, the total quantity of water used is equal to 0.236 m³.

■ Input from water-related sectors per physical unit of output from water-related sectors, as well, in other words m³ per m³ of output. Table 4-18 shows that there are no flows within the water sectors, because we have considered each of them independent, allocating water directly to the different economic sectors. The water-utility sector could play the role of both distributor and collector, in which case there will be a quantity input from recycling and reuse to the water utility, and this will be distributed to the sectors of the economy that use recycled water.

The direct-input (technology) coefficient matrix, represented in Table 4-18, will be referred to in the following analysis as Matrix A.

Direct and Indirect Purchases

As described in Chapter 3, matrix A illustrates the direct purchases made by each sector from all the other intermediate sectors per each DH or m³ worth of output. In addition to the first-round effects, there are second-, third- and subsequent-round effects which cannot be captured by the matrix A. For example, for irrigated sugar cane, each DH increase in final demand sales requires these direct first round output increases as shown in matrix A: 0.400 DH from sugar cane, 0.020 DH from industry and 0.241 m³ from surface water and 0.026 m³ from groundwater. These increases require further increases in output from each sector in terms of second-round effects. For instance, the second-round effects on irrigated sugar cane can be computed as the sum of the required first round increases (column 8) multiplied by the corresponding sector's sales to manufacturing as shown in Row 8 of Table 4-18, i.e., as shown in Table 4-19.

The full table of second-round effects is calculated by computing A2, in the same manner as for the other effects. In order to capture these other indirect effects, we determine the inverse of the Leontief Matrix, i.e., $(I-A)^{-1}$, represented in Table 4-20. This table shows direct and indirect or first round and production-induced effects of a one DH sale on the final demand, and of one m³ of water allocated to the final demand. For example, each additional DH from the sale of irrigated sugar cane to final demand would result, after all rounds of economic reactions have been felt throughout the economy, in

TABLE 4-19
Illustration for the Case of Sugar Cane

Required First-Round Increase by Sugar Cane	Sector Sales Sugar Cane	Second-Round Effect
0.400 DH	0.400 DH	0.16 DH
0.020 DH	0.00022 DH	0.00000154 DH
0.241 m³	0 m³	0 m³
0.026 m³	0.181 m³	0.0047 m³

1.92 DH in total irrigated production. This is computed by summing the coefficients of the sugar beet column for irrigated agriculture production (Table 4-20), in 0.307 DH rain-fed agriculture, 0.033 DH from livestock and 1.0179 DH from industrial production. Also, it results in 0.268 m³ of irrigated water and 0.0001 m³ of recycled water and finally 0.0287 m³ of groundwater through return flows. Therefore, each entry in Table 4-20 represents a detailed multiplier indicating an expected response to the stimulus of a sale of one additional DH (Dipasquale and Polenske, 1980).

Closed Matrix to Households

The previously described input-output table yields a model in which only the productive sectors of the economy and productive water activities are assumed to be endogenous to the system. This implies that all the final-demand sectors are determined by factors outside the regional productive system. Because the model can respond to changes generated from the outside, that is, from the final demand sectors, it is called an "open model." However, this design does not suffice in some cases; and the model can therefore be set up to make certain factors of final demand, such as households, exports, or others, internal to the model. Traditionally, analysts make households internal in this way, in which case the household sector is therefore considered endogenous to the economy. This is important because economic activities will represent one of the parameters of the income level of a household, and household income will be spent locally on the 18 economic goods, including water. Adding row 19 implies that all the household income is spent at the national level. We therefore create a new Table 4-21 by adding a new row to Table 4-18, corresponding to household income, and a new column for household consumption. The new matrix with households enclosed will be referred to as matrix A*.

TABLE 4-20

Inverse of the Leontief Matrix

Quadrant I—DH/DH

	WHEAT	BARLEY	MAIZE	OTHCER	LEGUME	FODDER	SGRBT	SGRCN
WHEAT	1.1060	0.0162	0.0166	0.0222	0.0142	0.0167	0.0234	0.0257
BARLEY	0.0025	1.0715	0.0056	0.0168	0.0021	0.0160	0.0227	0.0328
MAIZE	0.0009	0.0019	1.1541	0.0040	0.0011	0.0036	0.0053	0.0069
OTHCER	0.0006	0.0014	0.0012	1.1766	0.0005	0.0034	0.0047	0.0070
LEGUME	0.0014	0.0021	0.0020	0.0023	1.0747	0.0014	0.0017	0.0016
FODDER	0.0018	0.0043	0.0039	0.0114	0.0016	1.5601	0.0147	0.0219
SGRBT	0.0019	0.0046	0.0042	0.0127	0.0016	0.0120	1.6248	0.0247
SGRCN	0.0008	0.0023	0.0021	0.0069	0.0006	0.0066	0.0090	1.6797
SNFLW	0.0002	0.0004	0.0003	0.0007	0.0002	0.0006	0.0010	0.0012
OINDCRI	0.0011	0.0016	0.0015	0.0021	0.0014	0.0016	0.0029	0.0023
VEGET	0.0057	0.0109	0.0100	0.0194	0.0077	0.0162	0.0206	0.0296
CITR	0.0068	0.0167	0.0152	0.0446	0.0063	0.0419	0.0576	0.0856
AGR-RAIN	0.5793	0.8852	0.8219	0.7642	0.9347	0.3785	0.3074	0.1932
LVSTK	0.0085	0.0126	0.0121	0.0198	0.0105	0.0168	0.0330	0.0266
INDUSTRY	0.3844	0.4805	0.4706	0.4988	0.5100	0.3594	1.0179	0.3041
WATER NETWORK	0.0209	0.0653	0.0589	0.2068	0.0119	0.2002	0.2682	0.4231
SANITATION & REUSE	0.0000	0.0000	0.0000	0.0000	0.0000	0.0000	0.0001	0.0000
RETURN FLOWS	0.0022	0.0070	0.0063	0.0221	0.0013	0.0214	0.0287	0.0453

Quadrant III—m³/DH

For label meanings, please refer to legend in Table 4-16.

Source: Corresponds to the Inverse of matrix $(I - A)$, where A is Table 4-18

Quadrant II—DH/m³

SNFLW	OINDCRI	VEGET	CITR	AGR-RAIN	LVSTK	INDUSTRY	WATER NETWORKS	SANIT-REUSE	RETURN FLOWS
0 0106	0 0039	0 0149	0 0156	0 0145	0 0187	0 0229	—	0 0227	0 5796
0 0028	0 0016	0 0075	0 0107	0 0013	0 0226	0 0090	—	0 0089	0 7537
0 0010	0 0005	0 0024	0 0027	0 0009	0 0107	0 0037	—	0 0036	0 1586
0 0006	0 0003	0 0013	0 0022	0 0004	0 0151	0 0011	—	0 0011	0 1606
0 0015	0 0004	0 0012	0 0015	0 0022	0 0005	0 0013	—	0 0013	0 0367
0 0020	0 0009	0 0042	0 0069	0 0011	0.0497	0 0037	—	0 0036	0 5046
0 0021	0 0011	0 0050	0 0078	0 0010	0 0021	0 0049	—	0 0048	0 5692
0.0010	0 0005	0 0023	0 0041	0 0002	0 0008	0 0015	—	0 0015	0 3191
1 0415	0 0001	0 0006	0 0005	0 0002	0 0004	0 0010	—	0 0010	0 0267
0 0025	1 1560	0 0027	0 0019	0 0014	0 0019	0 0059	—	0 0058	0 0488
0 0065	0 0020	1 7344	0 0114	0 0076	0 0021	0 0033	—	0 0033	0 6843
0 0079	0 0037	0 0165	1 5772	0 0044	0 0065	0 0140	—	0 0138	1 9763
0 6395	0.1385	0 2932	0 4454	1 0154	0 0607	0 0383	—	0 0378	4 4582
0 0078	0 0062	0 0311	0 0204	0 0099	1 0227	0 0719	—	0 0711	0 5625
0 3347	0 2868	1 4596	0 7512	0 5011	1 1295	3 6678	—	3 6263	4 2868
0 0266	0.0118	0 0537	0 1175	0 0015	0.0175	0 0049	1 0000	0 0048	0 4816
0 0000	0 0000	0 0001	0 0001	0 0000	0 0001	0 0003	—	1 0003	0 0003
0 0028	0 0013	0 0057	0 0126	0 0001	0 0013	0 0004	—	0 0004	1 0512

Quadrant IV—m³/m³

TABLE   4-21

Partially Closed I-O Table with Respect to Households (Wages and Consumption)

	WHEAT	BARLEY	MAIZE	OTHCER	LEGUME	FODDER	SGRBT	SGRCN	SNFLW
WHEAT	0.088	—	0.001	—	—	—	—	—	—
BARLEY	—	0.061	—	—	—	—	—	—	—
MAIZE	—	—	0.132	—	—	—	—	—	—
OTHCER	—	—	—	0.147	—	—	—	—	—
LEGUME	—	—	—	—	0.068	—	—	—	—
FODDER	—	—	—	—	—	0.355	—	—	—
SGRBT	—	—	—	—	—	—	0.378	—	—
SGRCN	—	—	—	—	—	—	—	0.400	—
SNFLW	—	—	—	—	—	—	—	—	0.040
OINDCRI	—	—	—	—	—	—	—	—	0.001
VEGET	—	—	—	—	—	—	—	—	—
CITR	—	—	—	—	—	—	—	—	—
AGR-RAIN	0.512	0.791	0.679	0.562	0.853	0.182	0.109	—	0.593
LVSTK	—	—	—	—	—	—	—	—	—
INDUSTRY	0.024	0.008	0.013	0.018	0.012	0.023	0.138	0.020	0.004
WATER NETWORK	0.017	0.057	0.048	0.167	0.009	0.123	0.158	0.241	0.023
SANITATION & REUSE	—	—	—	—	—	—	—	—	—
RETURN FLOWS	0.002	0.006	0.005	0.018	0.001	0.013	0.017	0.026	0.003
HOUSEHOLD	0.007	0.008	0.032	0.016	0.018	0.096	0.083	0.087	0.005

For label meanings, please refer to legend in Table 4-16

Source: Adding the row corresponding to Household from Table 4-17 to Table 4-18

OINDCRI	VEGET	CITR	AGR-RAIN	LVSTK	INDUSTRY	WATER NETWORKS	SANIT-REUSE	RETURN FLOWS	HOUSEHOLD
-	—	—	0.010	0.010	0.005	—	—	0.432	0.027
-	—	—	—	0.018	0.002	—	—	0.656	0.015
-	—	—	0.000	0.008	0.001	—	—	0.122	0.002
-	—	—	0.000	0.012	0.000	—	—	0.123	—
-	—	—	0.002	—	0.000	—	—	0.023	0.004
-	—	—	0.000	0.031	—	—	—	0.292	—
-	—	—	0.000	—	0.001	—	—	0.333	—
-	—	—	—	—	0.000	—	—	0.181	—
-	—	—	0.000	—	0.000	—	—	0.023	0.001
0.135	—	—	0.001	—	0.001	—	—	0.032	0.002
-	0.421	—	0.004	—	0.000	—	—	0.358	0.007
-	—	0.355	0.001	—	0.002	—	—	1.197	0.012
0 112	0.146	0.246	—	—	0.002	—	—	2.441	0.080
-	—	—	—	—	0.020	—	—	0.455	0.034
0.051	0.207	0.090	0.133	0.299	0.719	—	0.989	—	0.405
0.009	0.028	0.071	—	0.005	0.000	—	—	—	0.000
-	—	—	—	—	0.000	—	—	—	—
0.001	0.003	0.008	—	—	—	—	—	—	—
0.020	0.087	0.081	0.076	0.066	0.094	2.540	0.160	—	0.349

The augmented matrix A* has a structure similar to matrix A, with the exception that each round of economic reaction incorporates both an addition to the income of households and an increase in output of the local sectors to satisfy the requirements caused by the local expenditure of household income. Thus the inverse matrix $(I - A^*)^{-1}$ shown in Table 4-22 includes an income multiplier and consumption effects.

Multipliers and Ratios

The previously defined matrices provide a first indication of which direct, indirect, and induced effects are the most significant in determining the size of sectoral output and income multipliers. Based on the generated water input-output table of 18 sectors and both the open and the closed-to-household matrices, we can generate four multipliers: output, income, employment, and water-use.

Output Multipliers

The details contained in matrix A* and the inverse matrices allow for the construction of a table of output multipliers such as Table 4-23. In this table economic effects and water-induced effects are distinguished for the 18 sectors. For example, each 1,000 DH of output from the rain-fed agriculture sector can be expected to result in 150 DH in direct or first-round output effects in all sectors, 1410 DH and 1.65 m³ in indirect effects, and 540 DH and 2.04 m³ in consumption-induced effects; this gives a total multiplier of 3100 (adding 1000, 150, 1410 and 540.) DH and 3.70 m³, and therefore a "flow-on" of 2100 DH and 3.70 m³ (defined from 3100 minus the initial effect of 1000.) The effects for all the other sectors are shown in Table 4-24. Using the shadow price of water generated from the water-resource model, the effect on the water-related sectors can be evaluated in value terms; the output multipliers are as shown in Table 8-28. If we look at rainfed agriculture, there is a total output effect of 3,110 DH, with a flow-on of 2,110 DH. For the water utilities, for each m³ of output, there is a total output effect of 11.89 DH and a flow-on of 11.27 DH.

Sugar beets and sugar cane seem to have the highest output multiplier, through the indirect effect. By looking at the second- or third-round matrix, we can see that the effect is accumulating through the use of both sugar beet and sugar cane as inputs to the sugar refining and processing industry, which plays an important role in the Moroccan economy. Irrigated vegetables have also a large output multiplier, which essentially results from the consumption-induced effect of 6,500 DH for each 1,000 DH of output. Regarding industry, for each 1,000 DH of additional output, there is 5,410 DH of flow-on effect. By looking at the different levels of each round, we can trace the source of the flow-on effect resulting. With regard to industry, analyzing both the second- and third-round effects, which corresponds to examining the coefficient corresponding to industry of matrices A-2 and A-3, it appears that the flow-on effect results from the indirect effect accruing at the third round, as it brings 4,934 DH of additional effect.

Using information from the base scenario, MEIAH-1 results show that the cost of increasing water availability, either by water-loss-reduction programs or by an increase in efficiency will be 5.50 DH/m³. The water-related activities have to be dealt with differently, as an additional 1,000 m³ of output of water requires an investment of 5,500 DH. The effect of an additional 1,000 m³ of output is evaluated in Table 4-24; in order to compare this with the other sectors, we will need to look at the multiplier effect of 1,000 DH, which will result in 1,189 DH of total output effect, with 1,127 DH of flow-on from the initial effect. Regarding the return flows, the interpretation is different, as the return flows are a result of an infiltration or drainage of an average of 18% of the water used in the system. To obtain 1,000 m³ of additional output from the return flows category necessitates an addition of 55,500 m³ of water supply, which represents 305,250 DH of additional investments, because it is actually part of a larger quantity. Therefore the last row of Part I in Table 4-24, can be read as if an additional 1,000 DH invested will result in 87 DH of total effects and 85 DH of flow-on effect, essentially resulting from the indirect and consumption-induced effect (dividing the table entry by 305.25 DH/m³). A similar factor is applied to the recycling and reuse categories, where the effect is much lower than the return flows, with a factor of 5. This explains the relatively large size of the output multiplier of the water related activities.

Overall, by looking at the column of the consumption-induced effects shown in part I of Table 4-24, there is a substantial induced effect from closing the model with respect to household income, mainly for the production consumed domestically, such as fodder for livestock , citrus and other orchard crops, and sugar beets and sugar cane used locally by households and for industrial processing.

Income Multipliers

In addition to output multipliers, income multipliers are computed and recorded in Table 4-24, where both the economic and water-induced effects

T A B L E   4 - 2 2
Leontief Inverse of the Partially Closed I-O Table
with Respect to Households

	WHEAT	BARLEY	MAIZE	OTHCER	LEGUME	FODDER	SGRBT	SGRCN	SNFLW
WHEAT	1.119	0.042	0.043	0.082	0.030	0.082	0.109	0.141	0.025
BARLEY	0.009	1.084	0.019	0.046	0.010	0.048	0.064	0.089	0.010
MAIZE	0.002	0.005	1.157	0.010	0.003	0.011	0.014	0.019	0.003
OTHCER	0.001	0.002	0.002	1.178	0.001	0.005	0.007	0.010	0.001
LEGUME	0.003	0.005	0.005	0.009	1.076	0.009	0.012	0.015	0.003
FODDER	0.003	0.006	0.006	0.016	0.003	1.566	0.022	0.032	0.003
SGRBT	0.003	0.006	0 006	0.016	0.002	0.016	1.630	0.031	0.003
SGRCN	0.001	0.003	0.003	0.008	0.001	0.008	0.011	1.682	0.001
SNFLW	0.001	0.001	0.001	0.003	0.001	0.003	0.004	0.005	1.042
OINDCRI	0.003	0.005	0.005	0.010	0.003	0.010	0.014	0.017	0.004
VEGET	0.010	0.020	0.019	0.040	0.013	0.039	0.051	0.070	0.011
CITR	0.015	0.033	0.032	0.081	0.016	0.083	0.110	0.157	0.017
AGR-RAIN	0.623	0.974	0.912	0.965	0.986	0.600	0.595	0.582	0.687
LVSTK	0.029	0.054	0.055	0.114	0.035	0.121	0.168	0.209	0.030
INDUSTRY	0.878	1.488	1.501	2.782	1.100	2.884	4.295	4.736	0.871
WATER NETWORK	0.023	0.069	0.063	0.216	0.014	0.211	0.282	0.441	0.029
SANITATION & REUSE	0.000	0.000	0.000	0.000	0.000	0.000	0.000	0.000	0.000
RETURN FLOWS	0.002	0.007	0.007	0.023	0.001	0.022	0.030	0.047	0.003
HOUSEHOLD	0.308	0.628	0.642	1.423	0.368	1.573	2.042	2.762	0.334

For label meanings, please refer to legend in Table 4-16

Source: Corresponds to the Inverse of matrix $(I - A^*)$, where A^* is Table 4-21

ƆINDCRI	VEGET	CITR	AGR-RAIN	LVSTK	INDUSTRY	WATER NETWORKS	SANIT-REUSE	RETURN FLOWS	HOUSEHOLD
0.012	0.056	0.064	0.026	0.039	0.056	0.229	0.070	0.793	0.090
0.006	0.027	0.034	0.007	0.033	0.025	0.112	0.032	0.858	0.044
0.001	0.007	0.008	0.002	0.013	0.007	0.024	0.009	0.181	0.010
0.001	0.002	0.003	0.001	0.016	0.002	0.006	0.002	0.166	0.002
0.001	0.006	0.007	0.004	0.003	0.005	0.027	0.007	0.062	0.011
0.002	0.008	0.011	0.002	0.051	0.006	0.019	0.008	0.523	0.008
0.002	0.007	0.011	0.002	0.003	0.007	0.013	0.008	0.581	0.005
0.001	0.003	0.005	0.000	0.001	0.002	0.004	0.002	0.323	0.002
0.000	0.002	0.002	0.001	0.001	0.002	0.008	0.003	0.035	0.003
1.157	0.008	0.008	0.003	0.005	0.010	0.030	0.012	0.076	0.012
0.005	1.749	0.028	0.012	0.009	0.015	0.081	0.020	0.760	0.032
0.009	0.042	1.607	0.012	0.019	0.035	0.142	0.043	2.108	0.056
0.166	0.431	0.608	1.055	0.131	0.150	0.772	0.197	5.177	0.304
0.019	0.096	0.097	0.028	1.055	0.125	0.362	0.146	0.900	0.143
0.603	3.026	2.605	0.951	1.925	4.945	8.797	5.444	12.474	3.463
0.013	0.060	0.125	0.003	0.021	0.010	1.036	0.012	0.515	0.014
0.000	0.000	0.000	0.000	0.000	0.000	0.001	1.000	0.001	0.000
0.001	0.006	0.013	0.000	0.002	0.001	0.003	0.001	1.054	0.001
0.197	0.976	1.155	0.280	0.496	0.796	5.481	1.133	5.102	2.158

TABLE 4-23

Output Multipliers—Distinguishing Economic and Water Effects

Output Multiplier	Initial Effect		Direct Effect		Indirect Effect		Consumption Induced		Total Multipliers		Flow-on***	
	Economic Initial Effect	Water Related Demand	Eco-sector Direct Effect (DH/DH*)	Water Activity Direct Effect (m³/DH**)	Economic Indirect Effect (DH/DH*)	Water Sector Indirect Effect (m³/DH**)	Eco-cons. Induced Mult (DH/DH*)	Wat-cons Induced Multiplier (m³/DH**)	Total Economic Sectors Multipliers (DH/DH*)	Total Water Related Multipliers (m³/DH**)	Total Economic Multiplier (DH/DH*)	Total Water Multiplier (m³/DH**)
WHEAT	1.00	—	0.62	0.02	1.48	0.004	0.60	0.002	3.70	0.03	2.70	0.03
BARLEY	1.00	—	0.86	0.06	1.65	0.009	1.22	0.005	4.73	0.08	3.73	0.08
MAIZE	1.00	—	0.82	0.05	1.70	0.013	1.24	0.005	4.77	0.07	3.77	0.07
OTHCER	1.00	—	0.73	0.18	1.87	0.044	2.76	0.010	6.36	0.24	5.36	0.24
LEGUME	1.00	—	0.93	0.01	1.63	0.003	0.71	0.003	4.28	0.02	3.28	0.02
FODDER	1.00	—	0.56	0.14	1.88	0.086	3.05	0.011	6.48	0.23	5.48	0.23
SGRBT	1.00	—	0.62	0.17	2.52	0.122	3.96	0.015	8.11	0.31	7.11	0.31
SGRCN	1.00	—	0.42	0.27	2.02	0.201	5.35	0.020	8.80	0.49	7.80	0.49
SNFLW	1.00	—	0.64	0.03	1.42	0.004	0.65	0.002	3.71	0.03	2.71	0.03
OINDCRI	1.00	—	0.30	0.01	1.30	0.003	0.38	0.001	2.98	0.01	1.98	0.01
VEGET	1.00	—	0.77	0.03	2.80	0.028	1.89	0.007	6.47	0.07	5.47	0.07
CITR	1.00	—	0.69	0.08	2.17	0.051	2.24	0.008	6.10	0.14	5.10	0.14
AGR-RAIN	1.00	—	0.15	—	1.41	0.002	0.54	0.002	3.11	0.00369	2.11	0.00369
LVSTK	1.00	—	0.38	0.01	1.97	0.013	0.96	0.004	4.30	0.02	3.30	0.02
INDUSTRY	1.00	—	0.75	0.00	3.10	0.005	1.54	0.006	6.39	0.01	5.39	0.01
WATER NETWORK	—	1.00	—	—	—	1.000	10.63	0.040	10.63	2.04	10.63	1.04
SANITATION & REUSE	—	1.00	0.99	—	2.82	1.005	2.20	0.008	6.00	2.01	6.00	1.01
RETURN FLOWS	—	1.00	6.67	—	8.46	1.533	9.89	0.037	25.02	2.57	25.02	1.57

* For the water related activities the economic-sector effects are in DH/m³
** For the water related activities, the water activity effects are in m³/m³
*** Flow-on effect = total effect – initial effect
For label meanings, please refer to legend in Table 4-16.
Source: Output multipliers computed using Table 4-20 and 4-22

TABLE 4-24

Input-Output Multipliers—Base Scenario

		Initial Effect	Direct Effect	Indirect Effect	Consumption Induced	Total Multipliers	Flow-on	Ratio Type I = Direct + Indirect / Initial	Type II = Tot Effect / Initial	Type III = Flow-on / Initial
Output Multiplier						**PART I**				
DH/DH	Wheat	1 00	0 63	1 48	0 60	3 71	2 71			
	Barley	1 00	0 89	1 66	1 22	4 77	3 77			
	Maize	1 00	0 85	1 70	1 25	4 80	3 80			
	Other Cereals	1 00	0 82	1.90	2 76	6 48	5 48			
	Legume	1 00	0 94	1 64	0 71	4 29	3 29			
	Fodder	1 00	0.63	1 92	3 05	6 60	5 60			
	Sugar Beet	1 00	0 71	2.58	3 97	8 26	7 26			
	Sugar Cane	1 00	0 55	2 12	5 36	9 04	8 04			
	Sunflower	1 00	0 65	1 43	0 65	3 73	2 73		Ratios are not	
	Other Industrial Crop	1 00	0 30	1 31	0 38	2 99	1 99		defined for the	
	Vegetables	1 00	0 79	2.82	1 90	6 50	5.50		output multiplier	
	Citrus	1 00	0.73	2 19	2 24	6 17	5 17		because the	
	Rainfed Agriculture	1 00	0 15	1 41	0 54	3 11	2 11		initial effect is	
	Livestock	1 00	0 38	1 97	0 96	4 32	3.32		equal to one.	
	Industry	1 00	0 75	3 11	1 55	6 41	5 41			
DH/m³	Water Network	0 62	—	0 62	10 65	11 89	11 27			
	Sanitation & Reuse	0 62	0 99	3 44	2 20	7 25	6.63			
	Return Flows	0 62	6 67	9 41	9 91	26 61	25 99			
Income Multiplier						**PART II**				
DH/DH	Wheat	0 01	0 09	0 06	0 06	0 21	0 20	21 18	30 76	29 76
	Barley	0 01	0.21	0 08	0.12	0 42	0 41	37 76	54 06	53 06
	Maize	0 03	0 18	0 12	0 12	0 45	0 42	9 17	13 89	12 89
	Other Cereals	0 02	0.47	0 19	0 27	0 94	0 93	40 45	57.86	56 86
	Legume	0 02	0.09	0 08	0.07	0 26	0.24	9 65	14 56	13 56
	Fodder	0.10	0 36	0 37	0 30	1 12	1 02	7 59	11 67	10 67
	Sugar Beet	0 08	0.45	0 49	0 38	1 41	1 33	11 46	17 10	16 10
	Sugar Cane	0.09	0 65	0 63	0.52	1 88	1 80	14 79	21 79	20 79
	Sunflower	0 00	0.11	0 05	0 06	0 22	0.22	32 55	46 75	45 75
	Other Industrial Crop	0 02	0 04	0 05	0.04	0 15	0 13	4 65	7.53	6 53
	Vegetables	0 09	0.14	0 31	0 18	0 72	0 64	5 19	8.29	7 29
	Citrus	0 08	0 24	0 30	0 22	0 83	0 75	6 60	10 28	9 28
	Rainfed Agriculture	0 08	0.01	0 12	0 05	0 26	0 18	1 72	3.41	2 41
	Livestock	0 07	0 05	0 18	0 09	0 39	0 32	3.49	5 90	4 90
	Industry	0 09	0 07	0 30	0 15	0 61	0 52	3 91	6 50	5 50
DH/m³	Water Network	2.54	—	2 54	1 03	6 11	3 57	1 00	2 41	1 41
	Sanitation & Reuse	0 16	0 09	0 43	0 21	0 90	0 74	3 28	5 61	4 61
	Return Flows	—	0.43	1 93	0 96	3 32	3 32	—	—	—

continued

TABLE 4-24

Input-Output Multipliers—Base Scenario

	Initial Effect	Direct Effect	Indirect Effect	Consumption Induced	Total Multipliers	Flow-on	Ratio Type I = Direct + Indirect / Initial	Type II = Tot Effect / Initial	Type III = Flow-on / Initial
Employment Multiplier				**PART III**					
Wheat	0 00	0 03	0 01	0 01	0 05	0 05	8.90	11 45	10 45
Barley	0 00	0 04	0 02	0 01	0 08	0 07	12 13	15 89	14 89
Maize	0 02	0.04	0 03	0 01	0 11	0 09	3 59	5 26	4 26
Other Cereals	0 01	0 04	0 03	0 03	0 12	0 11	7.44	11 40	10 40
Legume	0 01	0 04	0 02	0 01	0 08	0 07	5 58	7 28	6 28
Fodder	0 06	0 04	0 10	0 03	0 24	0 17	2 28	3 83	2 83
Sugar Beet	0 05	0 04	0 10	0 04	0 24	0 18	2 63	4 46	3.46
Sugar Cane	0 06	0 05	0 11	0 06	0 27	0 21	2 77	4 85	3 85
Sunflower	0 00	0 03	0 01	0 01	0 05	0 05	13 16	16 54	15 54
Other Industrial Crop	0 01	0 01	0 02	0 00	0 04	0 03	1.97	3 31	2.31
Vegetables	0 06	0 03	0 09	0 02	0 21	0 15	2 29	3 67	2 67
Citrus	0 05	0 04	0 08	0 03	0 20	0 15	2 34	3 82	2 82
Rainfed Agriculture	0 05	0 00	0 05	0 01	0.11	0 06	1 11	2 23	1 23
Livestock	0 01	0 00	0 02	0 01	0 04	0 04	2 47	4 43	3 43
Industry	0 01	0 01	0 02	0 02	0 06	0 05	4 43	8 09	7 09
Water Network	0 09	—	0 09	0 12	0 31	0 21	1 00	3 27	2 27
Sanitation & Reuse	0 14	0 01	0 17	0 02	0 34	0 20	1 20	2 37	1 37
Return Flows	—	0 26	0 27	0 11	0 64	0 64	—	—	—
Water-Use Multiplier				**PART IV**					
Wheat	0 02	0 02	0 03	0 00	0 07	0 05	—	—	—
Barley	0 06	0 06	0 08	0 01	0 21	0 15	2 20	3 33	2 33
Maize	0 05	0 06	0 07	0 01	0 19	0.13	2 38	3.55	2 55
Other Cereals	0.18	0 20	0 24	0 02	0 64	0 46	2.38	3 49	2 49
Legume	0 01	0 01	0 02	0 01	0.04	0 03	2.46	3 95	2 95
Fodder	0 14	0 17	0 25	0 02	0 58	0.45	—	—	—
Sugar Beet	0 17	0 23	0 34	0 03	0 77	0 60	3 27	4 43	3 43
Sugar Cane	0 27	0 35	0 55	0 04	1 21	0 94	3 37	4 51	3.51
Sunflower	0 03	0 03	0 03	0 00	0 09	0 06	2.18	3 36	2.36
Other Industrial Crop	0 01	0 01	0 01	0 00	0 04	0.03	—	—	—
Vegetables	0 03	0 04	0 07	0 01	0.16	0 13	3 64	5 06	4.06
Citrus	0 08	0 10	0 15	0 02	0 34	0 27	3.17	4.37	3 37
Rainfed Agriculture	—	0 00	0 00	0 00	0 01	0 01	—	—	—
Livestock	0 01	0 01	0 02	0 01	0 05	0 04	—	—	—
Industry	0 00	0 00	0 01	0 01	0 02	0 02	54 94	112 51	111 51
Water Network	1 00	—	1 00	0 07	2.07	1 07	—	—	—
Sanitation & Reuse	0 12	0 00	0 13	0 02	0 27	0 15	—	—	—
Return Flows	0 20	0 33	0 89	0 07	1 49	1 29	—	—	—

are summed in value terms. In addition, three types of ratio are calculated. Type I provides the ratio of both the direct and indirect effect divided by the initial effect, Type II provides more comprehensive estimates of the changes in the output than Type I multipliers to changes in income resulting from an exogenous change in final demand through households. In fact, the Type II ratios assess the whole effect of the investment, meaning direct, indirect and consumption induced effect, relatively to the initial effect. Thus it gives a more complete estimate. Finally, Type III evaluates the flow-on effect compared to the initial effect.

To obtain the income multiplier, we divide the output coefficients from the direct and indirect matrices by the level of income per unit of output, which is given by the row corresponding to the wage and salary of Table 4-16. This transformation provides the link between the sectoral output and the income generated through that output. The method is to convert the coefficients of the matrix A and the open and closed inverse matrices into income coefficients by multiplying these elements by the coefficients related to household income. The income equivalent of the direct coefficient is represented in Table 4-24. Each column is determined by multiplying the direct coefficient by the corresponding income coefficient. For example, for wheat they are calculated as 0.088×0.067 for sector 1, 0.0×0.067 for sector 2, etc. The income equivalent of the open inverse is obtained in the same way. For the matrix closed to households only the intermediate quadrant is used.

We note that in labor-intensive sectors, such as sugar beets, sugar cane, and vegetables, where household income represents a high proportion of the total output, the direct income change will be higher than in capital-intensive sectors with strong inter-industry links. Also, as the sugar beet and sugar cane are tightly linked to the sugar processing industry at the second and third rounds, the indirect effects are very high as well. In fact the total multipliers for sugar beets, sugar cane, citrus plantations, and vegetables are respectively: 1.41, 1.88, 0.83, and 0.72 DH of income per DH of output, compared to wheat production of 0.21 DH of income per DH of output. Also, the three income multipliers, from Part II of Table 4-24, can be viewed as a measure of association. For example, each DH of income "accruing" to employees in industry and services is associated with 5.50 DH in household income in sectors that have flow-on output effects from the industry and services sector.

Employment Multipliers

Using the same method as for the output multiplier, matrix A, the open and closed inverse matrix is transformed to an employment equivalent. This is done by multiplying the appropriate matrices by the employment coefficient described in Table 4-25. The agricultural sector covers 40% of the population, industry covers 20% of the employment, and the rest is in services and administrations.

This employment is further disaggregated by type of agriculture, based on the labor required for each crop, and could be used to define an employment equivalent matrix. The three types of employment multipliers are shown in Part III of Table 4-24, and because of the small numbers, they are shown in terms of one new job per one thousand additional DH of output. The multipliers show, for example, that each 100,000 DH of output in industry and services is responsible for one job in the sector itself, for another job in the direct effect, two jobs in the indirect effect, and two jobs in the consumption induced effect, which represents a total effect of 6 new employment opportunities, with 5 due to the flow-on effects of the industry and services. The multipliers differ from one sector to another, depending on the level of labor necessary to produce the additional quantity of output sought. For instance, typical of labor intensive products, an additional 100,000 DH of output of sugar cane requires 27 additional person-years of labor.

Employment multipliers are very important for employment intensive sectors, where it is valuable to see how any change in the output affects job availability. It is expected that the employment multipliers for the agricultural

TABLE 4 - 2 5
Employment Coefficients

Sector	Percentage of Labor	Labor (Millions)
Agriculture	39.00%	5.85
Livestock	3.00%	0.45
Industry & Services	55.00%	8.25
Water Utilities	2.70%	0.405
Water Collection	0.30%	0.045
Total	100.00%	15.00

Source: Based on "Annuaire Statistique du Maroc, 1995" (Royaume du Maroc, 1995)

sectors will be very high. However, considering the low incomes in the agricultural sector, it will be misleading to look at the employment effects only.

Water Use Multipliers

Water use multipliers record the quantity of water consumed by each sector of the economy, and by the water-related sectors, for each extra unit of output. It is important to distinguish between the economic sectors and the water-related sectors in the analysis. Contrary to previous multipliers, for the economic sectors the higher the effect, the lower the water efficiency of the sector. However the interpretation is different for the water sectors. It is drawn from the logic of transivity. For each cubic meter of output of the water-related sectors, the water used is larger because it accounts for the return flows which are being pumped from the ground or the recycled water re-use in industry. For the water-use equivalent coefficient matrix, the open and closed inverse is obtained using the same method as for income and employment multipliers. Each column of the newly defined water-use coefficient table is determined by multiplying the coefficient by the water use coefficients represented in Table 4-26.

The water-use multipliers are summarized in the last part of Table 4-24. An additional 1,000 DH of output, on average, that is equally distributed among different agricultural production activities in all the irrigated agricultural sectors, will result in an increased demand of 360 m³ of water. However, an additional 1,000 DH of investment in industry, results in the use of 20 m³. Sugar cane and sugar beets are the most water-intensive irrigated products. The water-use multiplier effect of livestock is 0.05 m³ for each additional DH of output, which could take the form of meat, leather, etc. One-third of it is due to the high livestock water demand, the second third is from a direct effect, and the last third is the indirect effect through the use of water in the agriculture and industry input.

Summary and Conclusion of Multiplier Analysis

Based on inspection of the multipliers, several specific conclusions can be drawn concerning output, income, and employment impacts of actions in the economic and water-related sectors.

■ The output, income, employment and water-use multipliers are considerably greater for industry and services and for high-return, less water intensive crops, than for the heavy water-use crops.

TABLE 4 - 2 6
Water Use Coefficients, 1995

		Water Use in m³ per DH of output	Water Use in m³ per $ of output
m³/DH or m³/$	Wheat	0.0191	0.1719
	Barley	0.0633	0.5697
	Maize	0.0526	0.4734
	Other Cereals	0.185	1.665
	Legume	0.0103	0.0927
	Fodder	0.136	1.224
	Sugar Beet	0.175	1.575
	Sugar Cane	0.267	2.403
	Sunflower	0.026	0.234
	Industrial Crops	0.0103	0.0927
	Vegetables	0.0314	0.2827
	Citrus	0.079	0.711
	Rainfed Agriculture	0	0
	Livestock	0.0054	0.049
	Industry	0.000192	0.00173
m³/m³	Water Network	1	1
	Sanitation & Reuse	0.12	0.12
	Return Flows	0.2	0.2

Source: Output of the water model MEIAH-1

■ The induced effects are important for the income multiplier in all the sectors. Also, the indirect effects are the largest for the output effects in all the sectors, as well as for the employment effects, and, for some sectors, for the income effects. For the water-use multiplier, the flow-on effects seem to be very important.

■ The multipliers for sugar beets and sugar cane are larger than those for irrigated vegetables, and are much higher than for the other irrigated agricultural products or for rainfed agriculture. This is essentially due to the fact that these latter three components have much higher returns and use less water than sugar beets and cane, and certain other crops.

■ Looking at the water network, it appears that the multiplier effect of additional outputs results mainly from the consumption-induced effects.

Macro-Economic Value of Water

Economic Effects

The structure of the newly defined water input-output table allows an analyst to estimate the change in the total output, and the value added from a given change in the final demand for the goods and services domestically produced. Although some sectors produce mainly for export, such as industry and services or irrigated agriculture sending out cereals and vegetables, other sectors, such as rainfed agriculture and livestock, are mainly producing for domestic use. Empirically recognizing the inter-linkages among sectors is a major strength of the input-output table. The problem is often to determine the level of output needed in order to meet the final demand. The water input-output structure enables the determination of the level of economic and water resources required to satisfy the final demand. To determine the combination of inputs that will maximize the gross national product, the linear-programming model described in Chapter 3 can be used.

A Linear Programming Approach

Linear Programming (LP) is used to compute the optimal value, which maximizes the gross national output, and meets the constaints on resource availability and other constraints on production in each sector. By varying these constraints, such as water availability, the value of the additional resources is evaluated. The objective function, in the present analysis, is the national value added. This is a row vector representing the payments of industries, services, and agriculture made to wages, salaries, profits, government, capital, land taxes, and tariffs. The sum of the elements of this vector is an approximation of the gross national product from the payments side, rather than from the purchase side of the accounts. Maximizing this function is similar to maximizing gross national output in the most profitable way given resource constraints.

The previously defined relationship that links the Leontief inverse to the supply and demand vectors (Leontief Relation $[I - A]^{-1}.Y = X$) corresponds to the basic input-output balance equations which link the final demand and the total sectoral output taking into consideration the intersectoral linkages captured by the inverse matrix of Table 4-20. In the LP, the input-output balance equation requires that the total gross output less intermediate demand be greater than or equal to final demand deliveries. It is important to note that the first fifteen sectors are in value terms, while the last ones correspond to the water-related activities. With combined input-output linear programming (IOLP), the requirements for water use are explicit in the model structure. In solving IOLP, we will determine the optimal level of output for each sector in order to ensure a optimum level of the gross national output. Manipulating the IOLP model allows estimation of the value of water to the economy as a whole, given these constraints and the objective of maximizing gross regional product. The IOLP has 18 decision variables and 17 constraints, and is expressed as follows:

Maximizing the objective function:

$$Z = Va. X \quad \text{(in BDH)}$$

Subject to:

Upper and lower bounds of the final demand:

$$Y' \geq [I - A].X \geq Y \quad \text{(in BDH and BCM)}$$

Constraints on water demand and supply:

$$\sum_i w_i X_i \leq 28.764 \quad \text{(in BCM)}$$

The lower value of the final demand corresponds to the situation in 1997. This final demand is projected to the year 2000, which represents its upper bound. The water coefficients are determined from the previously described tables and are redefined in Table 4-27. The water constraint is based on an average year, with 28.754 BCM of water available. Note that this quantity of water corresponds to the water supplied by the utility system of 172 MCM and 268 MCM from the return flows, added to the large contribution supplied directly from precipitation and groundwater, which enters the input-output table as a primary input.

Scenario Analysis

For the "business-as-usual" base scenario case, the year 2000 is taken to be an average rainfall year, and the total quantity of water available is 28.754 BCM. This quantity of water yields a total value added of around 447 billion DH from the eighteen sectors considered. The constraints on the final demand capture the interlinkages between these sectors, and the water availability constraint plays an important role in the inter-sectoral water allocation of the limited resource available. Finally, the maximization model generates a level of output, taking into consideration the different constraints. Table 4-28 illustrates the level of output from each sector. The final demand met by this level of output is determined using the Leontief relationship and is recorded in Table 4-28.

TABLE   4-27

Water Use Coefficients and Value Added per Unit of Output

Economic Sectors	Value Added in DH per Unit of Output	Water Requirement in m³ per Unit of Output	Final Demand for 1995 in Billion DH and Billion m³	Final Demand Forecasted for 2000 in Billion DH and Billion m³
Wheat	0.307	0.026	14.537	17.715
Barley	0.073	0.086	7.099	8.929
Maize	0.093	0.071	0.891	1.145
Other Cereals	0.058	0.250	0	0.077
Legume	0.051	0.014	1.770	2.139
Fodder	0.223	0.183	0	0.182
Sugar Beet	0.188	0.236	0	0.208
Sugar Cane	0.195	0.361	0	0.113
Sunflower	0.326	0.035	0.578	0.708
Industrial Crops	0.668	0.014	1.199	1.459
Vegetables	0.174	0.042	6.116	7.563
Citrus	0.148	0.107	6.710	8.800
Rainfed Agriculture	0.332	0.134	33.818	45.318
Livestock	0.240	0.021	15.068	18.146
Industry	0.245	0	327.439	393.057
Water Network	2.540	0.052	0.143	0.172
Sanitation and Reuse	0.160	0	0	0.268
Return Flows	0	0	0	0

Source: Computed from the water input-output table shown in Table 4-16

Sensitivity to Water Availability

The results of the linear programming model are highly dependent on the level of available water. When the water constraints become binding, an economy wide value of water is represented by the shadow price of the water availability constraint. The marginal cost of water also reflects the fact that there is a sector in the economy that is being affected by the low level of water availability. The water constraint is binding when the quantity of water available drops to 19.8 BCM, and where the shadow price of water is 2.331 DH/m³. The first sector affected is sugar cane in meeting the final demand for 1995.

The shadow price of water increases with the decrease in water availability, highlighting the value of water in periods of shortages. The results of looking

TABLE   4-28

Output of the IOLP Model

		Total Output in Billion DH for the Economic Sectors and m³ for Water Activities	Level of Final Demand in Billion DH for the Economic Sectors and m³ for Water Activities
Billion DH	Wheat	29.478	17.715
	Barley	14.005	8.929
	Maize	3.581	1.145
	Other Cereals	0.844	0.077
	Legume	2.498	2.139
	Fodder	2.838	0.182
	Sugar Beet	3.028	0.208
	Sugar Cane	0.333	0.113
	Sunflower	0.749	0.708
	Industrial Crops	3.561	1.459
	Vegetables	13.974	7.563
	Citrus	19.370	8.800
	Rainfed Agriculture	89.220	45.318
	Livestock	48.681	18.146
	Industry	1,515.892	393.057
Billion m³	Water Network	4.774	0.172
	Sanitation and Reuse	0.268	0.268

at the behavior of the model for a set of water availabilities are recorded in Table 4-29. The table shows the value of water at a given level of water availability, the range within which the value remains the same, and also the sector of the economy affected by the water shortages. The economic sectors are affected one by one, starting with the more water intense, and the least contributive to the GNP. The shadow price of water ranges from 2.331 DH/m³ for 19.8 BCM to as high as 92 DH/m³ for 15.4 BCM. If we employ the concept of reliability used by water planners, and take a water reliability of 75% (i.e., the level of flow exceeded 75% of the time), which is equivalent to 17.4 BCM of water available, the economic value of water at this availability is 3.64 DH/m³. This value is almost ten times higher than the price now paid for water for agricultural use. In the urban sector, only some cities, such as Casablanca, Rabat, and Marrakech pay at this rate. At the optimal level of

TABLE 4-29

Shadow Price of Water and Strategic Sectors

Water Availability (BCM)	Shadow Price of Water (DH per m³)	Affected Sector	Range (BCM)
19.78	2.331		19.73–19.78
19.7	2.364	Sugar Cane	19.72–19.68
19.59	3.013	Other Cereals	19.59–19.675
19.55	3.042	Sugar Beet	19.55–19.59
19.2	3.047	Fodder	19.20–19.55
19.1	3.291	Barley	19.10–19.20
17.5	3.426	Maize	17.5–19.0
16.975	3.638	Rainfed Agriculture – Return Flows	16.975–17.25
16.925	3.692	Citrus	16.92–16.97
16.912	5.603	Legumes	16.912–16.92
16.75	6.219	Sunflower	16.75–16.9
16.38	7.498	Wheat	16.38–16.55
16.25	12.718	Vegetables	16.25–16.375
16.222	25.019	Livestock	16.222–16.225
16.221	48.846	Industrial Crops	16.221–16.2215
15.43	78.720	Water Utility	15.43–16.22
15.424	92.094	Industry & Services	15.424–15.425

Source: Results of the sensitivity analysis of the IOLP model to water availability

output, represented in Table 4-29, Morocco's total value added through water supply is 436.8 BDH.

If we compare the result of the sensitivity analysis to the previously defined base scenario, sugar cane seems to be the most affected, as the production is equal to only 40% of what it is in the base scenario. Rainfed agriculture is also affected, with production dropping to 85% of the original level. Since sectors of high return and low use of water, such as industry and services, are still producing almost the same quantity, 1,505 billion DH, they are therefore still using the same quantity of water. By the same token, the output of water recycling remains the same, as the industrial sector is the only sector that reuses water. Water shortages affect the sectors one after the other. From Table 4-29, it seems that industry and services, as well as industrial irrigated crops are the last sectors to be affected by water shortages. In fact, the water used for these sectors is very low compared to other sectors. However, it is surprising to note that wheat is not affected among the first sectors, but rather stands in the eleventh position, just below vegetables.

The situation becomes critical, when all the sectors of the economy are affected, and the model, as formulated, becomes infeasible, meaning that in the situation that it shows, fundamental requirements cannot be met. At 14.8 BCM, which represents an extreme drought year, economic growth is seriously affected by water scarcity and neither the final demand for 1997 nor the 2000 forecast could be met. The production functions of the 18 sectors become infeasible one at a time. First livestock, then citrus and vegetables, then cereals and sunflowers, and finally rainfed agriculture, cannot perform their tasks. The last to be affected is the water utility, which goes out of action when there is only 2 BCM of water available, which is an extreme stress situation that is unlikely to happen in Morocco. This last observation can be made because the structure of the water utility in Morocco is not directly hit by water shortages. It is not that it does not come under stress, but that there will always be enough water to meet domestic household demand, if necessary through restricting water to other sectors.

Economy-Wide Demand Curve

As seen, the shadow price of water varies tremendously with water availability. The information recorded in Table 4-29 is plotted graphically in Figure 4-15. In this case, this value of water is at the macroeconomic level, and is different from the economic value of water generated by the water model. The objective function of the combined IOLP model represents not only the benefits from the sale of the production, but also the value added to each sector from capital investment, land use, tariffs, and household income. Thus, it provides a broader evaluation of water.

Elasticity of the Demand Curve

By undertaking a statistical regression of the data used to generate the macroeconomic demand curve, we can determine the elasticity of this demand curve. We have tried to fit the macroeconomic demand curve using a function of the form:

$$Q = b \, Pe$$

Figure 4-16 shows the fit of the demand curve, where the coefficients are $b = 19.6$ and $e = -0.06$. However, if we focus on the plausible range of water

FIGURE 4-15
Economy Wide Demand Curve for Water

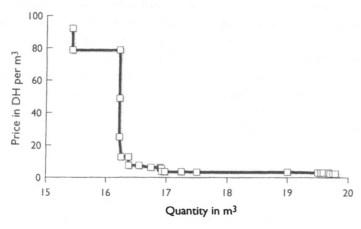

Source: Results of the sensitivity analysis of the IOLP model to water availability as summarized in Table 4-29

FIGURE 4-16
Regression—Economy Wide Demand Curve

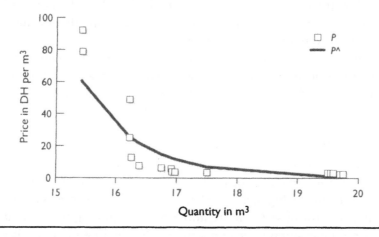

availability, starting from a very dry drought period with 16 BCM as the quantity of available water, the demand curve generated has different coefficients. The price elasticity becomes −0.18 for water, which is much higher than the previous value. This elasticity represents the response of the economy to the increase in the price of water.

Interpretation

This type of analysis helps assess the extent to which the water market is under-priced and what effect price increases could have on the economy. For the 75% reliability in the water availability, the economy-wide value of water is equal to 3.64 DH/m^3. The results of the analysis can be used to determine the positive economic effects of increased expenditures on water resources and infrastructure, especially since the shadow prices can be used as an input in cost-benefit analyses by adjusting them to become accounting prices. This analysis can also be used to see which sectors are the most sensitive to fluctuations in water availability, especially water scarcity.

Conclusion

The application of the MEIAH model to Morocco can assist policy analysis and the evaluation of policy options, both with regard to the technical handling of water, and at the strategic national economic level. The "business-as-usual" base scenario developed and used in this chapter represents the existing situation. It has been seen how MEIAH-1 outputs are used to contribute to the macroeconomic framework of MEIAH-2 using the water input-output table, which can be thought of as the first part of MEIAH-2. Urban shadow prices of water are seen to be higher than the agricultural shadow prices, by a factor of four in some cases, confirming that the highest economic return comes from urban water use.

The computation of the set of multipliers—output, income, employment and water use—shows that industry and services offer an area for future investment which is favorable in terms of new employment, additional income and minimized water use. Low-water-use irrigated crops are promising in terms of increases in output and income. The input-output linear programming (IOLP) confirms the sensitivity of the agriculture sector to water scarcity, as it is the first sector to be affected by low water availability, especially its more water-intense crops. The macro-economic value of water as generated by the model highlights the large gap between the prices currently charged and the cost of water. More importantly, according to the model's results, the economy seems to be responsive to changes in water price. It will be seen in the subsequent chapter that agricultural production and international trade are shaped by existing cropping patterns and international market constraints, and that MEIAH can estimate the results of varying policy in those domains. The existing base situation portrayed in this chapter is environmentally unsustainable due to the over-exploitation of groundwater and the lack of treatment of effluents, which will also be discussed in the following chapter.

Change in the GNP is one important indicator of growth for the countries of the world, and its links with water availability are of particular importance in forecasting the effects of future water shortages and drought periods. The difficulty remains that, at the political level, the interrelationships of the water sector and the national economy are obscured, with the result that it is hoped that the "invisible hand" will produced optimum results. Such unsophisticated procedures must yield in the future to governmental strategies that have broader horizons in view. The following step in this study will therefore look at different scenarios corresponding to policy options and investment structures different from the present "status quo."

5

Economic Analysis and
Policy Implications

Policy choices are studied by using the MEIAH model to evaluate different scenarios. A scenario is a package of parameter variations and decision variable constraints that is internally consistent. It presents, in the computer's language, the features of a possible situation or line of policy in the real world. To repay study, a scenario should also be realistic, meaning that the policies it expresses could be implemented within an appropriate range of time and capital. In Chapter 4, parameters representing a "business-as-usual" situation in the case of Morocco, which we call the Base Case scenario, were analyzed by MEIAH-1 and MEIAH-2. In the Base Case scenario, which we may now call Scenario A, the input parameters reflected existing policies in Morocco, including an absence of environmental monitoring and targets. This, of course, shaped the potential optimums generated by the models in that circumstance.

Moving Beyond the Scenario of the Present to Evaluate Possible Future Scenarios

The present chapter shows how MEIAH is used to study potential policy reforms, whose costs and effects are brought out by the model's economic analysis. The policy options are at three levels: the local, the national government, and the international setting. After reassessing the current and predicted real situation in Morocco, we move beyond the existing base case and in Scenario B consider what would emerge if Morocco were to place a significant emphasis on the sustainability of the environment. The focus then moves to changing cropping-patterns and trade policies, of which different combinations will be packaged into Scenarios C, D, and E. (The five scenarios are summarized in Table 5-1.)

TABLE 5-1
Summary of the Five Considered Scenarios

A. Business-as-Usual Scenario	No measures for environmental protection Tight cropping pattern policy Trade Barriers (both imports and exports) No change in water systems' efficiency or reduction in water losses
B. Environmentally Sustainable Scenario	Upper bound on groundwater extraction Minimum discharge to the ocean from river flow is required Tight cropping pattern policy Trade Barriers (both imports and exports) No change in water efficiency or reduction in water losses
C. Domestic Policy Reforms	Environmental sustainability 50% change allowed in cropping pattern policy Trade Barriers (imports and exports) retained No change in water system efficiency
D. Macroeconomic Reform	Environmental sustainability Globalization—Free trade 50% change allowed in cropping pattern policy No change in water system efficiency
E. Water, Trade and Food Security Nexus	Environmental sustainability Free Cropping Pattern Policy Globalization —Free trade

Generating multipliers, as MEIAH does, is a way to highlight for policymakers the pros and cons of intersectoral allocation policies, and may thus help in making economically justified but politically unpopular decisions. As an exercise to illustrate this capacity, toward the end of this chapter we test how a million dirhams of capital could be best invested for the national welfare, using the model's analysis of multipliers and ratios among different sectors of the economy. We give special attention to the consequences of alternative investments for employment, which is important in every country.

Sustaining the Environment
Economic development and environmental issues are often closely related. Patterns of development that erode the environmental resources on which

development must rely are obviously unsustainable. Environmental degradation caused by development can undermine development itself. Developing countries must be wary of pressure to over-exploit their natural resource base and to undervalue the resulting environmental degradation. In particular, the degradation and depletion of fresh water resources is posing increasing threats to economic development. In the case of Morocco, over-exploitation of groundwater is depleting aquifers and threatening saline intrusion. Undervaluing environmental degradation is also jeopardizing the quality of water through the discharge of both domestic and industrial effluents into rivers, raising the cost of treatment of the water. In the Sebou river basin, the concentration of paper industries and tanneries is threatening the health of people and animals living along the river.

The protection of the environment is an essential part of development, and to achieve such protection, it must be taken into consideration in planning. The MEIAH model behaves differently when environmental sustainability enters as a constraint. In the construction of Scenario B (and also Scenarios C, D and E which follow) the following environmental constraints are therefore added to the "business-as-usual" base case Scenario A.

- ■ Groundwater extraction should not exceed the sustainable yield, which has been calculated by a Dutch research group (Nedeco, 1994). The sustainable yield is set as a constraint.

- ■ Saline intrusion constraint: a minimum flow from the river to the ocean is set to protect fresh water quality in coastal aquifers.

- ■ Biological Oxygen Demand (BOD) should be held to an acceptable standard in the Sebou river, where data are available. (However, in the scenarios that follow the climatic conditions are assumed to be normal rather than drought-affected. In that case the Sebou BOD standard is not violated and the constraint is not activated in the model.)

Environmental Scenario Analysis

To prevent groundwater depletion, a sustainable extraction limit should be set for all groundwater aquifers. Groundwater costs less than surface water for urban use, since it does not need expensive filtration. Therefore, extraction for urban use in several aquifers exceeds the sustainable yield, for example, in the Souss basin due to over-exploitation by hotels. Avoiding the contamination of coastal aquifers by saline intrusion necessitates a minimum flow at the end of each river as it enters the ocean. Upstream water diversions from the river should take into consideration the minimum quantity of water that the river needs downstream.

MEIAH output, Scenario B: Adding such environmental constraints to the model reduces the water available from both surface sources and aquifers, in the first case due to requiring a minimum outflow of the river to the ocean, and in the second because an upper bound is set for extraction. With these environmental constraints, the value of the objective function becomes 24.5 Billion DH, which is 6% less than the aggregated benefit of the base case, Scenario A. Although the inter-sectoral water allocation remains the same percentage-wise, there is a net decrease of the water supplied by 5% to agricultural uses and 3% to urban uses. The 1.6 BCM of groundwater extracted represents half of the groundwater used in the base Scenario A, bringing about a 14% reduction in the total water available in the base scenario. Note that some aquifers, such as Touronienne, Dir Beni Mellal, and Beni Moussa, that were hardly used when no constraint was applied, are pumped to their sustainable yield, as shown in Figure 5-1.

FIGURE 5-1

Groundwater Extraction in MCM per Year

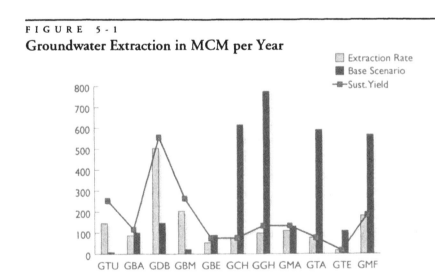

GTU = Turonienne; GBA = Beni Amir; GDB = Dir Beni Mellal; GBM = Beni Moussa; GBE = Berrechid; GCH = Chaouia; GGH = Gharb; GMA = Mamora; GTA = Tessaout Aval; GTE = Temara; GMF = Meknes-Fes.

Source: MEIAH-1 output—Scenario B, environmentally sustainable

Due to the constraint on groundwater extraction, the system makes use of more surface water in Scenario B than in the base Scenario A. Despite the saline intrusion constraint, 23.4 BCM are used, rather than being allowed to flow out to the ocean. Rather curiously, the effects of the trade barriers and the cropping constraint are such that in the green Scenario B we do not see more surface water being allocated in order to increase agricultural production. Also, the monthly average of the total reservoir storage in the region is drawn down to 677 MCM, compared to 1,045 MCM in the base case Scenario A.

These constraining factors translate into a much higher value, or shadow price, for water in green Scenario B, since the low cost groundwater source is limited to about half its yield in the base scenario. Both agriculture and urban areas have to look for another source of supply to make this up. Therefore, any additional cubic meter of water for the overall system will result in an additional 4.28 DH of output for the urban sector and 0.19 DH from agriculture. For the urban sector, the economic value is three times higher when environmental considerations are in force, while the economic value of water to agriculture is lower. This could have been predicted as there is more constraint on the quantity of water available, and because the economic returns are higher for urban than they are in agriculture, the limited quantity of water available is such that the shadow price of water will be much higher for urban than it is for agriculture.

The cropping pattern in Scenario B is unchanged from that in the base Scenario A. It continues to reflect the tight cropping pattern imposed by domestic agricultural policy. The same applies to agricultural trade, which continues to be constrained by export and import quotas and barriers. Figure 5-2 shows the level of domestic production and agricultural trade under green Scenario B.

The Sebou basin is particularly affected by effluents in the river, from both households and industrial establishments. The level of biochemical oxygen demand (BOD) in the stream is closely linked to the quantity of water in the stream. However, for the fiftieth percentile of climatic water availability considered in this scenario, that is to say in a year of average rainfall, although the level of BOD at localities directly affected by the paper industry and tanneries reaches 557 milligram per liter, after dilution by the Ouergha (SS7) and Zloul (SS8) tributaries, the Sebou drops down to 0.4 mg/l, by the time the river flows to its end node. In this situation, the BOD constraint does not become active in Scenario B.

FIGURE   5 - 2

Agriculture Production and Trade

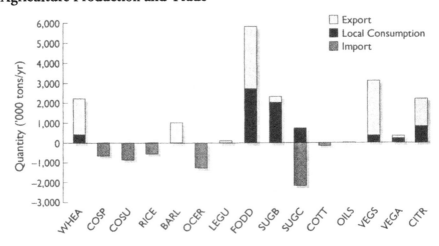

WHEA = wheat, COSP = spring corn, COSU = summer corn, BARL = barley, OCER = other cereals;
LEGU = legume; FODD = fodder; SUGB = sugar beet; SUGC = sugar cane; COTT = cotton;
VEGS = spring vegetables; VEGA = autumn vegetables; CITR = citrus plantations.

Source: MEIAH-1 output—Scenario B, environmentally sustainable

The sustainability of the environment should represent a priority in the actions of the government. Throughout the following economic analysis and strategic consideration in this book, the constraints on the environment are maintained. In contrast to the BAU base Scenario A, Scenario B represents the green base scenario, and the following Scenarios C, D, and E, are built upon it, incorporating and carrying forward its constraints.

Domestic Policy Reforms

The focus of international organizations and policy analysts has shifted towards the effectiveness of the government and of domestic reforms as a key factor in achieving a good pace of economic development. It is indeed important to understand the interaction between domestic institutions and policies, and development. Setting the appropriate rules for economic development shapes the whole economy.

To assess how the water sector might behave if potential policy reforms were applied to it, the following hypothetical new assumptions were adopted for onward applications of the DSS as constructed for Morocco.

■ *A reduced or eliminated cropping pattern constraint:* the water's optimal allocation to the different crops for each irrigated area (either large or small) is determined by the water-resource model.

■ *Free trade:* no barriers to the export and import of the agriculture production.

■ *Water transfers:* in this application, the model assumes only those inter-basin canals which exist today. Conveyance costs reflect present operation and maintenance costs. It recognizes existing links from reservoirs to irri-gated areas or cities: for the Oum Er Rbia river basin, there are several canals from the Daourat and Imfout Reservoirs to the Doukkala Large Irrigation Area (GH), to the El Oualidia Small/Medium Irrigation Area (PMH), and to the two coastal cities of El Jadida and Safi. Further upstream on the river, water is transfered to the city of Marrakech. This is similar to the previous scenario A (the base case) as the quantity transferred to these three cities have been entered into the model as a constraint.

When these assumptions are applied in Scenario C, the economic value of water is seen to be the main force driving inter-sectoral allocation, domestic cropping patterns and, thereby, the structure of Morocco's balance of trade. When we test the effects of relaxing barriers to international agricultural trade in Scenarios D and E, we see that the optimal solution is greatly affected. In some cases, we incorporate a range of adjustment in policy parameters, rather that simply a fixed amount of change.

MEIAH allows the evaluation of the impact of water-related policies, as well as of some macro-level policies indirectly related to the water sector. The complexity of the analysis will vary with the range of priorities and interde-pendencies and will provide the underpinnings for formulating public policy. Figure 5-3 gives a summary of the scenarios used in this book's analysis of MEIAH's usefulness. It also includes a set of non-water sectoral policies, which directly or indirectly affect the water sector or are affected by it.

Not All Policy Options Are Analysed Here

In Scenarios C,D, and E we set out MEIAH's evaluation of changing crop-ping patterns and international trade rules. However, many other policy adjustments could be made the basis of scenarios. Options which we have not selected for detailed review by means of MEIAH nonetheless merit mention, and the suggest the following considerations. Some water-management tools are analyzed from an aggregated production perspective. An example of such

FIGURE 5-3
Evaluated MEIAH Scenarios for Selected Water Resource Options

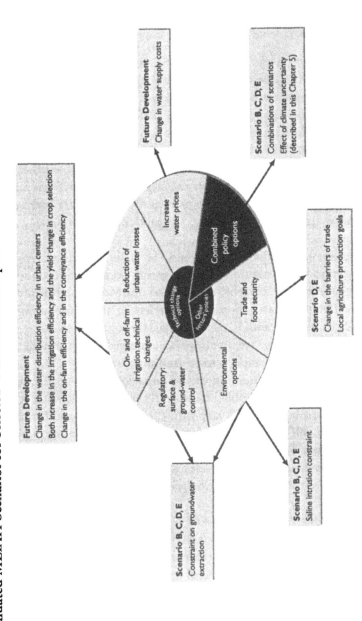

The scenarios B,C,D and E are described in this Chapter. Also, please refer to Table 5-1.
Source: Adapted from Figure 3-7 in Chapter 3

a tool is water policies encouraging an efficiency-oriented improvement in on-farm and off-farm irrigation technology. Such an increase in efficiency has a cost which must form part of the evaluation, but by saving water it will generate an additional supply of water. That additional water supply from this unconventional source could be allocated either within the irrigation sector itself or to the closest urban center. As a second example, urban-system efficiency could be increased more rapidly than is currently planned by the water utility in Morocco; this acceleration could be considered a policy option, taking into consideration its cost. Thirdly, water recycling, which makes more water of a lower quality available by recycling urban return flows, needs to be given consideration. All these options require a benefit/cost analysis.

From the water supply point of view, scenarios evaluating various reservoirs already existing or planned for the future provide guidance for future investments. Also, several studies have been undertaken of the possibility of transferring water from the Sebou river to the Oum Er Rbia Basin, for urban use in Casablanca. This is also considered a policy option.

As mentioned earlier, in the three-basin area there are two types of irrigated areas: small and medium ones (PMH) which are mostly private and have high per hectare yields, and large-scale areas (GH) where advanced irrigation techniques, such as sprinkler and micro-irrigation techniques are used. Although the water efficiency is higher for GH, the higher yield per hectare of the PMH is considered a more successful production return. It is therefore important to look at the impact of policies on yield increases, which can be achieved, for example, through soil improvement or changes in the fertilizers.

From a macroeconomic point of view, several national reforms affect the water sector, either directly or through a multiplier effect. For example, food and trade policy options, other than the broad ones to which we give detailed attention below, could be captured by running a group of scenarios (with a sensitivity analysis to measure the effects of each) on the amounts of trade to be permitted (import and export). Also, changes of the lower bound constraint on different forms of agricultural production will result in some changes in the water-allocation system, as well as in the economic returns from the irrigation sector. Regarding the environment, in addition to limiting groundwater extraction to a sustainable yield, and requiring a minimum flow to the rivers and the sea to overcome saline intrusion, local standards could be set to regulate industrial effluent. Alternative hydropower objectives could shape the reservoir release rules, and hence change flows in the rivers.

Cropping-Pattern Policy—Scenario C

As the agricultural sector consumes the majority of the mobilized water in Morocco, changes in agriculture have a great effect on water allocation, affecting the economic value of water, and therefore the cost to the government of subsidies. In the following paragraph, we first assess the response of the model to a change in the cropping-pattern policy. Then, after analyzing the possibilities of inter-basin transfers and the infrastructure required, the cost of water subsidies to the government is estimated.

The enormous impact of governmental decisions on development is well illustrated by the MEIAH model's analysis of a policy change at the farm level. Maintaining, in the instructions given to the model, the requirements of a sustainable environment, in Scenario C we consider the effects of allowing changes of up to 50% in the cropping pattern for both large scale (GH) and small/medium scale (PMH) irrigated areas.

In Scenario C the value of the net benefit for the three-basin region increases by 13% to 27.6 BDH, due to the shifts in agricultural production. Figure 5-4 compares domestic irrigated agricultural production under these more "freed up" conditions with a scenario where the cropping pattern remains the same as it has been since 1995. When governmental authority in this field is moderated and farmers have more choice, there is a net decrease

FIGURE   5 - 4

Water Allocation Among the Different Crops in Agriculture

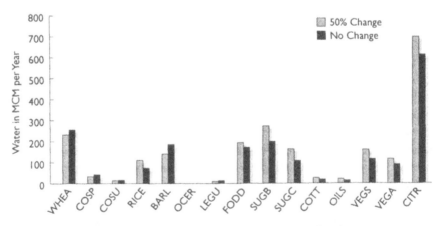

Source: MEIAH-1 output—Scenario C: 50% change in cropping pattern allowed

in the water used for cereals and corn, and more water is allocated to citrus, vegetables, and sugar. Water re-allocation is reflected in the quantities of foods produced. Because in this scenario there is no change in international trade policies, exports and imports remain the same and are not affected by such a domestic policy change.

In general, shadow prices are greatly affected by changes in cropping patterns. In this case, MEIAH's output for Scenario C tells us that the economic value of water throughout the economy increases because of these shifts within agricultural production. Remembering that in this scenario only a 50% change is allowed in the cropping pattern, the value of water in the urban area increases from 4.28 to 4.81 DH/m^3 and the agricultural value is multiplied almost by a factor of 5 to 0.93 DH/m^3. This is because the extra unit of water for agriculture will be allocated to a crop with a higher return when this is permitted within the new 50% margin of change. Consider the cases of Casablanca and its neighboring large irrigation area (Doukkala GH). For the Casablanca urban area, if the water supplied is increased by a unit, the objective value will rise above that of the green base Scenario B by 0.33 DH/m^3 (the price becomes 6.20 DH/m^3 rather than 5.87 DH/m^3). The change is even more noticeable for Doukkala GH, where the shadow price increases from 0.87 DH/m^3 under Scenario B to 2.40 DH/m^3 under Scenario C, when more allocation is allowed to crops with a higher return.

Although in Senario C a 50% cropping shift is allowed in irrigated areas, the scenario does not relax the tight constraints on trade, due to the minimum domestic consumption that must be met, and we do not see in the model's output a large change in overall agriculture production.

Global Balance and Inter-Basin Transfers

The three river basins of the studied region are differently endowed with water among themselves. In 1990, they were able to meet demand with their existing supply, but it is clear that future expectable water availability will not be enough to satisfy rising demand. According to some forecast studies, by the year 2020, the Oum Er Rbia basin will be in deficit. Four (4.0) BCM will be locally demanded and 296 MCM should be transfered to the Haouz, for irrigation as well as for urban use. Together for the Oum Er Rbia, these correspond to a total demand of 4.3 BCM; while the resource availability will be only 4.1 BCM, resulting in a deficit of 154 MCM (Table 5-2). Similarly, in forecasts for 2020 for the Bou Regrag and Coastal region, there is only 970 MCM of resource facing a demand of 1.9 BCM, creating a deficit of 920

TABLE   5 - 2

Government Estimate of Water Balance in the Basin in 2020

Basin	Demand in MCM	Water Available in MCM	Balance
Sebou	4,120	4,890	770
Bou Regrag and the Coastal Areas	1,890	970	−920
Oum Er Rbia	4,281	4,127	−154
Total	10,291	9,987	−304

Source: "Plan Directeur Integre"—Royaume du Maroc, 1992

MCM. In the case of the Sebou basin, however, there is an expected surplus of 770 MCM.

Despite the Sebou surplus, these forecasts imply an overall deficit in 2020 of 304 MCM in the three-basin region. This is a signal to improve the management of the resource. Here is a set of steps which illustrate the kind of response that could be made:

We see that there is a need to reduce the demand for water for the small-scale irrigated areas (PMH) in the coastal region, such as Chaouia (coastal aquifer) and the zone south of Rabat (Compare Figures 3, 6, and 7 in Appendix 1). A 10% increase in the water efficiency for the PMH in Chaouia will make it possible to save 10 MCM, which is of particular value because it is near the high-demand Casablanca urban area.

According to the water model, tightening the efficiency of the water distribution network in the cities of Rabat, Sale and Mohamedia by 5% per year, would make it possible to save 4.4 MCM by the year 2000, and therefore 20 MCM by the year 2020. This calculation is based on a price elasticity of -0.3 for urban uses, and -0.55 for agriculture (Rogers and Bouhia, 1997). In the Oum Er Rbia river basin, there is a large potential for water-loss reduction. For example for the three large-scale irrigated areas (GHs) of Doukkala, Haouz, and Tadla, a 10% increase in efficiency starting in our base year 1997 would make it possible cumulatively to save 136 MCM by the year 2000.

Further water-loss reduction programs in cities could save more water. Casablanca, for example, is projected to consume 123 MCM in the year 2000, and 179 MCM in 2020. A loss-reduction program aiming at 2% increase in water efficiency per quinquennium, would bring down the forecast water demand to 158 MCM for 2020. Casablanca's remaining deficit of 35 MCM could be covered by water saved from Doukkala irrigation. Transfers are planned from Sebou to the other basins. These are economically viable for urban use in Casablanca and Mohamedia, but will not be economically justifiable for agricultural use with its lower return.

In order to balance the supply and demand accounts, there is a need to increase the water availability in Oum Er Rbia by 154 MCM, or to reduce its demand an equivalent amount. If we look at the water balance in the region as a whole, an overall efficiency increase in the system of 3.7% will save 154 MCM, achieving the desired balance between supply and demand in the region of study.

Change in the intersectoral allocation of water could also take place through a slight change in the pricing of water in urban and/or agriculture areas. Using the demand curve for agriculture developed in Appendix A, an increase in the water charge to farmers by 0.3 DH/m^3, will result in a reduction of the water demand in the Doukkala, for example, by 20 MCM per year. A similar quantitative change in urban water use, for example in Casablanca, would require a greater price increase, of more than 1 DH/m^3.

Cost to the Government and Pricing Policies

In the water model, the cost of water depends on its source and the level of treatment needed. The average extraction cost of groundwater is 0.30 DH/m^3; the treatment cost of this water ranges between 0 for irrigation to 1 DH/m^3 for potable water. Transporting surface water costs between 0.5 and 1.5 DH/m^3, depending on the distance and the type of canals, while treating surface water for urban use costs about 2.5 DH/m^3. Therefore, the overall cost of water lies between 0.30 to 1.30 DH/m^3 for agriculture and between 0.5 to 4 DH/m^3 for urban water use. In terms of development of new sources, the marginal costs for new groundwater will, on average, be lower than those for new surface water.

Water charges to users in Morocco are substantially below the actual costs of water, excepting only a few urban situations. In irrigation, the costs of water far exceed the economic value of water as represented by the shadow price for irrigation water generated by the model. This is 0.19 DH/m^3, under current policies. Even without environmental protection measures, the economic return of water from agricultural use is 0.36 DH/m^3, which is still low in comparison to the cost. The large difference between the cost of water at 0.19 DH/m^3 and the price paid by both farmers and some urban centers results in heavy costs to the government. MEIAH's analysis of both the BAU Base Scenario A and the environmentally sustainable green Base Scenario B indicates the cost to the government from water subsidies in agriculture amount to 1.9 Billion DH for the "business-as-usual" case, and up to 2.6 Billion DH if priority is given to environmental protection. For urban use, sector subsidy policies ensure the balance between the cost and the price of water. In environmentally sustainable situations, comparing the price paid for water with its economic value, there is a large difference that stands to be taken care of by the government. This deficit exists both in agricultural (1.76 billion DH) and urban use (1.66 billion DH).

International Policies: Scenarios D and E

Domestic policies of the government, no matter how sophisticated, tell only half the development story. Government also plays an important role by setting the rules and creating the institutional setting for international trade, including tariffs, export subsidies, import quotas, voluntary export restraints, and local-content requirements. In Morocco, trade policies are based on import quotas, that is to say, on direct restrictions on the quantity of a good that may be imported. For exports, the quantity of domestic products directed to the international market is limited by GATT/WTO commitments and by bi-lateral policy agreements with purchasing countries. Any change in import quotas or export limitations for agricultural goods will have a great effect on domestic production, and therefore on the water used for irrigated cropping. In this section, two scenarios are analyzed. Both assume free trade, but the first, Scenario D, follows Scenario C in allowing only a 50% change in the domestic cropping pattern, while the second, Scenario E, assumes both that free trade is in effect, and that farmers have entire freedom in deciding what to plant for the domestic/international market. In this case, the economic returns on water dictate both the forms of local production and the balance of trade.

Scenario D: Free Trade with 50% Freeing of Cropping Patterns

Relieving international trading of its present restrictions, while limiting cropping changes to 50% and maintaining the environmental sustainability rules of the green Base Scenario B, leads to a net increase in the aggregated benefit for the year 2000, raising the objective function to 31.6 Billion DH. This primarily results from a shift in the balance of trade from a deficit of 5.57 Billion DH for the environmentally sustainable green Base Scenario B, to a trade surplus of 0.27 Billion DH. Agricultural exports increase from 8.70 to 12.55 Billion DH and Morocco imports 12.27 Billion DH of agricultural goods. These gains are also driven by the 50% change in cropping pattern which this scenario permits in irrigated agriculture. Figure 5-5 illustrates the level of trade and local production for each of the 15 types of irrigated crops in Scenario D. Since this scenario allows only a limited flexibility of 50% from the fixed cropping pattern, a large shift to imported commodities could not take place. A limited increase of imports was observed, in corn, sugar cane, and cotton. National production of wheat drops somewhat, while on the export side, Moroccan production of rainfed barley, which could not be directed to the international market in the "business-as-usual" scenario due to trade barriers, shows a significant increase in the quantity of exports.

In Scenario D, due to the higher return on water from agriculture now that it is freer to go to the most profitable crops, there is a 1% increase in the allocation of water to agriculture. A similar change occurs in the shadow prices of water, where the agricultural value rises to 1.29 DH/m^3 from 0.36 DH/m^3 in green Base Scenario B. The shadow price of water across both the agricultural and urban sectors increases as well, but by a smaller magnitude,

FIGURE 5-5

Crop Production and Trade—Free Trade Scenario

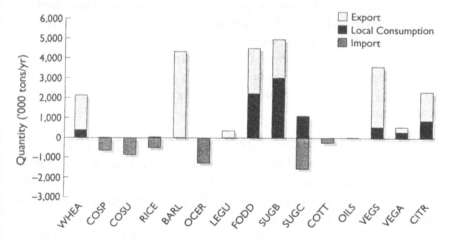

Source: MEIAH-1 output—Scenario D: 50% change allowed in the cropping pattern and relaxed international market barriers

to 4.44 DH/m^3. Groundwater extraction increases by 1.6%, staying within the sustainable extraction range. However, due to a 16% drop in average reservoir storage, the benefit from hydropower generation drops by 40% to 17.48 Billion DH. There is a tradeoff to be evaluated between releasing the water for agricultural production and storing it to increase hydropower generation. In this Scenario D, the benefit of the extra unit of water to agricultural use seems to be higher than the benefit from the sale of electricity generated by the reservoir.

Scenario E: The Relationship Among Water, Trade, and Food Security

Food security should be considered from a global point of view, not purely the domestic level. A national population can enjoy security of its food supply without having to aim for food self-sufficiency, meaning the entirely domestic production of all its food requirements. Using international agreements as well as efficient domestic production, a country should meet it domestic consumption needs without jeopardizing the sustainability of its natural resources, which could be a consequence of pressing for fully domestic production. Countries are often reluctant to shift from entirely domestic self-sufficiency, maintained and directed by the "visible hand" of the government to reliance on the "invisible hand" of the market, especially when this market extends beyond the national territory directly controllable by the government. However, in this section we consider Scenario E, representing this latter situation. We posit a perfectly open situation, where both the cropping pattern and the level of trade are determined by the market, including elements of the market which are international. We do maintain, in Scenario E, the constraints from the green Base Scenario B that protect the environment. It could even be considered that the market liberties we give to this scenario increase its productivity to a degree that pays for its environmental sustainability.

Scenario E Analysis: The case of open trade and free cropping pattern

Under Scenario E, the total net benefit to the region doubles to 44.7 BDH, as a result of a tremendous change in the balance of trade. Morocco would be exporting 19.6 BDH of agriculture production, and agricultural imports drop to 7.5 BDH. The balance of trade in Scenario E becomes highly positive (12.1 BDH). This is essentially due to the shift in domestic production from low-return, water intensive crops, to less water intensive crops with higher economic return. The region no longer produces spring corn, rice, barley and cotton, which are imported from the international market (Table 5-3). The water saved from this production change is allocated to both spring and autumn vegetables, as well as citrus, both of which are largely export crops. A total of 7.346 million tons of vegetables is exported, compared to 2.861 million tons for the green Base Scenario B. Figures 5-6 and 5-7 highlight the changes between the two scenarios in the production of seven crops.

As a result of the increase in the economic returns of water allocated to agriculture, in Scenario E the shadow price of water to agriculture increases to 1.88 DH/m^3, which intensifies the gap between the rising shadow price, i.e., the economic value of water, and the low cost of water to the farmer. The increase is smaller in urban use, as the trade and agricultural reforms do not affect the already high return from urban water use, and the shadow price of water remains at a relatively unchanged level of 4.50 DH/m^3.

Targeting Priority Investments

The concern of the government is not only to foster national economic growth, but also to avoid social distortions arising from policy reforms. In

TABLE 5-3

Agriculture Sector: Local Production and Trade under Scenario E

	Local Production in '000 Tons	Imports in '000 Tons	Exports in '000 Tons
Wheat	6.43	0	1,103.60
Corn Spring	0	679.49	0
Corn-Summer	0.22	869.2	0
Rice	0	594.09	0
Barley	0	0	4,261.28
Other Cereals	0	1,269.69	0
Legumes	70.66	0	423.17
Fodder	382.82	790.23	0
Sugar Beat	3,457.47	0	2,680.71
Sugar Cane	2,031.61	0	0
Cotton	0	261.08	0
Oil Seeds	592.10	0	739.59
Vegetables-Spring	1,817.58	0	5,148.13
Vegetables-Autumn	1,720.35	0	2,198.65
Citrus	1,423.89	0	2,356.65

Source: MEIAH-1 output—Scenario E: open trade and free cropping pattern

FIGURE   5-6

Cropping Pattern—Policy Reform Scenario E

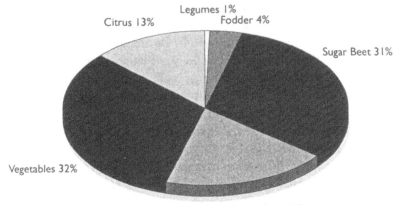

Source: MEIAH-1 output—Scenario E: open trade and free cropping pattern

FIGURE   5-7

Cropping Pattern—Green Base Scenario B

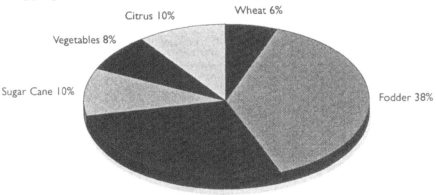

Source: MEIAH-1 output—Scenario B: green base scenario

Morocco, 40% of total employment is offered by agriculture. Any change reducing jobs in the farming sector may do social damage. Therefore, work lost from agriculture should be replaced by jobs in other sectors of the economy, such as industry or services. Investments must be targeted taking such socio-economic implications into consideration.

A good policy reform cannot take place without an effective institutional environment and a well considered investment plan. Developing countries cannot afford capricious or risky investments, and a therefore an analytic instrument which brings out the consequences through several cycles in all the affected spheres of a proposed placement of funds is of value. After assessing the water model's predictions of results from several policy changes aimed at economic growth, we see that targeting strategic sectors for priority investment can have positive effects throughout an economy.

MEIAH lets us evaluate strategic investments in the different sectors of the economy. Consider the multiplier effect of additional output from any of the 18 sectors of the economy which may arise from revised allocation of water. The additional output can be thought of as new investment in the sector, which itself yields an additional output. For a proposed investment, MEIAH can generate figures describing the output, income, employment, and water-use multiplier effects to be expected—initial, direct, indirect, consumption induced, and effects from the flow-on of the economy (as defined in Chapter 3 and described in Chapter 4). Thus, through the determination of strategic sectors, MEIAH is a tool to assess the value of projects.

How Best to Invest a Million DH?

The input-output model developed for Morocco makes it possible to assess the multiplier effects expectable from any change in sectoral output. Thus, it can be used to determine the impact of an investment on different socio-economic indicators in each sector. It could be used, as an illustration, to target the best investment of a million DH.

First, we consider the primary input for each sector per unit of output, also equivalent to the total value added per unit of output recorded in Table 5-4. For each sector, this coefficient indicates the necessary investment for each unit of output. Using an algebraic transformation, that is dividing 1 Million by the corresponding cell of Table 5-4, Table 5-5 summarizes the additional output resulting from the 1 Million DH of investment for all the economic sectors.

For water-related activity, the water-supply curve is such that we can assume that the marginal cost of any additional unit of water is 5 DH/m³. This is, in fact, the cost of reducing water losses. Water losses are so high in the system that ample amounts of water are available to be realized by such investments in conservation. This implies that an investment of 1 million DH in improving the water-system's efficiency will mobilize 200,000 m³ of water, and we carry that value forward in our calculations.

From Table 5-5, we can see that the difference between the industrial and agricultural sectors in the level of additional output from a 1 million DH investment is almost a factor of ten. We can use these coefficients with the previously generated multipliers to look at the impact on output, income, employment, and water use of additional output. We obtain Table 5-6 by multiplying the coefficients of Table 5-5, by the corresponding cell from Table 4-24 in Chapter 4 of the total multipliers and the flow-on effect. From these results, there are three possible strategic investments corresponding to three main sectors: agriculture, industry and services, and the water sector. Each investment yields a different outcome, in terms of output and additional income and the number of job created. In the following sections, the investment analysis is taken up, one at a time, for the water sector itself, the agricultural sector, and the industry/services sector, respectively.

Investing in the Water Sector

By the water sector, we mean the utilities and other organizations that mobilize (or "produce") water and distribute it to consuming sectors. As just seen,

TABLE 5-4

Value Added per Unit of Output

Sectors	Value Added per Unit of Output
Wheat	0.944
Barley	0.947
Maize	0.956
Other Cereals	0.846
Legume	0.991
Fodder	0.887
Sugar Beet	0.854
Sugar Cane	0.777
Sunflower	0.978
Other Industrial Crop	0.991
Vegetables	0.974
Citrus	0.934
Rainfed Agriculture	0.485
Livestock	0.618
Industry	0.062

Source: This corresponds to the last row of the coefficient matrix in Table 4-17 of Chapter 4

investing one million DH in loss-reduction in the water sector is equivalent, at a cost of 5 DH/m³, to an increase in mobilized water of 200,000 m³. This new quantity of water when put at the service of the economy would result in a total output increase of 2.38 million DH, of which 89.6% is from the consumption-induced effect. Both from the initial and direct effect, an additional 0.25 Million DH results from the intersectoral allocation of the water. Beside the fact that 19 new jobs will be created initially at the water utility level to mobilize this quantity of water, the indirect effect which captures the linkages of the water sector with the other sectors of the economy would result in 19 other jobs. Finally with the consumption-induced effect, a total of 62 jobs will result from this additional quantity of water. Going back to the water cycle, within a one-year period of time, 20% of the water allocated to the irrigated agriculture sector comes back to that sector through return flows. Also, 80% of the water used in industry is recycled within the produc-

TABLE 5-5

Additional Output Resulting from 1 Million DH of Investment in Each Sector

Sectors	Additional Output
Wheat	1,059,159 DH
Barley	1,055,776 DH
Maize	1,045,976 DH
Other Cereals	1,182,305 DH
Legume	1,008,661 DH
Fodder	1,127,740 DH
Sugar Beet	1,170,815 DH
Sugar Cane	1,287,340 DH
Sunflower	1,022,164 DH
Other Industrial Crop	1,008,652 DH
Vegetables	1,026,955 DH
Citrus	1,070,634 DH
Rainfed Agriculture	2,062,284 DH
Livestock	1,619,221 DH
Industry	16,074,959 DH
Water Supply	200,000 m³

Source: Each cell correspond to 1,000,000 divided by the cell of Table 5-4, except for Water Supply where it is 200,000 m³ divided by the corresponding value in Table 5-4

TABLE 5 - 6

Multiplier Effect of 1 Million DH Investment in Each Sector

	Initial Effect	Direct Effect	Indirect Effect	Consumption Induced	Total Multipliers	Flow-on
Output Multiplier						
Wheat	1,059,159	669,518	1,568,593	633,013	3,930,282	2,871,123
Barley	1,055,776	940,987	1,748,538	1,286,719	5,032,019	3,976,243
Maize	1,045,976	889,714	1,780,880	1,304,593	5,021,163	3,975,187
Other Cereals	1,182,305	967,945	2,241,721	3,266,554	7,658,525	6,476,220
Legume	1,008,661	946,105	1,649,817	720,139	4,324,722	3,316,061
Fodder	1,127,740	706,217	2,162,236	3,445,190	7,441,383	6,313,643
Sugar Beet	1,170,815	831,959	3,022,580	4,643,339	9,668,692	8,497,878
Sugar Cane	1,287,340	708,376	2,731,794	6,904,514	11,632,024	10,344,684
Sunflower	1,022,164	665,014	1,457,534	663,664	3,808,376	2,786,212
Other Industrial Crop	1,008,652	305,171	1,317,566	385,697	3,017,086	2,008,434
Vegetables	1,026,955	810,718	2,892,620	1,946,480	6,676,774	5,649,819
Citrus	1,070,634	780,745	2,349,064	2,402,244	6,602,687	5,532,052
Rainfed Agriculture	2,062,284	314,523	2,907,688	1,122,651	6,407,147	4,344,863
Livestock	1,619,221	616,110	3,194,085	1,558,380	6,987,796	5,368,575
Industry	16,074,959	12,130,987	49,920,209	24,969,999	103,096,153	87,021,194
Water Network	123,800	—	123,800	2,130,190	2,377,790	2,253,990
Income Multiplier						
Wheat	7,131	90,411	60,619	61,230	219,391	212,260
Barley	8,131	217,696	89,301	124,461	439,590	431,459
Maize	33,950	185,766	125,496	126,190	471,402	437,453
Other Cereals	19,265	556,083	223,282	315,967	1,114,597	1,095,332
Legume	17,804	91,237	80,581	69,657	259,279	241,475
Fodder	108,308	407,376	414,610	333,246	1,263,539	1,155,232
Sugar Beet	96,688	530,779	577,073	449,140	1,653,680	1,556,992
Sugar Cane	111,386	836,411	810,933	667,858	2,426,589	2,315,203
Sunflower	4,864	107,337	51,007	64,195	227,402	222,538
Other Industrial Crop	19,795	39,838	52,186	37,308	149,126	129,331
Vegetables	89,539	143,154	321,256	188,279	742,228	652,688
Citrus	86,796	253,795	319,356	232,364	892,309	805,514
Rainfed Agriculture	155,977	27,250	240,603	108,592	532,422	376,444
Livestock	106,591	73,961	297,852	150,739	629,142	522,552
Industry	1,516,340	1,125,360	4,803,534	2,403,664	9,848,898	8,332,558
Water Network	507,995	—	507,995	205,949	1,221,939	713,944

continued

TABLE 5-6

Multiplier Effect of 1 Million DH Investment in Each Sector *(continued)*

	Initial Effect	Direct Effect	Indirect Effect	Consumption Induced	Total Multipliers	Flow-on
Employment Multiplier						
Wheat	5	29	12	7	53	48
Barley	5	47	17	14	83	78
Maize	22	42	36	15	115	93
Other Cereals	12	53	39	37	141	129
Legume	11	44	20	8	83	72
Fodder	70	48	111	39	267	197
Sugar Beet	62	48	115	52	278	216
Sugar Cane	72	58	141	77	348	276
Sunflower	3	32	9	7	52	49
Other Industrial Crop	13	8	17	4	42	29
Vegetables	58	36	96	22	211	154
Citrus	56	40	90	27	214	158
Rainfed Agriculture	100	3	108	13	224	124
Livestock	18	8	37	17	81	62
Industry	105	85	379	279	848	743
Water Network	19	—	19	24	62	43
Water Use Multiplier						
Wheat	20,248	20,461	26,564	4,447	71,719	51,472
Barley	66,796	65,731	81,037	9,040	222,604	155,808
Maize	55,060	58,109	72,971	9,165	195,306	140,245
Other Cereals	218,326	233,641	286,848	22,949	761,765	543,438
Legume	10,373	10,274	15,257	5,059	40,963	30,590
Fodder	152,980	195,393	285,235	24,204	657,812	504,832
Sugar Beet	204,566	266,124	402,330	32,622	905,642	701,076
Sugar Cane	344,115	455,048	704,390	48,508	1,552,060	1,207,945
Sunflower	26,543	25,556	32,382	4,663	89,144	62,601
Other Industrial Crop	10,361	10,963	14,280	2,710	38,314	27,953
Vegetables	32,281	43,421	74,022	13,675	163,399	131,118
Citrus	84,565	108,053	159,829	16,877	369,324	284,759
Rainfed Agriculture	—	1,290	5,193	7,887	14,370	14,370
Livestock	8,827	22,252	37,080	10,948	79,107	70,280
Industry	3,086	16,861	152,697	174,583	347,227	344,141
Water Network	200,000	—	200,000	14,958	414,958	214,958

Source: multiplication of the coefficients of Table 5-5 by the corresponding cell from Table 4-24 in Chapter 4

tion process. In addition to that, all the water used by households flows back into the water cycle after being used. The structure of the input-output table is such that it captures the indirect effects in a large number of rounds. This explains the large water-use multiplier and the 214,958 m³ flow-on effect for the water-supply utility.

Investing in Agriculture

Let us consider investing one million DH in the agricultural sector, both irrigated and rainfed, on a basis weighted by expected level of returns. Table 5-7 records the investment in each type of production, as well as the additional output resulting from that investment.

On average, this investment would result in 0.909 million DH of initial effect of the additional output. The total multiplier effect is equal to 4.865 million DH, of which a third is from the indirect effect, as we take into consideration the quantity used for industry, and a second third is from local food consumption by households. As shown in Table 5-8, this investment results in 0.586 million DH of income through wages and household returns, and the creation of 120 jobs in the agricultural sector. However, this

T A B L E   5 - 7

Agricultural Investment and the Additional Resulting Output

Sectors	Share of Million DH Investment	Additional Output in DH
Wheat	81,641	77,081
Barley	81,902	77,576
Maize	82,670	79,036
Other Cereals	73,137	61,860
Legume	85,728	84,992
Fodder	76,676	67,991
Sugar Beet	73,855	63,080
Sugar Cane	67,170	52,177
Sunflower	84,596	82,761
Other Industrial Crop	85,729	84,994
Vegetables	84,201	81,991
Citrus	80,766	75,437
Rainfed Agriculture	41,930	20,332

Source: This second column is computed by multiplying the second column by the column of Table 5-5 and dividing by a Million DH

investment would not happen without an additional water supply for irrigation, amounting to 212,657 m³. For a water-scarce country with no water surplus, another investment needs to be made to supply this quantity of water for irrigation. Referring to Table 5-8, another 1.063 Million DH must to be invested to supply this quantity of water.

Table 5-8 shows that the highest return crops are vegetables and citrus; they are at the origin of 122,131 DH of income and 32 new jobs, and have the least water requirement of 39,069 m³. Sugar beet and sugar cane, although they result in a higher total income effect of 187,447 DH and 29 new jobs, consume 111,700 m³ of water, almost three times the water demand of vegetables and citrus. Fodder is similar. These findings are parallel to those of Scenario E, described in the previous section, in which Morocco is open to the global economy, and the flexibility granted to domestic cropping pattern policies allows the water sector to behave as dictated by the market.

The use to be made of this analysis would depend on the government's goal: create new jobs, alleviate poverty by increasing household income, seek national growth through additional economic output or save water for future generations, by refraining, for example, from overpumping aquifers.

Investing in Industry and Services

Although the largest water consumer is agriculture, it represents only 16% of the total GDP; the remaining 84% is from industry and services. According to the SAM95, a million DH investment in industry and services would generate 1.607 million DH of additional output. The total output effect of such an investment is equal to 103 million DH. Almost half of it is through the indirect effect, and consumption-induced effects cover 24% of the total output effect. The income generated by this investment is of a factor of 9.8, mostly through indirect effects. This investment would create 848 jobs in industry and services, which includes some jobs in agriculture arising through the linkages, such as growing the beet sugar needed for the production chain of the sugar processing industry. However, the additional output generated by the million DH investment demands 345,227 m³ of water. The mobilization of such a quantity of water would require an additional investment in the water sector. However this quantity will result in only a 15% change in the total income that could have resulted from investing 1 million DH in industry and services. This water could be generated either by water-saving programs or through intersectoral allocation from agriculture. In the latter case, the newly created industrial/service jobs make it possible to overcome

TABLE 5 - 8

Multiplier Effect of 1 Million DH of Investment in the Agricultural Sector

	Initial Effect	Direct Effect	Indirect Effect	Consumption Induced	Total Multipliers	Flow-on
Output Multiplier						
Wheat	77,081	48,725	114,155	46,068	286,028	208,948
Barley	77,576	69,141	128,478	94,545	369,739	292,164
Maize	79,036	67,228	134,567	98,578	379,409	300,373
Other Cereals	61,860	50,644	117,290	170,911	400,705	338,845
Legume	84,992	79,721	139,017	60,680	364,410	279,418
Fodder	67,991	42,577	130,360	207,708	448,637	380,646
Sugar Beet	63,080	44,824	162,848	250,169	520,921	457,841
Sugar Cane	52,177	28,711	110,723	279,848	471,459	419,282
Sunflower	82,761	53,844	118,012	53,735	308,352	225,590
Other Industrial Crop	84,994	25,715	111,024	32,501	254,233	169,240
Vegetables	81,991	64,727	230,943	155,405	533,066	451,075
Citrus	75,437	55,012	165,516	169,263	465,228	389,791
Rainfed Agriculture	20,332	3,101	28,666	11,068	63,167	42,835
Total Agricultural Sector	909,307	633,970	1,691,599	1,630,478	4,865,353	3,956,046
Income Multiplier						
Wheat	519	6,580	4,412	4,456	15,966	15,447
Barley	597	15,996	6,562	9,145	32,300	31,702
Maize	2,565	14,037	9,483	9,535	35,620	33,055
Other Cereals	1,008	29,095	11,682	16,532	58,317	57,309
Legume	1,500	7,688	6,790	5,869	21,847	20,347
Fodder	6,530	24,560	24,997	20,091	76,178	69,648
Sugar Beet	5,209	28,597	31,091	24,198	89,095	83,886
Sugar Cane	4,515	33,901	32,868	27,069	98,352	93,838
Sunflower	394	8,691	4,130	5,198	18,412	18,018
Other Industrial Crop	1,668	3,357	4,397	3,144	12,566	10,898
Vegetables	7,149	11,429	25,649	15,032	59,259	52,110
Citrus	6,116	17,882	22,502	16,372	62,872	56,757
Rainfed Agriculture	1,538	269	2,372	1,071	5,249	3,711
Total Agricultural Sector	39,308	202,081	186,934	157,713	586,035	546,727

continued

TABLE 5 - 8

Multiplier Effect of 1 Million DH of Investment in the Agricultural Sector *(continued)*

	Initial Effect	Direct Effect	Indirect Effect	Consumption Induced	Total Multipliers	Flow-on
Employment Multiplier						
Wheat	0	2	1	1	4	3
Barley	0	3	1	1	6	6
Maize	2	3	3	1	9	7
Other Cereals	1	3	2	2	7	7
Legume	1	4	2	1	7	6
Fodder	4	3	7	2	16	12
Sugar Beet	3	3	6	3	15	12
Sugar Cane	3	2	6	3	14	11
Sunflower	0	3	1	1	4	4
Other Industrial Crop	1	1	1	0	4	2
Vegetables	5	3	8	2	17	12
Citrus	4	3	6	2	15	11
Rainfed Agriculture	1	0	1	0	2	1
Total Agricultural Sector	25	32	44	18	120	95
Water Use Multiplier						
Wheat	1,474	1,489	1,933	324	5,219	3,746
Barley	4,908	4,830	5,954	664	16,356	11,448
Maize	4,160	4,391	5,514	693	14,758	10,597
Other Cereals	11,423	12,224	15,008	1,201	39,857	28,434
Legume	874	866	1,286	426	3,452	2,578
Fodder	9,223	11,780	17,197	1,459	39,659	30,436
Sugar Beet	11,021	14,338	21,676	1,758	48,793	37,772
Sugar Cane	13,947	18,444	28,550	1,966	62,907	48,959
Sunflower	2,149	2,069	2,622	378	7,218	5,069
Other Industrial Crop	873	924	1,203	228	3,229	2,355
Vegetables	2,577	3,467	5,910	1,092	13,046	10,468
Citrus	5,958	7,613	11,262	1,189	26,023	20,064
Rainfed Agriculture	—	13	51	78	142	142
Total Agricultural Sector	68,589	82,447	118,166	11,455	280,657	212,068

the job loss problem created in the agriculture sector by withdrawing the small amount of water needed.

Choice of Investments

Water scarcity constrains the range of possibilities of water-resource expansion at an affordable price. Therefore, the water-use multiplier ought to be taken into consideration in the choice of investments, and be included in national planning. It is clear that the marginal benefit, in terms of additional output, income, and employment, from investment in the agricultural sector is not as great as it is in industry and services. In fact, in agriculture the water required for the additional output requires a little more money than the amount originally invested to increase output. Nevertheless, investment in the water sector would allow an increase in the water availability, and generate indirectly both new incomes and new jobs. It is the role of policy makers to decide on the appropriated plan of investment, using these analytical indications as a guide in their decisions.

Strategic Conclusions

Applying the MEIAH model, both to the "business-as-usual" base Scenario A, and to the different policy scenarios, gives an overview of how the water sector's behavior has effects throughout the economy. It is misleading to focus too much on present water allocations to the different sectors, since these neglect the sustainability of the environment, and under present rules Morocco is experiencing very rapid depletion of its aquifers. Constraining groundwater extraction to avoid this would reduce the water pumped to half, but it is the only way to preserve the long term situation. Sustaining the environment should be a priority in national planning.

Opening Morocco to the international market seems to be the key to achieving the highest economic benefit, and will be even more beneficial if the tight cropping policy is relaxed. The latter point is established when we see that under the condition of free international trade, MEIAH gives different results when only a fifty percent change is allowed in the cropping pattern and even more different ones when cropping decisions are entirely unconstrained. Given partial or complete cropping freedom, agricultural production shifts towards more vegetables and citrus, which are then exported to the international market. In this circumstance, crops with high water requirements and low returns, e.g., wheat, barley and rice, are imported, rather than being grown under irrigation in Morocco. With both trade and cropping constraints removed, we see a net increase in the shadow price of water in agriculture, as additional water is applied to the highest-return crops, and we note that a free market will shift the balance of trade from a deficit to a positive value.

MEIAH gives policy analysts, national and international, a tool to evaluate the implications of a set of investments or policy decisions. In this application to the case of Morocco, it has brought out the potential of the industry and services sectors to repay investment not only with high returns, but also the creation of new employment. This offers an escape from jobs in agriculture which have become insecure due to the increasing water scarcity. Of course, such a move toward industry and services must be part of a long-term plan, which cannot be successful without a parallel educational reform to prepare future generations with new skills and interests. For irrigated agriculture, the investment analysis of MEIAH-2 converges towards the same results as MEIAH-1, showing the benefits of a shift towards low-water use, high-return crops. Thus, it implies that there are rewards for adopting flexibility in cropping pattern policies and for considering an an internationalizing reform of trade to harvest these differentials in productivity.

6

Conclusions and Future Development

This study, throughout its length, has sought to show the concrete utility of an approach which has often been considered overly theoretical and unrealistic. This chapter, in particular, points out how a mathematical hydro-economic model can help decision-makers who are coping with many pressures, including political ones. After a brief recapitulation, we discuss the application of the MEIAH DSS to Morocco and to other countries, and we then look at MEIAH as a point of departure for research and new thinking about water planning for sustainable socio-economic development, where water is considered as an economic good that necessarily holds an important place in national planning.

Goals and Objectives of this Study

The main goal of this study was to place the handling of water resources in its proper position as an integral and important part of overall economic management, particularly in water stressed countries. The MEIAH system is targeted to high-level decision makers, policy analysts and strategic planners. In a particular note of realism, it is supplemented with a stochastic simulation that takes into account annual environments of sharply varying levels of precipitation and flow. It thereby saves a large amount of time and effort othewise devoted to independently programming and simulating this real-world factor.

The application of MEIAH is an interactive process, which emphasizes the collaboration of different stakeholders. Throughout the development of the model a continuous dialogue was maintained with different governmental bodies and international organizations, including elements of the governments of Morocco, Tunisia, Cyprus, Egypt, Malta, Lebanon, Yemen, and the World Bank and the European Investment Bank, to ensure coherence and the incorporation of different and often conflicting perspectives.

Conclusions and Recommendations

Morocco must allocate its scarce water needs for the highest economic return. This cannot take place without a water network structure which can move water within the country, and more importantly without some flexibility of cropping patterns, which are highly linked to international trade policies. MEIAH's results bring out the need to move from a constraining goal of "domestic self-sufficiency" in some agriculture production to a more flexible target of "food security," which permits the country to specialize in the crops it grows best, exporting a major share of production and covering the remaining national demand by importing food from abroad. Expanding its food market thus beyond the national frontier, and giving freedom and flexibility for market-based cropping decisions at the farm level, will allow Morocco to move beyond its existing balance of trade and reach a higher socio-economic level of welfare.

As shown in the study, a small increase in the water efficiency of the irrigation system will allow the reallocation of the water saved to nearby urban areas. This type of project should be given priority in the agenda of investment, as it represents the lowest step in the marginal water supply curve, meaning that it is the least expensive way to obtain "new water." Other ways of obtaining additional water include loss prevention measures, groundwater extraction, geographical water transfers, and desalination, each in principle somewhat more expensive than the one before.

Water availability is jeopardized by pollution from both industrial and domestic effluents. Low water quality leads to high treatment costs, or defeats treatment efforts. In some parts of the Sebou river, the level of chemicals is such that the water cannot be used for drinking. There is a need to set standards for industrial discharges into rivers, to protect the quality of river water and reduce the costs of treatment.

The value of water to urban residents and enterprises, which is expressed in this study by the shadow prices of water generated by the model, is very high, although the price of water actually paid by city-dwellers and factories is far lower and does not reflect even the basic costs of supply. The situation is similar in the agricultural sector, where the quantities of water used and the water subsidies are much higher yet. Obtaining an intrinsically expensive commodity so cheaply provides no incentive for the efficient use of water by users.

When an economy changes or is perturbed, MEIAH's set of multipliers yields information on the resulting changes to be expected in income, in total output of the economy, in the number of jobs and in water use by the sectors concerned. These socio-economic results are used to evaluate the consequences of potential investments in different sectors of the economy. A similar investment will generate more job opportunities if made in industry than if it is placed in agriculture, and will also require less water to support an increase in production in the industrial sector than in agriculture. For example, one million DH of capital invested in agriculture will allow the creation of 120 new jobs, while the same amount invested in industry and services will provide 848 jobs, seven times the number. Investing directly in the water sector itself can increase water availability and indirectly create new jobs in sectors using water.

MEIAH's water input-output linear programming is an analytical tool that highlights the strategic sectors of the economy and generates an economy-wide value of water of 3.64 DH/m^3 for an amount of annual rainfall and flow which has been met or exceeded in 75% percent of past recorded years. This result not only stresses the scarcity of the resource but also gives a hint for the water pricing structure. MEIAH also indicates a good response of the economy to change in the water price, represented by an elasticity of −0.18.

In a water-stressed country, annual variations of precipitation and water flows in the rivers have large effects in the economy. These are well represented in Morocco by the variation in wheat production, as a result of changes in precipitation, as discussed in Appendix 4. The stochastic simulation part of the model evaluates the risks of planning in a situation of flow uncertainty, by determining changes in the net benefit, agricultural imports and exports, and the shadow prices of water when annual flows vary. The set of investment or policy options actually chosen will be a function of the risk that decision-makers find acceptable, depending on their risk tolerance, but MEIAH will give them information that they did not have before. It is worth noting that shadow prices in agriculture are more sensitive to water variability than in urban areas: we see a standard deviation of 0.17 DH/m^3 in agriculture compared with 0.09 DH/m^3 in urban use. Despite the stochasticity of the shadow price, the mean urban economic value of water, at 4.60 DH/m^3, remains close to twice as high as its mean agricultural value, 2.86 DH/m^3.

Implementation of the MEIAH Model
What Is the Model and Who Is It For?

There are several governmental bodies and ministries in every water-stressed country that discuss water every day and formulate plans and strategies for its management. This model is intended to give those officials and all relevant stakeholders and political groups common data and predictions in order to analyze a set of options and scenarios. Scenario analysis provides an improved understanding of the responsiveness of the economy to any change coming from the water sector or from macroeconomic factors. Its common acceptance will be a step forward toward coordinated decision making.

The image of drought that has frequently devastated areas in Morocco was very present during the design of MEIAH. Early planning and management of the water resource could have avoided the emergency projects that became imperative when drought struck. For example, in 1995, water was shipped from the area of Jorf El Asfar (near El Jadida) to Tangier, in the north of Morocco, at a cost of 50 DH/m^3, equivalent to US$6/m^3.

Often, policy-makers, knowing that 40% of employment is provided by the agricultural sector, are reluctant to take water away from agriculture, fearing to kill jobs. MEIAH provides precise estimates of the employment effects of water decisions. Morocco is a country with much potential for socio-economic development and industrial expansion. Investing in the industrial sector would offer employment opportunities to compensate for losses in the agriculture sector due to diminished water supply. A reduction of the water supplied to agriculture, moreover, could be offset by an increase in system efficiency both in the rural supply network and at the on-farm level, where the losses can reach 60%. MEIAH tells us that if a water conservation approach is taken in the agricultural sector, no job or other losses will result from re-allocation, but rather a more efficient use of the resource will emerge.

It is time today to understand the real economic value of water. Drought seems to have a greater and greater effect on the population and on agriculture production, not only because the situation may be climatically worse than it was decades ago, but also because the population has been increasing, raising both potable water demand and agricultural consumption. Due to the high subsidy in the water sector, the cost of supply of water to users does not reflect its economic value, and hence users feel little incentive to use water efficiently. If the objective of subsidizing water is to alleviate poverty, this has not been achieved, as water subsidies primarily benefit the rich.

Rural development is a primary objective for developing countries, and any plan linked to water should foster this goal. The development of rural areas means not only the expansion of irrigated areas, but also the use of advanced techniques, the increase of water efficiency and the use of scarce water so as to achieve its highest return. The latter point suggests the importance of giving farmers flexibility in the use of water to pursue the best return.

MEIAH has also been framed to raise the awareness of the international community. National problems of water are tightly linked with the international situation. How can a country be asked to move from food self-sufficiency to food-security without free and secure access to the international food market? How can a country be asked to relax its cropping pattern policies if there is no security of supply for non-locally grown agriculture goods? How can a country undertake a macro-economic reform without any response from the international market? It is clear that the problem cannot be solved at the local level or even at the national level, without bringing international factors into play.

How Can Such a Model Be Used?

In a country with a difficult water situation, a group of researchers could be trained to use MEIAH, using its results to assist members of the cabinet in their political-level decision-making. This is mainly crucial when preparing strategies for drought years. Alternatively, the MEIAH model could be applied by a think-tank or a water planning group staffed by academics, researchers, governmental officers and representatives of the various users of water in the country employing MEIAH. With it, such a group can develop a water strategy, formulate an action plan, and target priority investments.

Such a group of technical persons making a national application of MEIAH can expand or change the data in the model for more accurate results. They will also maintain a continuous awareness of the assumptions that underlie the model, checking and altering them as needed. The interface is built in such a way that it is possible to review the data while analyzing the results. The use of Excel spreadsheets makes it possible to create and evaluate alternative scenarios and generate graphs and figures of what seems relevant to examine. The MEIAH model is user-friendly, such that MEIAH's equations and computation details that lie behind the interface need not be mastered in detail by the decision maker, unless he or she so desires to go into them. Good communication between analysts and decision-makers undoubtedly plays an important role in achieving productive application of research such as this.

Application of the Model to other Countries

Although the author's home country, Morocco, was present in mind while designing this model, other countries of the Middle East and North Africa have similar circumstances, and MEIAH can easily be tailored to fit them. Several regional countries have expressed interest in such a model, including the Planning Bureau in Cyprus, and the Ministries of Water Resources of Lebanon and Turkey.

Drought is not the only problem of the water sector; at the other extreme, floods compromise the socio-economic prospects of large areas in East and Southeast Asia. The relationships between water and the general economy incorporated in MEIAH can help them in planning, as they can help industrialized countries look at the relationship of their water resource to traditional economic sectors.

Future Developments

For application in a variety of national and regional contents, the methodology of MEIAH would remain the same, but the model would need revision, new data would be used, and the water model ought to be hydrologically restructured in order to fit the considered system. There will certainly be a need for detailed information on the water sector, and an up-to-date social accounting matrix for the new country of application.

For MEIAH as Applied to Morocco

Throughout the chapters of this thesis, several assumptions have been made that could be reviewed and improved for more accurate results. Also, representing a whole region in a set of equations and constraints cannot be done without significant simplifications, and like the assumptions, these must be kept in mind by the user.

The first part of the MEIAH model covers only the three-basin area of Oum Er Rbia, Bou Regrag and Sebou, because of its high natural economic and social potential. According to the political division of Morocco mentioned in Chapter 4, there are eight different river basins. The five remaining river basins: Loukkos, Moulouya, Tensift, Souss-Massa and South of Atlas, could well be covered with a water resource model similar to MEIAH-1. Thus, coverage of the entire country would be based on observation, not extrapolation from a part to the whole.

There are several avenues of future development for MEIAH to make the DSS more comprehensive. With the provision of more data, a more detailed treatment of the urban water demand could be done, providing separate demand elasticities for each city or for sub-sets of this market. For agriculture, the different types of soil could be taken into consideration when estimating yields for the different types of crops (Edwards et al., 1990). Groundwater extraction, which this MEIAH treats as coming from a simple underground reservoir, could be modeled using finite elements techniques to capture the effects of several wells pumping from the same aquifer, modeling the water table effects of different levels of joint extraction. Regarding the water budget, soil moisture is assumed to be constant in the present MEIAH, and was not included in the water balance. The model could well be made to reflect variability in soil moisture, as this can affect agriculture production, and is of particular interest to the farmer.

Other components could be added to the objective function on the cost side, such as health impacts for both human beings and livestock due to environmental degradation (Dorfman et al., 1972). In fact, water pollution could be analyzed in more detail by individuating the chemicals and suspended solids in the industrial and domestic effluents. The health impact of the low quality of water could be evaluated, either when poor water is used for household needs, or when a low quality of irrigation water affects agriculture production. The MEIAH model could also be transformed into a dynamic model, which would be able to determine an optimal reservoir management regime, in terms of monthly storage and release levels. This would be of great interest for hydrological planning and would involve a yearly analysis of the region. Such a model would make it possible to investigate long-term drought security programs, clearly of great value in the face of high annual rainfall variability.

Limitations of the Input-Output Model

The structure of an input-output table is static and assumes that there is no technological change within five years of the planning. Creating a dynamic model would also overcome the limitations of this assumption by making it possible to take into consideration temporal changes in technical coefficients of the input-output matrix. In this study, moreover, the 15-sector input-output table is highly aggregated for industry, services and rainfed agriculture; more detail could be captured if these sectors were broken down into finer categories. The water sector in the input-output table, for example, could differentiate qualities of water, taking into account levels of pollution and treatment. Water activities could also be disaggregated by considering different types of water supply, such as potable water, different irrigation systems, and water coming from contrasting geographic areas.

Onward Creation of a Water CGE Model

The newly defined water input-output table could be used as a base to form a Water Social Accounting Matrix, which would include water as an input and commodity, differentiated according to source, as well as according to the activities related to water. Such a SAM can then be translated into equations which balance the different commodities, thus forming a Computable Generalized Equilibrium (CGE) model which integrated water. The hydrological cycle of water would appear using physical balance equations in addition to the traditional set of economic equations. A CGE model is more interactive than an input-output table, as it considers the production function of the economic commodities and involves a broader set of primary inputs (labor, capital, land, and in this case, water). The formulation of the CGE model is such that both quantities and relative prices are determined endogenously within the model. There have been several efforts to use a CGE model to assess the impact of environmental policies on an economy and an environment, but often to consider air quality rather than to incorporate a water sector. A new water CGE model would include hydrological equations which would link water, as one of the inputs to different economic activities, to its physical sources—precipitation and groundwater—capturing the return flows after being used. A set of simulations would evaluate the effects of hydrological changes and, inter-sectoral allocation on the economy as a whole through socio-economic indicators that cannot be determined using the input-output table.

For Morocco, a CGE has been developed and is already being improved. The same water balance accounts are translated into hydrological equations, and thereby water is considered from its sources to its final use, with due attention to return flows, losses in the system and evaporation. This is an ongoing research project in collaboration with the International Food Policy Research Institute (IFPRI) which seems to have great potential for Morocco.

It is my hope that similar projects can be implemented for other regions, where the management of too little or too much water is a significant factor in economic growth. The field of hydro-economics is just beginning to develop, and the present study invites the reader to take part in what is sure to be an ongoing and productive process.

Appendix *1*

Case Study of Morocco

In amplification of the briefer historical and economic description given at the beginning of Chapter 4, this appendix presents detailed background on the Kingdom of Morocco and its water situation, to which the MEIAH model was applied. Morocco is presented here primarily from an economic perspective, emphasizing on the need for macroeconomic reform, the promotion of rural well being, and greater integration with the expanding world economy. This appendix then offers an overview of the water sector in Morocco, focusing on the three-basin region of the Oum Er Rbia, Bou Regrag and Sebou (and two coastal) rivers. This region was used for the development of the first part of the model MEIAH.

The Moroccan Economy
Overview of the Water Sector
Morocco is distinguished among the countries of North Africa by the magnitude of its mountains, the extensiveness of its arable coastal lowlands, and its full exposure to the Atlantic Ocean. These geographical features highly influence the very diverse climatic conditions within the country, and result in a large variability of the water resources, both spatially and temporally.

Region of Study: Oum Er Rbia, Bou Regrag and Sebou River Basins
The zone of principal study for this book is a group of three major river basins—Oum Er Rbia, Bou Regrag and Sebou—and also includes some coastal rivers (Mellah, N'fifikh, Cherrat and Yquem) which are grouped as the coastal basins. This zone covers 13% of Morocco's land and has a 215 km coat on the Atlantic ocean. This region has seen substantial important water

resource development in the last few years. Figure A1-1 shows the location of the studied region in the map of all the country, and then it is zoomed to show in more detailed the flows of the rivers from the Middle and High Atlas mountains into the Atlantic Ocean.

A large share of the national water resource, as well as of population and economy, is concentrated in this group of basins. The Oum Er Rbia is the largest (highest volume) of Morocco's rivers, and the Sebou has the largest catchment area. Sixty percent of the potential water resource in Morocco is concentrated in the three-basin region, and it accounts for 60% of the national agriculture potential. The climate varies substantially from the north of the region to the south, giving the Sebou basin—surrounded by Medium and High Atlas mountains—high flows, whereas the water-starved Oum-Er-Rbia watershed (200 mm per year precipitation) attempts to meet its high urban demands (for cities like Casablanca) through expensive inter-basin transfers from the Sebou. However, the intense pollution of the Sebou river, due to the sugar industries around the Reservoir Garde de Sebou, the paper industries in the region of Kenitra and the tanneries in the Plateau of Fez and Meknes, jeopardizes the quality of the water and has major public health impacts. Despite the presence of several surface and groundwater reservoirs, there is intense competition in meeting demands for water uses in the Oum-Er-Rbia. These demands include agricultural ones, (numerous GHs and PMHs in the basin, and out-of-basin transfer to Doukkala and El-Oualidia) and urban needs (Casablanca, and out-of-basin transfer to Marrakesh, Safi and El Jadida).

The three basin region is an important part of the country and contributes significantly to the national economic activity, as it generates 68% of the national cereal production, 87% of legumes and 90% of the crops that require industrial processing (oilseeds, textiles, etc.). Regarding urban demand, 55% of Morocco's population (13.4 million people) is located in the region and up to 80% of Morocco's industrial establishments are situated in the dense urban areas of this zone. This includes the principal water consuming industries: phosphate, sugar and paper.

International agencies such as the World Bank, USAID and UNDP, have financed a number of projects in the region in water supply and irrigation development, and have supported studies by international consultants ("Etude du Secteur de l'Eau" by NEDECO). They are interested in the application of river basin approaches and in examining the macroeconomic consequences of the large water subsidies, especially in irrigation.

FIGURE A1-1
Morocco and the Region of Study

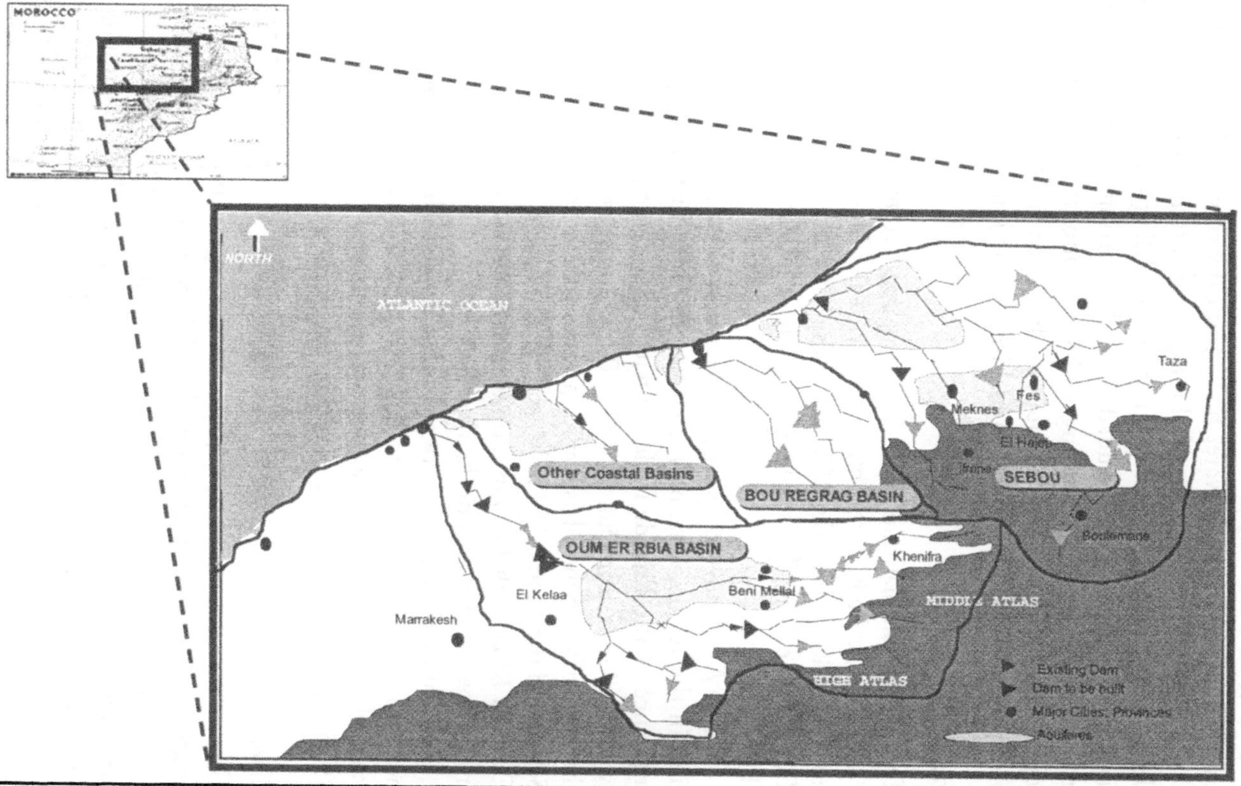

Water Supply

The rivers of this combined basin drain a catchment area of about 80,000 km². The rivers get their water flows from the snow melt of the High and Medium Atlas mountains, and through precipitation and surface drainage along the tributaries' watersheds. For this modeling work, the inflows to the river are assumed to be included from the starting points of the different tributaries. Some of the starting nodes have monthly flow data, while for some others the monthly distribution has been modeled on the monthly precipitation variations, since annual inflows are known.

Precipitation

The average annual rainfall in Morocco, apart from the mountain heights, varies from as high as 750 mm per year in the Mediterranean region of the north (Loukkos) to under 100 mm in the Saharan regions of Ouarzazate and Tafilalt in the south. The total precipitation for Morocco averages 150 billion m³ (BCM) per year.

Figure A1-2 shows the spatial distribution of the average annual precipitation in the region. One may note the 430 mm in Bou Regrag, where the influence of the altitude is clearly felt. The average precipitation varies between 760 mm near Oulmes and 500 mm in the coastal area, 750 mm over the total of the Sebou basin with a variation between 400 mm in the high Sebou and the plain of the Beht, and 1800 on the Rif mountains, 520 mm in Oum Er Rbia, with 1100 mm on the Middle Atlas Mountains and 300 mm in the downstream part of the river basin.

Annual precipitation has two distinct seasons, dry from May to September, and wet from October to April, as well as a very intense inter-annual variability. Table A1-1 shows the average annual precipitation for the year 1995 for selected meteorological stations in Morocco.

Groundwater

Groundwater aquifers are dispersed in the region and represent significant sources of water in perpetuity if exploited in a sustainable manner. The region contains 11 aquifers, of which two groups of four and three aquifers are inter-connected, located as shown in Figure A1-3. Maximum rates of sustainable extraction are represented in Table A1-2, totalling 130 MCM per year. Table A1-2 also shows the acronym of each aquifers as used in the programming in this study.

FIGURE A1-2
Rainfall Distribution

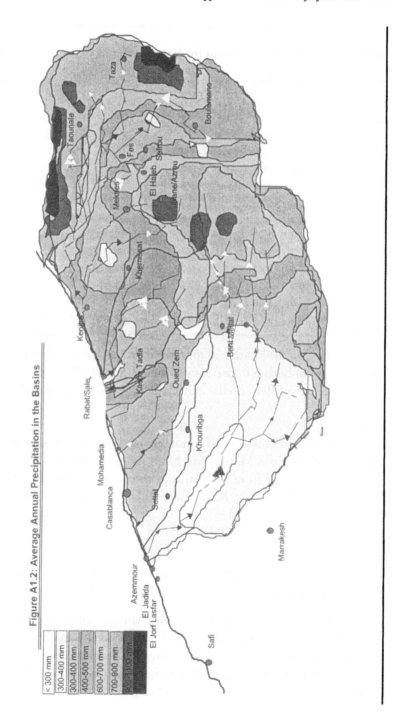

Figure A1.2: Average Annual Precipitation in the Basins

TABLE A1-1

Average Monthly Precipitation for Some Selected Centers in mm for 1995

Stations	Sept.	Oct.	Nov.	Dec.	Jan.	Feb.	Mar.	Apr.	May	Total
Agadir	0.9	1.0	2.4	10.0	0.0	21.4	70.1	5.1	4.5	115.4
Beni Mellal	5.2	19.0	17.4	1.8	0.0	42.4	4.6	59.9	1.9	152.2
Casablanca	4.9	35.7	27.8	2.0	4.8	41.0	11.0	20.8	0.0	148.0
El Jadida	1.9	4.6	28.4	11.0	17.2	34.8	21.8	23.2	0.0	142.9
Fes	25.3	28.0	23.2	1.0	1.6	32.8	36.2	23.5	10.0	181.6
Ifrane	52.1	43.4	56.1	5.6	4.9	79.6	134.0	96.9	10.5	483.1
Kenitra	2.2	49.3	85.6	0.6	12.2	38.8	15.4	39.8	0.0	243.9
Marrakesh	0.0	36.3	5.0	1.0	0.0	43.6	44.6	123.0	0.0	253.5
Meknes	22.3	96.5	16.2	0.7	6.0	50.7	28.5	51.8	6.4	279.1
Ouarzazat	1.5	51.3	0.0	0.4	0.0	0.0	34.3	65.7	0.4	153.6
Rabat-Sale	1.4	19.4	42.5	0.2	8.9	57.6	10.3	34.4	0.0	174.7
Safi	0.5	32.1	15.4	20.0	0.1	34.1	42.2	40.2	0.0	184.6
Tanger	56.0	39.8	76.7	3.0	33.4	23.6	54.6	45.9	4.2	337.2
Taza	25.5	49.8	42.3	10.6	8.0	18.4	21.1	41.1	3.5	220.3

Depending on the location of these aquifers, they are used for urban use or for irrigation, or for both purposes, as it is the case for Dir Beni Mellal, which both supplies the city of Beni Mellal and small and medium irrigated areas nearby.

Flows to the Rivers

Inflows to the region originate from small oueds (seasonally dry water courses) and streams from the Middle and High Atlas Mountains, from the mountains of the Rif, and from the plains of the center region through drainage. The Oum Er Rbia, Bou Regrag and Sebou region has been represented schematically in Figure A1-4. The inflows to the different rivers are represented by 22 nodes, identified as follows:

- 8 in the Sebou river basin: SS1 to SS8
- 5 for Bou Regrag and the coastal rivers: S1, S2, and SB1 to SB3
- 9 for Oum Er Rbia river basins: SO1 to SO9

The Directorate of Hydrology in the Ministry of Public Works has collected historical monthly inflow data for these river basins. After working to refine this raw data somewhat, the average of these historical inflows has been calculated for use in the model for the base case, where the inflows are assumed to be those of an average rainfall year.

FIGURE A1-3
Groundwater Sources in the Region of Study

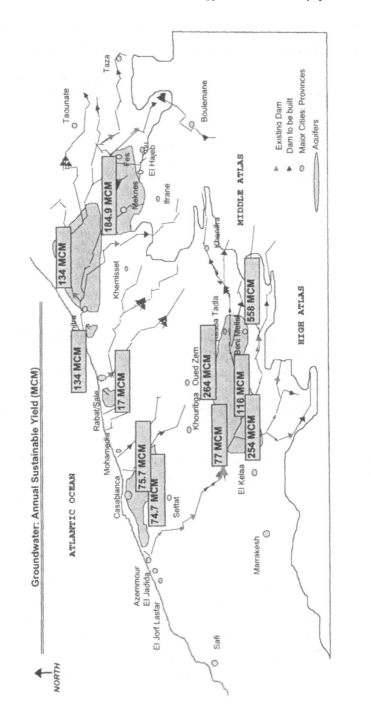

TABLE   A1-2

Sustainable Exploitation Yield for the Aquifers of the Region

Aquifers	Acronyms	Sustainable Extraction Yield in MCM
Turonienne	GTU	254.0
Beni Amir	GBA	116.0
Dir Beni Mellal	GDB	558.0
Beni Moussa	GBM	264.0
Berrechid	GBE	74.7
Chaouia	GCH	75.7
Gharb	GGH	134.0
Mamora	GMA	134.0
Tessaout Aval	GTA	77.0
Temara	GTE	17.0
Meknes-Fes	GMF	184.9

Table A1-3 gives the 75% reliabilities—the level of flows exceeded 75% of the time—for inflows from each node to the rivers as used in the optimization model. Month to month variability within the year is clear, as is the distinction between the two seasons. Figure A1-5 illustrates the flows of the starting point of Oued Tessaout, tributary of the Oum-Er-Rbia river.

Reservoirs

A striking characteristics of these river basins is the large number of reservoirs (17 dams with a capacity varying from 7 million m³ (MCM) to 3,730 MCM in Al Wahda) which are used for different purposes (urban, agriculture or both). About 25 further dams are planned for future construction by 2020. Figure A1-6 shows the distribution of these 17 existing and 25 planned reservoirs in the region. These reservoirs are for month to month storage for irrigation or urban use; their capacities are shown in Table A1-4.

Some of these reservoirs have installed hydropower capacity. In Morocco, 8% of the total electrical energy is from hydropower, and the largest part of this hydropower production originates from the three-basin region. The different hydropower capacities, varying from 8 to 300 MW, are also shown in Table A1-4, along with the constituents of hydro capacity, such as the water heights (heads) and turbine size. Also given are the acronyms for dams and reservoirs in the programming.

FIGURE A1-4

Hydrological Schematic of the Region

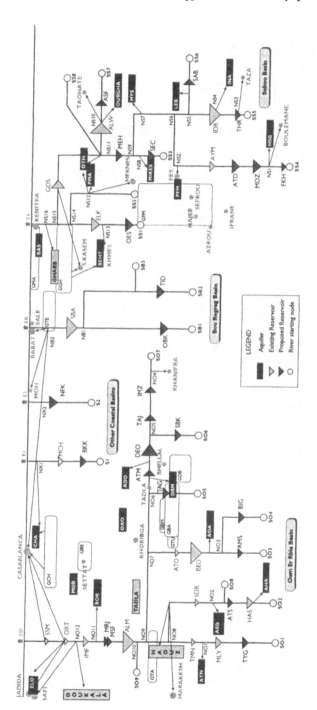

TABLE A1-3
Monthly Inflow to the River from the Different Tributaries—75% Reliability

		Sept.	Oct.	Nov.	Dec.	Jan.	Feb.	Mar.	Apr.	May	Jun.	Jul.	Aug.
Tessaout	SO1	2.69	2.90	3.12	4.29	4.92	5.02	7.90	9.10	6.69	3.93	2.54	2.24
Lakhdar	SO2	3.50	3.94	3.98	4.30	5.00	5.80	7.55	9.45	7.65	4.52	3.23	3.20
	SO3	3.52	3.23	3.77	3.95	4.79	6.99	15.95	19.85	11.68	5.86	3.78	3.18
Oued El Abid	SO4	2.14	1.89	2.20	2.71	2.76	4.31	12.05	15.60	8.64	4.10	2.29	1.92
	SO5	2.20	2.95	3.10	4.40	55.75	6.00	6.40	6.55	4.25	2.88	2.08	1.81
Derna	SO6	3.83	4.34	4.61	5.67	7.60	8.89	0.47	8.23	6.67	3.89	3.18	2.99
Srou	SO7	10.95	11.65	12.35	13.85	14.90	15.80	15.90	16.30	15.30	12.10	11.00	10.80
Fellat	SO8	3.11	4.41	7.28	3.11	0	0	0	0	0	0	1.67	2.45
	SO9	3.28	3.99	4.78	4.71	6.56	6.72	8.24	11.16	9.92	4.62	3.09	2.77
Mellah	S1	0.21	0.20	0.38	0.37	1.03	0.33	0.30	0.31	0.30	0.31	0.04	0.04
N'fifikh	S2	0.13	0.12	0.26	0.26	0.70	0.24	0.21	0.22	0.18	0.19	0.03	0.03
Grou	SB1	0.34	0.57	1.35	1.76	2.85	3.20	2.76	2.13	1.45	0.52	0.22	0.17
Bou Regrag	SB2	0.32	0.68	1.91	2.49	3.77	3.38	3.67	2.66	1.78	0.56	0.19	0.16
	SB3	0.42	1.35	1.99	3.89	5.56	5.88	5.42	3.79	2.73	0.87	0.33	0.29
Beht	SS1	1.91	2.48	4.09	6.24	8.33	7.73	9.15	7.84	4.85	3.14	1.27	0.93
Rdom	SS2	0.63	1.02	1.86	3.09	2.70	2.91	2.75	2.46	1.56	0.90	0.39	0.26
Mikkes	SS3	0.90	1.29	1.07	1.68	2.34	1.94	2.41	2.74	2.27	1.22	0.81	0.58
Guigou	SS4	5.17	5.96	6.66	8.10	10.65	13.85	21.60	24.10	19.10	12.40	6.97	5.29
Inaoun	SS5	0.88	1.59	3.49	7.22	9.13	12.55	12.19	12.33	7.63	2.70	1.08	0.62
Lebene	SS6	5.85	17.19	21.00	27.40	32.40	35.71	44.30	48.38	35.29	24.23	8.05	5.95
Ouergha	SS7	13.59	17.19	21.00	27.40	32.40	35.71	44.30	48.38	35.29	24.23	17.13	13.74
Zloul	SS8	10.10	11.25	0	0	6.35	0	0	52.65	42.75	25.85	19.15	18.00

Source: Nedeco 1994, and "Plan Directeur de l'Eau," 1995

FIGURE A1-5

Flow in the Oued Tessaout Tributary of Oum Er Rbia

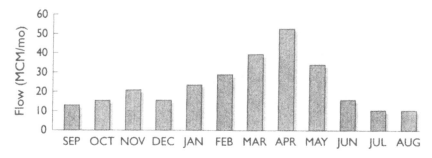

Source: Royaume du Maroc, 1994 and 1995

Agriculture Sector

Morocco's irrigation sector is well-developed. Irrigation accounts for 85% of the mobilized water resources and its history is very linked with that of water resources development. Of the 71 million hectares of Morocco, 21 million are classified as rangeland and 9 million as cultivable land. Irrigated agriculture covers almost one million hectares, and is divided into 500,000 hectares of Large Scale Irrigated areas (GHs) administered by the Ministry of Agriculture (ORMVA), and 400,000 hectares of Small and Medium Irrigated areas (PMHs), operating with traditional systems under governmental guidance and support. About 100,000 hectares are operated by the private sector.

In the Oum Er Rbia, Bou Regrag and Sebou region, the water demand for irrigation is to satisfy both PMH and GH. PMH cover 95,110 ha along the valley (Sebou, Inaouene, Beht, Ouergha, Medium and Low Sebou) and in the plain of Meknes-Fez. PMH demand 580 MCM per year, as shown in Figure A1-7. PMHs are dispersed in the region and are primarily irrigated by private wells. (Much of the current data, such as yields and net benefits for PMH, are averages for the whole country, not specific to the three-basin region.)

GHs are found in four different areas: Doukkala, Gharb, Haouz and Tadla, which are shown in Figure A1-8. Four GHs are irrigated from the mobilized water of the region of study, of which three from the Oum Er Rbia basin: Doukkala (located in the south of the region is supplied through interbasin-transfer by the Canal of Doukkala), Tadla and Haouz. The fourth GH—Gharb—is located in the coastal area of the Sebou river. These irrigated areas are managed by four corresponding ORMVA, and each has been

FIGURE A1-6
Existing and Planned Reservoirs of the Region

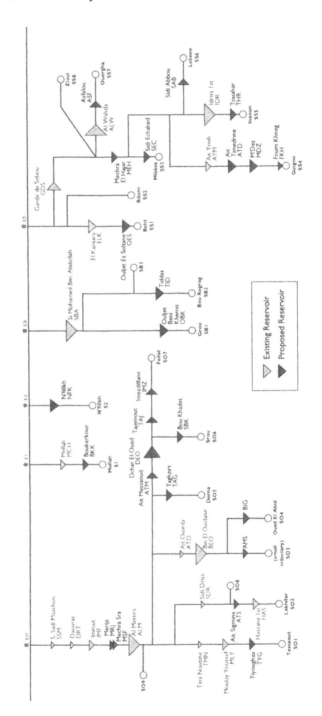

TABLE   A1-4

Characteristics of the Reservoirs

Reservoirs	Acronyms	Maximum Capacity in MCM	Hydropower Capacity in MW	Maximum Head in m
Imezdilfane	IMZ	70	62	60.41
Taskdert	TAS	20	38	42.14
Tajemout	TAJ	7	28	36.42
Bou Khadet	SBK	439	4.8	70
Dchar El Oued	DEO	740	84.7	96
Ait Messaoud	ATM	13	6	34
Taghzirt	TAG	239	8.7	150
Bou Inougoudane	BIG	143	19.8	83
Amesfrane	AMS	84	110.1	76.2
Bin El Ouidane	BEO	1,300.3	135	104
Ait Ouarda	ATO	110	458	172.2
Hassane 1st	HAS	262.6	67	181.1
Ait Sigmine	ATS	110	—	80
Sidi Driss	SDR	3.7	77	48.26
Tiyoughza	TYG	145	10.9	110
Moulay Youssef	MLY	175.2	24	82.5
Timi Noutine	TMN	5.3	—	28.78
Al Massira	ALM	2,759.8	128	57.5
Mechra Sfa	MSF	22	29	40.3
Merija	MRJ	20	31.4	40.43
Imfout	IMF	18.2	31.2	36
Daourat	DRT	9.5	17	20.6
S. Said Maachou	SSM	1.5	20.8	33.23
Boukerkour	BKK	60	1.8	60
Mellah	MCH	8.2	7.1	31.32
N'fifikh	NFK	50	1.3	12
Ouljet Beni Khemis	OBK	600	—	172.49
Tiddas	TID	600	—	120
Si Mohamed Ben Abdellah	SBA	486	—	60
Ouljet Es Soltane	OES	208	16.4	77
Al Kansera	ELK	265.8	14.4	44.8
Sidi Echahed	SEC	170	8	70.65
Foum Khneg	FKH	40	—	37.17
M'Dez	MDZ	600	52	97
Ait Timdedrine	ATD	3	148	34
Ait Youb	AYM	110	239	115.72
Touahar	THR	40	24	43.36
Idriss 1st	IDR	1,185.8	40.6	54
Sidi Abbou	SAB	70	5	35
Bab Ouandar	BAO	390	38	131.54
Rhafsai	RHA	290	30	105.32
Tafrant	TAF	290	21	102.99
Mechra El Hajar	MEH	18	7	19
Asfalou	ASF	320	20	112
Al Wahda	ALW	3,730.5	248	992.9
Garde de Sebou	GDS	40.1	—	37.19

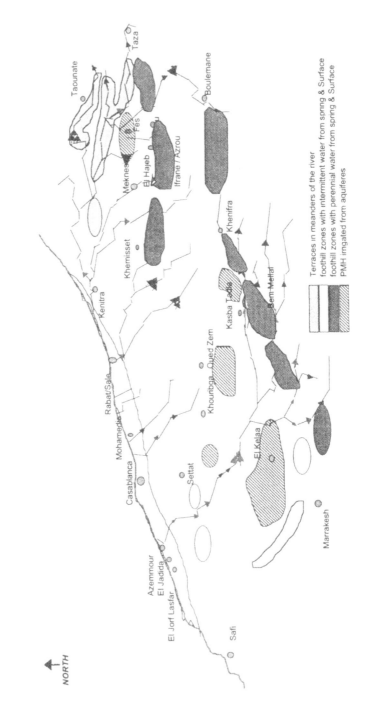

FIGURE A1-7
Small and Medium Irrigated Areas in the Region of Study

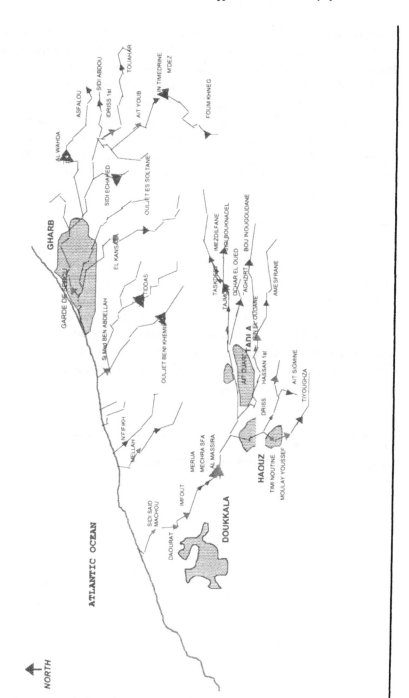

FIGURE A1-8

Large Scale Irrigated Areas in the Region of Study

through many irrigation projects financed by international cooperation (World Bank). Several advanced irrigation techniques, such as sprinklers, are well diffused these areas. Each of the four GH has its characteristics in terms of the type of water supply sources, which are reflected in the different characteristics of each in terms of yield, labor, land, agriculture production and water requirement. There are several expansions planned by the year 2020 of both PMH and GH (Figure A1-9). Table A1-5 provides their irrigated area figures for 1995, and proposed irrigated areas for 2010 and 2020, and acronyms as used in the model. Note the ambitious plans to expand irrigation which are reflected in this table.

Irrigation Water System

The efficiency of an irrigation system depends on its size: for the large scale irrigated areas, the distribution irrigation efficiency is 86%, while in small and medium scale areas, efficiency is 53%. At the on-farm level, although GHs use more advanced technologies, efficiency seems to be higher for PMHs with 75%, compared to 69% in the large scale irrigated areas.

The water supplied for irrigation is either from groundwater aquifers or from the rivers. In either case, there is some cost for the pumping or for the diversion of the surface water. Table A1-6 summarizes this cost of supplying the water for each type of irrigated area.

FIGURE   A1-9

Irrigated Area in the Basin vs. All Morocco

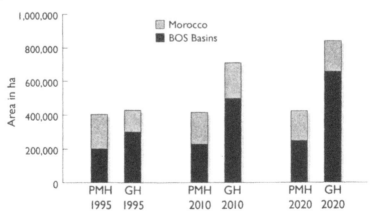

Agriculture Production

There are nineteen different types of production grown in this area: wheat (WHEA), spring corn (COSP), summer corn (COSU), rice (RICE), barley (BARL), other cereals (OCER), legume (LEGU), fodder (FODD), sugar beet (SUGB), sugar cane (SUGC), cotton (COTT), oil seed production (OILS), spring vegetables (VEGS), autumn vegetables (VEGA), citrus plan-

TABLE A1-5

Irrigated Areas in Hectares

Name	Acronym	1995	2010	2020
Large Scale Irrigated Areas (GH)				
Gharb	GHA	89,678	137,045	220,400
Tadla	TAD	97,300	99,687	107,900
Haouz	HAO	53,550	134,590	202,700
Doukkala	DOU	61,300	127,003	125,300
Small and Medium Scale Irrigated Areas (PMH)				
Amont Dchar El Oued	ADO	7,878	8,941	9,700
Oued El Abid Ait Ouarda	OAO	1,381	1,567	1,700
Amont Timi Noutine	ATN	1,827	2,074	2,250
Amont Hassan 1st	AHA	2,761	3,134	3,400
Amond Sidi Driss	ASD	10,558	11,982	13,000
Dir Beni Mellal	DBM	29,318	33,274	36,100
Amont Oued El Abid	AOA	1,624	1,843	2,000
Moyen Oum Er Rbia	MOR	4,954	5,623	6,100
Bas Oum Er Rbia	BOR	1,015	1,152	1,250
El Oualidia	ELO	3,980	4,516	4,900
Chaouia	CHA	27,931	31,699	34,391
Beht	BHT	6,189	7,024	7,620
Inaouene	INA	9,242	10,489	11,380
Haut Sebou Guigou	HSG	14,099	16,001	17,360
Moyen Sebou	MYS	6,538	7,420	8,050
Bas Sebou	BAS	6,538	7,420	8,050
Ouergha	OUG	18,923	21,476	23,300
Mikkes	MIK	1,218	1,383	1,500
Lebene	LEB	3,427	3,890	4,220
Plateau Fez Meknes	PFM	28,425	32,260	35,000
Piedmont Moyen Atlas	PMA	4,719	5,355	5,810
Other PMH	OTH	8,121	9,217	10,000

TABLE   A1-6

Cost of Irrigation Water Supply

		Surface Water Cost in DH/m^3	Groundwater Cost in DH/m^3
Large Scale Irrigated Areas			
Gharb	GHA	0.20	0.35
Tadla	TAD	0.19	0.36
Haouz	HAO	0.18	0.49
Doukkala	DOU	0.32	0.35
Small and Medium Scale Areas		0.2225	0.3875

tations (CITR), other cash crops (OCSH), greenhouse bananas (GHBN), greenhouse vegetables (GHVG), and others (OTHR). Yields vary for each GH, and among the PMH. Water requirements for each type of crop depend on the type of soil and the climate of the irrigated area. Table A1-7 provides the characteristics of each crop, in terms of monthly water requirement, based on a research done by NEDECO, the World Bank and the Ministry of Agriculture. Yields depend also on the soil, and the climate. Cropping pattern policies, implemented through a system of subsidies, are very specific, each type of agricultural production having a certain hectarage allocated to it. Figure A1-10 shows the overall cropping pattern in the region. In the MEIAH model reported in this study, this cropping pattern is used for the "business as usual" Scenario A in Chapter 4, and then is relaxed in order to analyze different scenarios in Chapter 5.

International Trade

Food consumption is satisfied by both domestic production from irrigated and rainfed land, and international imports. Table A1-8 shows domestic demand for the year 1995. Irrigated production represents 40% of the value added in agriculture, and the rest is from rainfed agriculture, as shown by Figure A1-11 at the national level.

International trade is highly regulated. Both imports and exports are constrained by certain agreements with other countries, which are taken into consideration for the "business as usual" scenario of Chapter 4. Table A1-9 gives exports prices for agricultural production, as well as the import prices as set through the GATT agreements (Alaoui, 1994).

TABLE A1-7
Crop Monthly Water Requirements in mm per Month

	Sept.	Oct.	Nov.	Dec.	Jan.	Feb.	Mar.	Apr.	May	Jun.	Jul.	Aug.
WHEA	0	0	0	7.0	28.0	32.0	51.0	55.0	0	0	0	0
COSP	169.0	142.0	0	0	0	0	0	0	0	0	38.0	0
COSU	0	0	38.0	100.0	169.0	142.0	0	0	0	0	0	0
RICE	0	0	294.6	294.6	294.6	294.6	0	0	0	0	0	0
BARL	136.2	78.0	31.0	16.0	18.0	19.0	39.0	73.0	143.7	142.0	172.0	178.0
OCER	136.2	78.0	31.0	16.0	18.0	19.0	39.0	73.0	143.7	142.0	172.0	178.0
LEGU	0	11.3	11.3	11.3	11.3	11.3	11.3	11.3	11.3	11.3	0	0
FODD	86.0	67.2	36.9	29.5	40.8	33.5	0	0	0	0	0	0
SUGB	0	4.0	6.0	10.0	23.0	25.0	48.0	73.0	116.0	120.0	64.0	0
SUGC	84.2	84.2	84.2	84.2	84.2	84.2	84.2	84.2	84.2	84.2	84.2	84.2
COTT	128.0	0	0	0	0	0	0	25.0	48.9	30.0	172.0	169.0
OILS	0	0	0	0	0	0	0	0	0	0	0	0
VEGS	93.8	32.7	1.4	4.6	32.5	33.4	0	0	0	60.7	113.0	143.7
VEGA	60.7	113.0	143.7	93.8	32.7	1.4	4.6	32.5	33.4	0	0	0
CITR	60.2	48.3	29.0	3.5	9.9	3.1	34.0	37.2	66.3	91.8	125.4	105.7

Source: computed from Nedeco, 1994—Agriculture and Irrigation, and other World Bank reports

Cropping Pattern in the Region

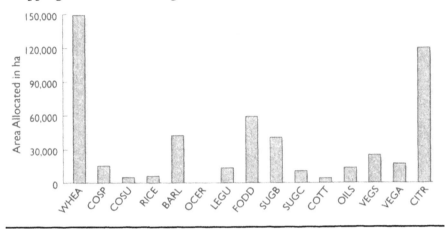

TABLE   A1-8

Agriculture Consumption for 1995

Agriculture Product	Acronym	Consumption in '000 Tons
Wheat	WHEA	3279
Corn Spring	COSP	1388
Corn Summer	COSU	1388
Rice	RICE	1023
Barley	BARL	49
Other Cereals	OCER	1664
Legume	LEGU	24
Fodder	FODD	1664
Sugar Beet	SUGB	4776
Sugar Cane	SUGC	4776
Cotton	COTT	228
Oil Seeds	OILS	170
Vegetable-Spring	VEGS	1002
Vegetable-Autumn	VEGA	453
Citrus	CITR	473

FIGURE A1-11

Rainfed Agriculture Production

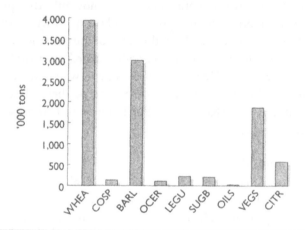

TABLE A1-9

Imports and Exports Prices for Agriculture Production

Agriculture Product	Acronym	Export Price in DH per ton	Import Price as of the GATT agreements in DH per ton		
			1995	2000	2005
Wheat	WHEA	1504	3104	2967	2816
Corn Spring	COSP	1528	2040	2002	1976
Corn Summer	COSU	1172	2040	2002	1976
Rice	RICE	2438	1600	1600	1600
Barley	BARL	871	1962	1827	1678
Other Cereals	OCER	1341	2369	2265	2157
Legume	LEGU	2867	200	200	200
Fodder	FODD	111	2625	2625	2625
Sugar Beet	SUGB	158	4750	4750	4750
Sugar Cane	SUGC	113	3296	3296	3296
Cotton	COTT	3942	1000	1000	1000
Oil Seeds	OILS	3886	4775	4775	4775
Vegetable-Spring	VEGS	831	2625	2625	2625
Vegetable-Autumn	VEGA	1098	2625	2625	2625
Citrus	CITR	1320	3000	3000	3000

Source: Anuaire Statistique du maroc, 1995

The benefit from the agriculture sector is computed as the area under the demand curve, taking into consideration levels of imports and exports. As shown in Figure A1-12, this benefit depends on not only the quantity of agriculture production imported or exported, and the quantity produced and consumed locally, but it also depends on the slope of the demand curve (slope of AA′), which differs from one crop to another. Based on a study done by Kutcher for the Master Plan of Development for Egypt, where the food regime could be assumed to be similar to that of Morocco, these elasticities are represented in Table A1-10 (Kutcher, 1980; Lofgren and Robinson, 1997; Metzel, 1992; and Stryker, 1991).

Urban Water Demand

Morocco's most populated cities are located in the region of study (mainly Casablanca and Rabat); major industrial establishments are also grouped in the vicinity of the large cities. The trend of population increase is very steep, and therefore water demand for the years 2010 and 2020 is expected to rise greatly in some urban centers, as shown in Figure A1-13 for the studied region. Figure A1-14 shows the trend in urban population. Also, per-capita consumption is expected to increase by the year 2020. Based on studies by the Potable Water Agency (ONEP), the changes in the per capita consumption, the total urban demand and the increase in the system efficiency are all summarized in Table A1-11.

FIGURE A 1 - 1 2
Agriculture Production Demand Curve

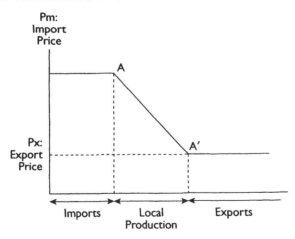

TABLE A1-10
Price Elasticity for Each Crop

Crop	Acronym	Elasticity
Wheat	WHEA	−0.55
Corn Spring	COSP	−0.07
Corn Summer	COSU	−0.68
Rice	RICE	−0.74
Barley	BARL	−0.20
Other Cereals	OCER	−0.38
Legume	LEGU	−0.63
Fodder	FODD	−0.38
Sugar Beet	SUGB	−0.57
Sugar Cane	SUGC	−0.57
Cotton	COTT	−1.00
Oil Seeds	OILS	−1.20
Vegetables–Spring	VEGS	−0.75
Vegetables–Autumn	VEGA	−0.75
Citrus	CITR	−1.40

FIGURE A1-13
Monthly Urban Household Water Demand in MCM

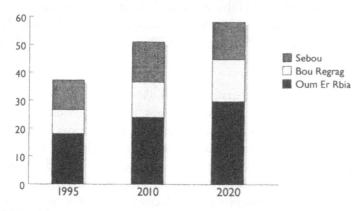

Source: ONEP, 1994

FIGURE A1-14

Population Trend, Millions, for Urban Areas

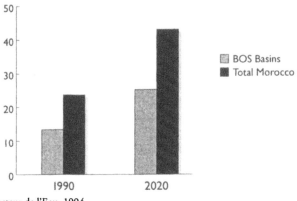

Source: Plan Directeur de l'Eau, 1994

Similarly, the monthly industrial water demand is expected to increase in the region as shown in Table A1-12. The industrial demand had been included in the urban demand.

There are several programs launched for water loss reduction and increases in the efficiency of the urban water network. The efficiency of the water network varies from 45% to 78%; the aim by the year 2020 is to reach an average efficiency of 76% (Table A1-11), through water saving measures and encouraging recycling in industry. For example, for Casablanca, there is a planned increase in the efficiency from 67% to 78% by the year 2020.

Urban Demand

If we consider a demand curve of water as shown in Figure A1-15 and a supply curve represented as a set of steps referring to different costs of supplying water by different means, these two curves cross at the optimum point for a quantity Qo and a price Po. The net benefit from water supply is then computed as the area under the demand curve, reduced by the cost of supplying the water, represented as the dashed area in Figure A1-15. The urban demand curve is generated for each city based on the consumption and price of 1995 (Katz and Rosen, 1994). The water demand elasticity is equal to –0.25, as determined by an unpublished study done by the World Bank on Casablanca and the vicinity.

TABLE A1-11
Urban Per Capita Water Consumption, Water Demand and Distribution Efficiency

	Per Capita Consumption (lpcd)			Total Urban Demand (m³/month)			Distribution Efficiency (%)		
	1995	2010	2020	1995	2010	2020	1995	2010	2020
Oum Er Rbia	55.4	82.1	83.6	20,906,180	28,247,513	34,725,175	70%	76%	77%
Khnifra	15.5	69.0	69.6	450,666	985,377	1,215,532	73%	77%	77%
Beni Mellal	20.6	67.2	69.8	1,151,763	2,260,265	2,791,752	72%	77%	77%
Khouribga	35.3	58.0	59.3	996,599	1,295,359	1,382,504	58%	71%	75%
Settat	61.7	82.9	84.3	1,574,360	1,481,219	1,815,060	74%	77%	78%
Mohamedia	104.0	102.0	102.7	1,667,205	2,577,377	3,157,749	72%	77%	77%
Casablanca	95.0	102.0	104.0	13,696,153	17,341,875	21,501,686	67%	78%	78%
El Jadida	55.8	93.3	95.3	1,369,434	2,306,042	2,860,893	71%	77%	77%
Bou Regrag & Costal	82.5	100.6	102.7	11,659,481	18,971,147	24,422,528	75%	79%	79%
Khemissat	42.0	66.7	68.6	443,644	894,913	1,108,175	78%	78%	78%
Kenitra	107.4	119.3	120.8	2,104,542	3,477,463	4,260,367	71%	79%	79%
Sidi Kacem	34.9	72.4	74.2	3,108,880	6,597,802	9,450,607	70%	76%	76%
Rabat	159.0	167.0	168.0	3,948,368	5,091,506	5,883,730	77%	80%	80%
Sale	69.0	77.5	82.0	2,054,047	2,909,462	3,719,649	79%	81%	81%
Sebou	62.1	103.2	104.5	11,099,240	15,777,870	15,000,314	69%	76%	76%
Boulemane	43.2	72.4	73.4	95,555	214,453	251,875	71%	77%	77%
Taza	30.1	77.5	79.2	769,747	1,338,806	1,634,885	69%	75%	76%
Taounate	37.6	76.4	76.6	470,767	295,498	363,236			
Sefrou	51.1	93.9	94.1	545,273	709,115	871,899	65%	76%	76%
Fez	71.5	108.0	108.5	5,558,640	8,242,860	9,986,924	70%	76%	76%
Ifrane	69.8	133.4	131.4	329,189	504,200	588,898	72%	76%	76%
El Hajeb	56.8	74.3	79.8	186,609	332,591	428,418			
Meknes	137.0	189.7	192.8	3,143,460	4,140,346	874,178	71%	74%	77%

TABLE A1-12

Industrial Water Consumption

Province	Acronym	Industrial Demand in MCM		
		1995	2010	2020
Casablanca	UCAS	1.174	1.734	2.114
El Jadida	UALJ	0.096	0.178	0.232
Safi	USAF	0.313	0.579	0.754
Marrakech	UMAR	0.237	0.437	0.570
Settat	USET	0.041	0.092	0.115
Khouribga	UKHO	0.044	0.075	0.088
Beni Mellal	UBEN	0.035	0.220	0.267
Khnifra	UKHA	0.034	0.068	0.082
Mohamedia	UMOH	0.492	0.837	1.02
Rabat	URAB	0.029	0.118	0.136
Sale	USAL	0.063	0.122	0.157
Kenitra	UKEN	0.165	0.263	0.32
Khemissat	UKHM	0.026	0.05	0.061
Sidi Kacem	USKA	1.589	4.193	6.13
Meknes	UMEK	0.061	0.269	0.328
Ifrane	UIFR	0.023	0.028	0.032
Fez	UFES	0.188	0.573	0.698
Sefrou	USEF	0.024	0.029	0.035
El Hajeb	UELH	0.012	0.020	0.024
Taounate	UTAO	0.008	0.016	0.020
Boulemane	UBOU	0.003	·0.009	0.011
Taza	UTAZ	0.023	0.055	0.067
Azrou	UAZR	0.003	0.009	0.011

The cost of supplying the water depends on the source as well as the distance of transfer if transfer is needed. Groundwater supply cost is equal 0.38 DH/m^3, which includes both the extraction cost and the treatment cost. Surface water supply cost includes the cost for treatment and an additional cost for transfers, which varies from 0 DH/m^3 to 4.5 DH/m^3.

Water Pollution and Environmental Considerations

Atlantic coastal aquifers suffer from saline intrusion if they are overdrawn. There is therefore a minimum outflow constraint that has to be met when the rivers empty into the ocean (around 63 MCM per year for Oum-Er-Rbia and Sebou). See Table A1-13.

FIGURE A1-15

Urban Demand and Supply Curve for Water

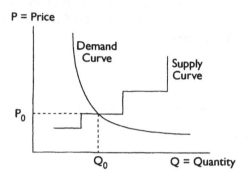

TABLE A1-13

Minimum Outflow to the Ocean to Prevent Saline Intrusion

	Minimum Yearly Outflow to the Ocean in MCM
Oum Er Rbia	63
Bou Regrag	30
Sebou	60

Industrial Pollution

Achieving regional goals in terms of water quality necessitates some investigation of pollution discharged into the region's water. It is only in recent years that researchers have focused on concerns that are a serious threat to the environment in some locations. In the Sebou river, the quality of water is starting to seriously threaten the health of the downstream populations. Tanneries, paper and sugar industries and urban wastewater are large sources of pollution on the river. Some studies have been conducted in locating and determining the different points of effluent discharge along the river (Figure A1-16). The main pollutants from these surveys are: biological oxygen demand (BOD), and chemical oxygen demand (COD), suspended solids and chrome. Due to data constraints, this version of the model looked only at the dilution concentration of BOD discharged from 10 industries grouped in five different points along the Sebou river (Table A1-14). For the purposes of MEIAH, for each industry along the Sebou river, information was gathered on the different sources of water used, and the pollutants resulting from the production process. For example, Figure A1-17 provides the characteristics for a paper factory in Kenitra.

FIGURE   A1-16
Sources of Pollution of Sebou River Basin

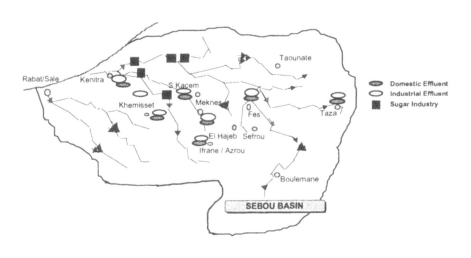

TABLE   A1-14
**Level of BOD Discharge from Each Industry Source:
Industrial Evaluation, 1995**

Type of Industry	Node on the Schematic	BOD Discharge in mg/l
Sunab-Sidi Slimane (sugar industry)	NS11	1900
Tannery – Meknes	NS12	800
Cellulose-Sidi Yahi du Gharb (sugar industry)	NS14	2758
Group of Sugar Processors	NS15	9500
CMCP-Kenitra (paper industry)	NS16	60

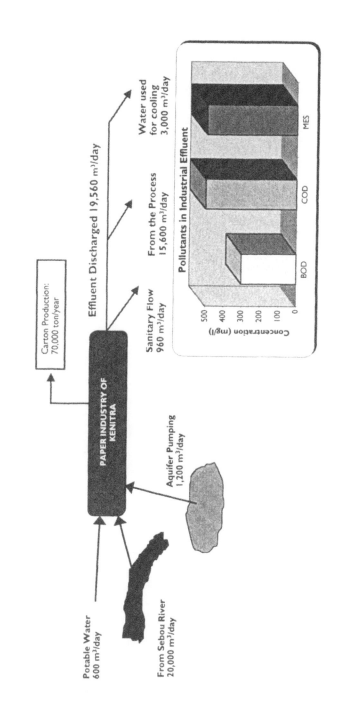

FIGURE A1-17
Pollution from a Paper Factory in Kenitra

Appendix 2

The MEAIH-1 Model:
A Decision Support System

This appendix provides the structure of the DSS for the analysis and allocation of water among different sectors.

The Water Resource Mathematical Programming Model

The nonlinear optimization model developed is a multi-faceted approach to water resource planning and management. The river basins studied involve multiple supplies (reservoirs, groundwater) and multiple demands. The model groups together hydrological, physical, social, agricultural, economic, environmental, mathematical and computer tools to analyze the nonlinear relationships among the parameters and the decision-variables in the region.

The water resource mathematical model, MEIAH-1, is a monthly model covering a 25 year period (1995 to 2020). It maximizes the aggregated net benefits (social surplus) to all users in the area (agriculture, urban, hydropower), constrained by the continuity of the system, water demand, land availability, and environmental, financial, macreoconomic or other considerations. It does this by determining optimal values of various decision variables including water flows, groundwater utilization, reservoir storage and releases, sectoral allocation, urban demands, cropping patterns, and hydropower generated on a monthly and yearly basis. Shadow prices can also be determined to estimate the scarcity of water. The model can be conveniently disaggregated into nine sections: continuity constraints, reservoir constraints, hydropower constraints, urban constraints, irrigation constraints, production and trade constraints, environmental constraints, policy constraints, and the objective function.

There is a wide range of parameters and variables that have to be defined for the formulation of the model and the definition of the constraints. There are eight distinguished variables which are used to define the system and the different parts of it. Table A2-1 displays these different variables, which will be used in the expression of the constraints as well as the objective function of the optimization model.

In addition to the decision variables, there is a large number of parameters that describe the situation and make it possible to express it in terms of mathematical relationships. Table A2-2 summarizes the parameters that will be used in the equations.

Continuity Constraints

The continuity constraints are included in the model to insure mass conservation. The studied region can be represented schematically using a set of nodes covering the important points of the system: inflow, demand, intersection, and reservoir. The continuity constraint expresses the fact that the water flows that enter a node (the sum of flows $Q(n1,n,t,y)$ that enter the node, n, from the connected nodes, $n1$, at month, t, and year, y) is equal to the flow that leaves the node, if it has not been stored or diverted, or lost. This relationship starts with the inflows to the river ($QINFLOW(n,t,y)$) at node, n (starting node of the river), and ends at the stream node, ne. Figure A2-1 summarizes the six types of nodes of the system: ns – starting nodes, nr – reservoir nodes, ng – groundwater nodes, nf – inflow nodes, nu – urban area, ni – irrigated area. Equations (1) to (5) correspond to the basic continuity relationships (note that the flows are defined when the connection exist between two nodes). The symbol "∀" means "for any."

TABLE A 2 - 1
Decision Variables for the Optimization Model

Decision Variable	Description
Z	Value of the objective function
$Q(n,n1,t)$	Water flow from node n to node $n1$ at time t (in Million cubic meters per month)
$RSTOR(n,t)$	Reservoir storage (MCM per month)
$IAREA(n,t)$	Land at node n for type of crop c (ha)
$HPGEN(n,t)$	Hydropower generation (KWH)
$QDDOMV(n)$	Domestic water demand as a varaiable (MCM per month)
$IMPORTS(c)$	National imports in 1000 tons
$EXPORTS(c)$	National exports in 1000 tons

TABLE A2-2

The Parameters of the Model

$A(n)$	Coefficient for head storage relation
$ATARIF(n,\text{type},y)$	Tariffs for agricultural water (DH per m^3)
$ALPHA(n,y)$	Demand curve coefficient
$BETA(n)$	Water demand
c	Crop type (wheat, corn, barley, rice, cereals, legumes, fodder, sugar beet, sugar cane, cotton, oils, vegetables, citrus)
$CAP(n)$	Capacity of reservoirs (MCM)
$CAPMAX(nr)$	Maximum capacity for the reservoir nr
$CTRAN(n,n1,y)$	Unit cost of transporting water from n to $n1$ in year y (DH per m^3)
$CGU(n,y)$	Unit cost of gw pumping for urban use (DH per m^3)
$CURIAREA(n,c)$	Current area (ha)
$CROPCAL(c,t)$	Cropping calendar 1-grown 0-not grown
$CRWATREQ(c,t,y)$	Crop water requirements (mm per month)
$DAG(c,y)$	Domestic agriculture consumption
$EFD(n,y)$	Distribution irrigation efficiency per area
$EFU(n,y)$	Distribution efficiency (fraction)
$EFF(n,y)$	On-farm irrigation efficiency
$Ehyp(n,t)$	Hydropower efficiency assumed
$EXPMAX(c)$	Maximum agriculture exports in 1000 tons
$EXPMIN(c)$	Minimum agriculture exports in 1000 tons
$GSTOR(n)$	Groundwater storage (MCM per year)
$GFRAC(t)$	Groundwater storage fraction available in month t (fraction)
$GF(ng,t,y)$	Renewable yield
gw	Groundwater
$HEADMAX(n)$	Maximum head in meters
$HPRICE(n,t,y)$	Net price for hydropower in DH per KWH
$HPCAP(n,y)$	Maximum capacity of reservoir in node n in year y (MW)
$IAMAX(n,y)$	Area of irrigated lands for both GH and PMH
$INVBETA(n)$	Inverse beta
$LPC(n,y)$	Per capita consumption in liter per day
$LFxFU(n,t)$	Load factor and factor of utilization assumed
LOS	Factors defining losses in storage
n	Nodes
$NPRICE(n,c,y)$	Price for crop c at n in year y (DH per ton)
$NATQAG(c,g)$	Domestic consumption in 1000 tons
$MINFLOW(n,n1,t,y)$	Minimum flow requirements (MCM per month)
$PEF(n,d)$	Percent wastewater (fraction)
$POP(n,y)$	Population per province and future trends
$PRINCR(c,y)$	Price increase fraction for crop c in year y
$PAGINC$	Percentage of agriculture increase

continued

TABLE A2-2

The Parameters of the Model *(continued)*

PAGINC	Percentage of agriculture increase
$P_X(c,y)$	Export price as function of the year
$P_M(c,y)$	Import price as the GATT agreement in DH per Ton
QAGMAX(cd,y)	Maximum national consumption
QAGMIN(cd,y)	Minimum national consumption
QSAG(c,g,y)	Quantity definition
QDAGR(c,y)	National demand for agriculture production in 1000 tons
QED(nu,n,t,y)	Effluent discharged to the river from household and industry salinity
QMIN(n,y)	Lower bound for computational purposes (MCM per month)
QDDOM(n,y)	Quantity of domestic demand (MCM per month)
QDIND(n,y)	Industrial Consumption (MCM per month)
QINFLOW(n,t,y)	Inflows into start nodes (MCM per month)
QLOSSF(n,n1,t)	Conveyance losses from n to $n1$ at time t (fraction of Q)
QSAL(n,t,y)	Min flow required for salinity control (MCM per month)
QLOS(nr,nn,t,y)	Loss fraction in the system
r	Discount rate
RCAP(n,y)	Maximum Capacity of reservoir in node n in year y (MCM)
RCOST(n)	Annualized cost of dam at n (MDh)
RFFU(n,n1,t)	Return flow fraction at time t — urban (fraction of QD)
RFFI(n,n1,t)	Return flow fraction at time t — irrigated (fraction of QD)
RLOSSF(n,t)	Fraction of storage changed — fcn of temp & pptn (fraction)
RSTOR(nr,t,y)	Reservoir storage
RLOS(nr,t,y)	Loss fraction
RFI(nn,nu,t,y)	Fraction of return flows
RFU(nn,nu,t,y)	Fraction of return flows
RFAGR(c)	Rainfed agriculture production in Morocco in 1000 tons
RSAG(c,g,y)	Revenue definition
SALES(c)	Gross production of a commodity
SWU(n,y)	Surface water cost for urban use (DH per m³)
SWA(n,y)	Surface water cost for agriculture use (DH per m³)
sw	Surface water
t	Month of year
type	Type of water source: groundwater or surface water
y	Year (1995, 2000, 2005, 2010, 2015, 2020)
YD(n,c,y)	Yield (tons per ha)
WR(ni,c,t)	Monthly water requirements per crop
WSAG(c,g,y)	Welfare segments
WS(nu,t,y)	Fraction of waste water in the urban area

F I G U R E   A 2 - 1

Continuity at the Nodes of the System at Month *t* and Year *y*

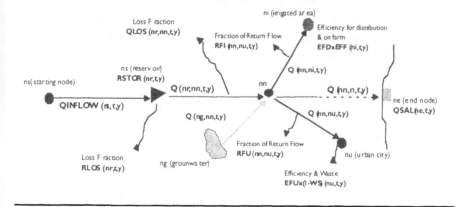

$$\text{Start Node Constraint}: \quad \forall(ns, t, y) \quad \sum_n Q(ns, n, t, y) = QINFLOW(ns, t, y) \tag{1}$$

$$\text{Continuity at Intermediate Nodes}: \quad \forall(nn, t, y) \quad \sum_n \Big(1 - QLOS(nn, n, t, y)\Big) Q(nn, n, t, y)$$
$$= \sum_n Q(nn, n, t, y) \tag{2}$$

$$\text{Continuity at Urban Nodes}: \quad \forall(nu, n, t, y) \quad Q(nu, n, t, y) =$$
$$\sum_{nl} \Big[EFU \times WS(nu, t, y) \times \Big(RFU(nl, nu, t, y) \Big) * \Big(1 - QLOS(nl, nu, t, y) \Big) \, Q(nl, nu, t, y) \Big] \tag{3}$$

$$\text{Continuity at the Irrigated Areas}: \quad \forall(ni, n, t, y) \quad Q(ni, n, t, y) =$$
$$\sum_{nl} \Big[EFD * EFF(ni, t, y) \times \Big(RFI(nl, ni, t, y) \Big) * \Big(1 - QLOS(nl, ni, t, y) \Big) \, Q(nl, ni, t, y) \Big] \tag{4}$$

$$\text{Continuity at the Reservoir Nodes}:$$
$$\forall(nr, t, y) \quad \sum_n \Big[\Big(\big(1 - QLOS(n, nr, t, y) \big) * Q(n, nr, t, y) \Big) + RSTOR(nr, t-1, y) \Big]$$
$$= \sum_n \Big[Q(nr, n, t, y) + \big(1 + RLOS(nr, t, y) \big) * RSTOR(nr, t, y) \Big] \tag{5}$$

Reservoir Constraints

One of the objectives of this model is to yield an investment schedule for reservoirs projects, and determine the optimal size $RCAP(nr)$ of the planned reservoirs, in addition to targeting an appropriate reservoir storage $RSTOR(nr,t,y)$, and release rule $Q(nr,t,y)$. An upper bound is set on the largest practical size for the dams $CAP(nr)$.

$$\text{Capacity Constraint:} \qquad \forall nr \qquad RCAP(nr) \le CAP(nr,y) \qquad (6)$$

$$\text{Storage Constraint:} \qquad \forall(nr,t,y) \qquad RSTOR(nr,t,y) \le RCAP(nr) \qquad (7)$$

Hydropower Constraints

The hydropower production process can be substantially defined using three decision variables, which are incorporated into the model: the flow $Q(nr,n,t,y)$ through the turbines of the power plant nr, the head associated with the flow, which is a function of average reservoir storage, $RSTOR(nr,t,y)$, and the installed hydropower capacity of the plant, $HPCAP(n)$ (which is zero when no hydropower is generated by the reservoir). These decision variables are linked to hydro-electric production through the following equation (8):

$$\text{Hydropower Generation} \qquad \forall(nr,t,y) \quad HPGEN(nr,t,y) =$$

$$7157.4 \ A(nr) \ Ehyp(nr,t,y) \sum_{n} \left[Q(nr,n,t,y) \left(\frac{RSTOR(nr,t,y) + RSTOR(nr,t-1,y)}{2} \right) \right] \qquad (8)$$

where $HPGEN$ is the energy produced, A is the head of the reservoir at the start of the period, $Ehyp$ corresponds to the power plant efficiency, and 7157.4 represents the unit conversion factor. The installed capacity is reduced by the load factor, and the factor of utilization of the plant ($LF \times FU$) sets an upper limit on the energy (9):

$$\text{Hydropower Capacity:} \qquad \forall(nr,t,y) \qquad HPGEN(nr,t,y) \le \frac{HPCAP(nr)}{LF \times FU(nr,t,y)} \qquad (9)$$

Urban Constraints

Due to the increasing urban population, the domestic demand for water $QDOM(nu,t,y)$ at each domestic demand node, nu, is rising. Similarly, the industrial demand for water $QIND(nu,y)$ tends to keep up with the income growth which shapes its future trend. This urban demand determines the water supplied to the corresponding nodes:

$$Urban\,Water\,Demand: \quad \forall(nu,t,y) \quad \sum_n EFU(nu,t,y)\big[(1-QLOS(nu,n,t))Q(nu,n,t,y)\big]$$

$$\geq QDOM(nu,t,y)+QIND(nu,t,y) \tag{10}$$

Irrigation Constraints

The irrigation constraints set the relationship between water and agricultural production. Due to the complexity of the agricultural sector (crops depend on water volume and quality, soil characteristics, solar radiation, etc.) simplifications had to be made to link the water flows to the cropping pattern in modelling the agriculture sector. Each irrigated area $IAMAX(ni,y)$ has its own characteristics in terms of yield of production $YD(ni,c,y)$ for each crop c, and the monthly water requirement $WR(ni,c,t)$. The area $IA(ni,c,y)$ under each type of crop represents the model decision variable. Taking into consideration the efficiency at the distribution level $EFD(ni,t,y)$ or at the farm level $EFF(ni,t,y)$, as well as losses in the system, two constraints are required:

$$Irrigated\,Water\,Demand: \quad \forall(ni,t,y)$$

$$\sum_n EFD \times EFF(n,t,y)\big[(1-QLOS(n,ni,t,y))Q(n,ni,t,y)\big] \geq \sum_c WR(ni,c,t,y)IA(ni,c,y) \tag{11}$$

$$Land\,Constraint: \quad \forall(ni,t,y) \quad \sum IA(ni,c,y)CROPCAL(c,t,y) \leq IAMAX(ni,y) \tag{12}$$

Production and Trade Constraints

Agriculture production in the region that comes both from irrigated and rainfed agriculture $RFAG(c,y)$ determines the sales $SALES(c,y)$ of national products.

$$Commodity\,Balance: \quad \forall(c,y) \quad SALES(c,y)$$

$$\leq \sum_{ni}\big(YD(ni,c,y)IA(n,c,y)\big)+RFAG(c,y) \tag{13}$$

The relationship between imports $IMPORTS(c,y)$, exports $EXPORTS(c,y)$, domestic consumption $DAG(c,y)$ and agriculture production shapes the local cropping pattern (14). Often, the government imposes some limits on trade which represent the upper bound for either imports or exports, or both.

Demand Balance: $\forall(c,y)$ $SALES(c,y) + IMPORTS(c,y) =$

$$EXPORTS(c,y) + \sum_{g}\left(QSAG(c,g,y)\,DAG(c,g,y)\right) \tag{14}$$

Environmental Constraints

Since the effluent discharged to the river $QED\,(nu,n,t,y)$ from households and industry jeopardizes water quality in the region, an upper bound on the concentration of chemicals needs to be maintained to insure environmental quality standards. (This is relevant for a pollution control equation that is not expressed in MEIAH at this point.) Similarly, due to salinity intrusion, a lower bound $QSAL\,(n,t)$ is set for a minimum flow at the coastal end of the rivers (15). Also, since the sustainability of groundwater is threatened by its overexploitation, groundwater pumping should not exceed the renewable yield $GF\,(ng,t,y)$ (16).

Saline Intrusion Constraint: $\forall(ne,t,y)$ $\sum_{n}Q(n,ne,t,y) \leq QSAL(ne,t)$ (15)

Groundwater Extraction: $\forall(ng,t,y)$ $\sum_{n}Q(ng,n,t,y) \leq GF(ng,t,y)$ (16)

Policy Constraints

The previously described constraints deal with the physical, environmental and economic aspects of water. Other policy and legal constraints could be added to insure the realism of the optimal solution. For example, the area under each type of crop should not exceed a 50% change from what was set by national planners. This constraint is employed in two scenarios of this study's Chapter 5. Many other constraints could be added to the system: financial constraints in terms of the budget, or in terms of a fixed goal for a certain type of crop. Also, a nonegativity constraint of the variables could be applied.

Objective Function

The general form of the objective function is the maximization of the aggregated net discounted benefit for the different water users in the region. This maximization is fourfold: First, household and industrial net benefits are determined by computing the area under the demand curve for water reduced by the cost of supplying the water to the corresponding demand nodes (water pumping, transfers, connections). Second, the net benefits from agriculture correspond in the social surplus from agriculture production. For a particular product, the demand curve is piecewise linear, where import and export prices (P_m and P_x) are fixed exogenously and set, respectively, the upper and lower price of the national production (where the domestic price is linearly decreasing as a function of quantity). The solution of the model will therefore correspond to the equilibrium of the agriculture market, taking into consideration the cost of supplying the water to the irrigated areas. The third component of the objective function corresponds to the benefit from the sale of hydropower. The capital and maintenance costs for new reservoir investment are discounted and divided over the construction period, and enter as a negative in the objective. These four components are determined for each block of five years, then discounted to the present.

$$
Z = \sum_{ord(y)} \frac{1}{(1+r)^{ord(y)}} \left\{
\begin{array}{l}
\left[
\begin{array}{l}
\sum_{j} \left(QAG(c,g,y)\,WS(c,g,y) + EXPORTS(c,y)\,P_x(c,y) - IMPORTS(c,y)\,P_M(c,y) \right) - \\[6pt]
\sum_{(ng,ni,t)\backslash I} \left[COST(ng,"gw",y) * Q(ng,ni,t,y) * (1 - QLOSSF(ng,ni,t,y)) \right] \\[6pt]
- \sum_{(nn,ni,s))} \left[ATARIF(nn,"sw",y) * Q(nn,ni,t,y) * (1 - QLOS(nn,ni,t,y)) \right]
\end{array}
\right] \\[18pt]
+ \left(
\begin{array}{l}
\sum_{nu} 12 * \dfrac{Alpha(nu)}{(1 - invBeta(nu))} * QDU(nu,y)^{(1 - invBeta(n))} \\[8pt]
- \left[\sum_{(ng,nu)} CGU(ng,y) * Q(ng,nu,t,y) \right] \\[8pt]
- \left[\sum_{((nn,nu,t)} CTRANS(nn,nu,y) * Q(nn,nu,t,y) \right]
\end{array}
\right) \\[18pt]
+ \left(\sum_{(n,t)\$nrbl(n,y)} [HPRICE(n,t) * HPGEN(n,t)] \right) - \sum_{nr} \left(RCOST(nr)\,\dfrac{RCAP(nr)}{CAPMAX(nr)} \right)
\end{array}
\right\}
\tag{17}
$$

Domestic and Industrial Net Benefit

The urban benefit corresponds to the area under the demand curve, reduced by the cost of supplying the water to different urban demand nodes. To define this net benefit, there is a need to revisit some basic economic concepts. The concept of demand curve of water has to be defined. As for any economic good, because water consumption is dependent and sensitive to water charges and prices, a demand curve can be generated, although a limited availability of data can be a problem. As generally considered, we have a constant elasticity "b" for which the demand curve has the form:

$$P = a\, Q^b$$

where: P = price for water in money per cubic meter
Q = quantity of water demanded in cubic meter
a = the coefficient of the demand curve
b = demand elasticity, which typically ranges between −0.18 and −0.48 for household and between −0.3 and −1.32 for industry

By defining the demand curve and overlapping it with the supply curve, we can have some understanding of efficient water use and efficient water allocation. Figure A2-2 shows graphically a demand curve of water and a water supply curve. The highlighted area refers to the economic surplus (here named the economic net benefit) which represents the sum of the producer and the consumer surpluses, and corresponds to the integrated area. Numerically, this is equal to:

$$CS + PS = \frac{a}{a(b+1)} Q^{(b+1)}$$

where: CS = consumer surplus
PS = producer surplus

On the Figure A2-2, P* and Q* refer to the optimal price and the optimal quantity where the demand curve and the supply curve intersect. The economic surplus is used in the objective function of the optimization model as the net benefit from domestic and industrial water use.

Agricultural Net Benefit

The agricultural net benefit also corresponds to the area under the demand curve, reduced by the cost of supplying the water for irrigation. There is an additional distinction that has to be considered, concerning the import and export levels of agriculture. Depending on the price of a crop in the international market, there will be either export or import of that crop, which will affect differently the net benefit. Similarly with domestic and industrial pro-

FIGURE A2-2

Supply and Demand Curve for Water

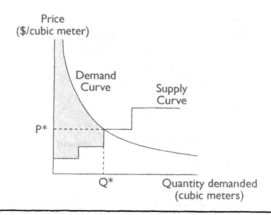

duction, we need the price elasticity of the different type of crops. Figure A2-3 shows the different possibilities for the world price of one type of production.

We can consider two different cases:

The first case is when domestic production is higher than domestic demand, in which case the additional production is directed to export and will be subject to the international price, which will be an additional benefit to the objective function of the model. According to the Figure A2-3, there will be a level of production of Q2, and the quantity (Q4 – Q2) will be exported to the international market. The net benefit will therefore be the selling of the level Q2 of production in the domestic market, reduced by the supply cost in addition to the quantity exported.

The second possibility is when there is only a small quantity of a crop produced locally or none, and the rest, or all of it, is imported at international prices. This will enter as a negative value in the objective function. In the Figure A2-3, it represents a production of Q1 locally (which can also be equal to 0) and the rest (Q3 – Q1) being imported from the international market to meet the local demand.

The inclusion of the level of imports and exports, as well as international prices, in the model gives a certain flexibility between whether or not to produce an agricultural good locally to meet domestic demand, or to obtain it in the international market. However, we should note that the macroeconomic constraint serves to tighten or loosen the flexibility regarding international markets and international prices.

FIGURE   A 2 - 3

Agriculture Production Supply and Demand Curve

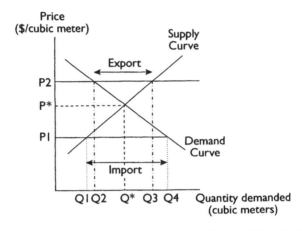

Hydropower Benefit

The price elasticity of hydropower is considered to be infinite. The benefit from hydropower corresponds to the net returns from the sale of the energy generated by the reservoir, with an installed hydropower capacity in the market. This is calculated by multiplying the price of energy by the quantity generated.

Model Implementation and Scenarios

The MEIAH-1 Water Resource Model, constructed using the set of equations (1) to (17) has been implemented using the GAMS (Generalized Algebraic Modeling System) programming language (Brooke, Kendrick and Meeraus, 1988). The studied region of Oum Er Rbia, Bou Regrag and Sebou River basins is represented in graphical way in Figure A2-4. It is represented schematically in Figure A2-5. The different types of nodes and how they are linked to each other are indicated, as are the different cities of the region as well as the irrigated areas. In this figure, reservoirs are represented by the triangles. Groundwater aquifers correspond to the dark areas on Figure A2-4, which shows how they overlap with the rivers and tributaries of the region.

As represented in Figure A2-5 there is a large number of nodes of various types, summarized in Table A2-3.

FIGURE A2-4

Region of Study: Oum Er Rbia, Bou Regrag and Sebou River Basins

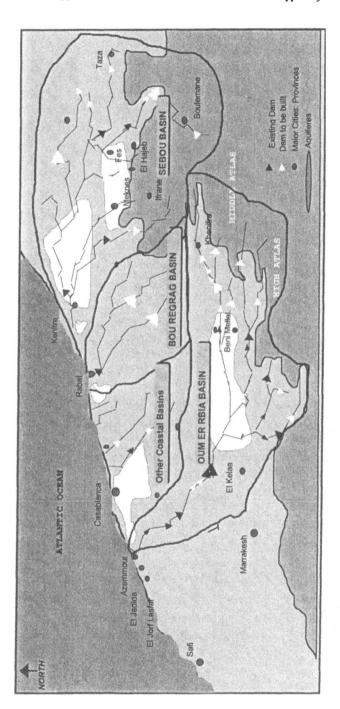

FIGURE A2-5
Schematic of the Oum Er Rbia, Bou Regrag and Sebou River Basins

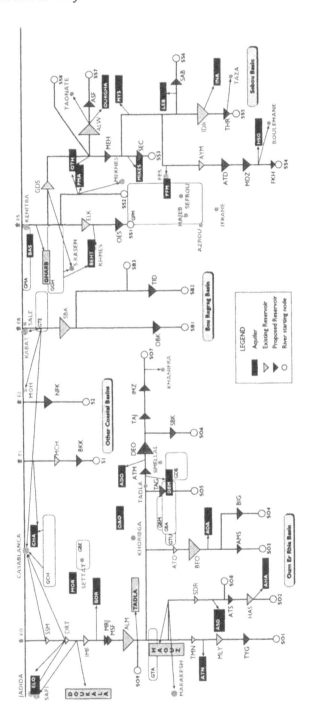

Computing Details

Taking into consideration these sets of nodes, and the different data at each node for each block of five years, using the system of looping, the previously described equations are defined for each of the nodes. In the current formulation, the number of variables in the model is 16,500 and the number of constraints is 14,600 (other than some bounds expressed separately). Some of the objectives and constraints are highly non-linear (for example, hydropower generation and areas under demand curves). This model runs for about two hours on a 200 MHz machine. It is interfaced with Microsoft Excel spreadsheets to display the inputs and outputs (live-linked to the GAMS). However, when the model is reduced to one year, the optimal solution is determined after 20 minutes of run. This is based on an interactive interface driven by a hierarchical menu. The interface is able to perform a range of functions, from first showing and changing the model parameters to running the model and defining the scenarios, and then displaying the outputs of the model in both tabular and graphical terms. The model is performed in MS-DOS for Windows.

The Generalized Algebraic Modeling System (GAMS) was initially developed at the World Bank; a similar package is the AMPL developed in the Bell Labs. The advantage of such a package is its fast and powerful capacity for

TABLE A2-3

Set of Nodes in the Region

Set	Type of Nodes	Number
ns	start nodes	22
ne	end nodes	5
nrn	new reservoir nodes without hydropower	4
nrnh	new reservoirs with hydropower	25
nro	old reservoir nodes without hydropower	3
nroh	old reservoir nodes with hydropower	14
nra	all reservoir nodes	46
nu	urban (domestic and industrial) demand nodes	23
gh	major irrigation project	4
pmh	small and medium irrigation project	22
ni	all irrigated areas	26
nn	other nodes	32
ng	groundwater nodes	11

solving optimization problems. All the files are written and read as ASCII text (from Windows) which makes it possible to use them in developing the interface. Also, the language used for GAMS gives an elegant and efficient way of representing the mathematical relationships. However, due to the fact that there is no graphical output provided with the GAMS model that could enable the representation of the large amount of information in an efficient way. Microsoft Excel spreadsheets are therefore used to display the information and to edit the input information.

Scenario Selections

The way this model is formulated provides opportunities to specify scenarios that a decision-maker wishes to investigate. The interface of the model provides a structure that helps policy analysts in the determination of the scenario. This is represented in Figure A2-6. It is a spreadsheet linked to other spreadsheets and then linked to the GAMS model itself.

For example, the parameters that could be varied in the scenarios include: the year (1995 to 2020), climate conditions (wet, normal, dry, very dry) which correspond to different levels of inflow reliability, possible connections (interbasin or intra-basin transfers), change in the price of water (national level domestic, industrial or irrigation water tariffs, or for a specific center or area) food security goals (national production or trade) and pollution standards. For the cropping pattern constraints for example, selecting the box referring to the cropping pattern will lead the person who is using the model to another spreadsheet, shown in Figure A2-7, which allows him to chose the agriculture production that he wishes to control. Similarly for the level of pollution, selecting the case referring to pollution, would lead him to the appropriate spreadsheet shown in Figure A2-8.

In addition to running different scenarios, this decision support system allows the user to view results graphically and schematically in an interactive manner. Both the input and the output data are displayed in a user-friendly manner—as a simplified Geographic Information System, in order to highlight the spatial and temporal distribution of results with regard to water supply and demands.

Model Output and Interpretation

One of the most important outputs of this water model is the shadow prices of water for each sector and for each node. The value of the shadow price is determined using the equations (10) and (11) that link the demand for water

FIGURE A2-6

Scenario Definition

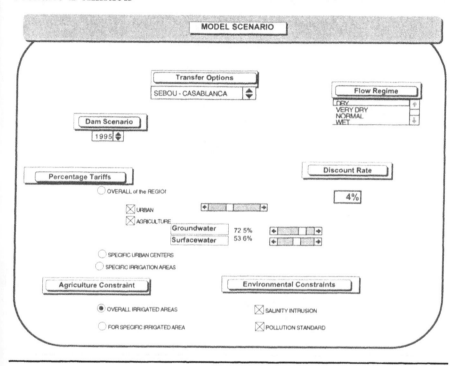

to the quantity supplied. Chapter 5 provides a thorough explanation of the different results for the chosen scenarios in this study applying MEIAH to Morocco.

Depending on the scenario chosen, this model generates a range of results. Two types of results may be highlighted from the current elaboration. First, there is a set of decision variables specifying the flows of water in the system from the sources of supply to the multiple users. Second, the economic consequences of specific policy changes, in the agricultural (trade, national production) or the urban (water tariffs, specific connections, measures for increasing efficiency) sectors are brought out.

For the supply side, the primary model results yield optimal water flows in the river, the quantity to be extracted from groundwater and the monthly releases from the reservoir. For a reservoir that has a power plant facility, the

FIGURE   A2-7

Scenario Set-up: Cropping Pattern

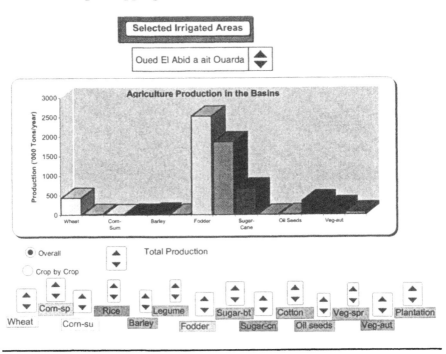

hydropower generated—computed by the model—depends closely on the amount of water storage and on the regime for monthly releases.

In the base Scenario A, where inflows to the river correspond to monthly averages, the objective and the set of constraints shape the overall water allocation in the region between the urban centers and irrigated areas. The computed shadow prices from equations (10) and (11) represent an estimation of the value of water. For example, Casablanca gets water from different reservoirs along the river, which yield a high shadow price of water (7 DH/m³), reflecting the scarcity of water in the region. For Rabat, the groundwater aquifer represents the main source of water for urban purposes and permits a very low shadow price.

The comparative advantage in trade or in national agricultural production appears in the cropping pattern for both large and small-to-medium irrigated areas, generated by the model for the 12 crops chosen. In order to highlight

FIGURE A2-8

Scenario Set-up: Environmental Considerations

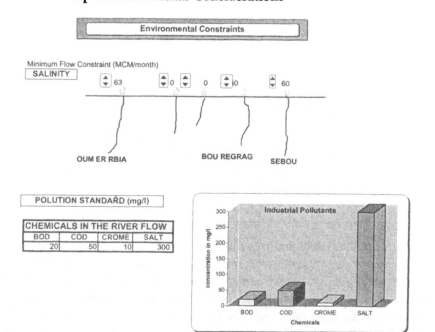

the impact of the agricultural demand function for the main agriculture production—wheat, barley, corn, other cereals, sugar beat and oil seeds—a cross-comparison between three scenarios is worth considering. A comparison of the Chapter 5 scenario where there is no constraint on the area under each type of crop with the current cropping patterns, shows that the the model tends to encourage high value crops that require less water (vegetables, sugar beet, oil seeds and cash crops). However, by setting a pattern of agriculture, already favored by planners, the model should not make a tremendous change in recommended crops, thus Scenarios C and D set a 50% possible change in the area under each type of crop. Under these scenarios, especially when trade is freed under Scenario D, exports tend to go to zero while imports increase, explaining the reduction of irrigated areas (Figure A2-9).

There are a number of parameters that depend upon MEIAH's variables and which are computed as model results. These include water losses, components of the objective function in terms of the costs and benefits, averages

FIGURE   A2-9

Trade and Agriculture Production—Scenario D

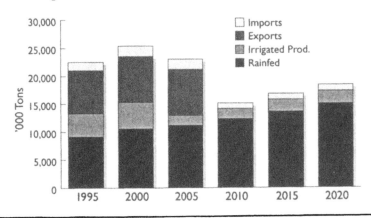

of the various variables and parameters to provide a synoptic view. To assess the impact of the uncertainty of such parameters, a simple, yet highly informative technique is available using the optimization model. This is Sensitivity Analysis on either hydrological parameters (such as inflows) or economic parameters (discount rates and subsidies in water tariffs). Sensitivity Analysis will inform the user of the response of the decision variables to alternative inputs. Such Sensitivity Analysis on both the hydrological and economic parameters involves running the model repeatedly for different values of the key parameters. Doing this is an important post-processing exercise that will help decision makers in targeting the appropriate national water policy, depending on how risk averse they chose to be.

Appendix 3

Background on the Input-Output Table used in MEIAH, and on Parallel Work by Others

This appendix provides certain background on the detailed Social Account Matrices (SAMs) which have been prepared for Morocco, and at its conclusion indicates how the SAM incorporated into MEIAH was prepared.

Based on the OECD's development of an 1990 input-output table for Morocco, Ian Golden of the World Bank created a SAM in which water was distinguished as one of the factors of production. As shown in Table A3-1, this matrix treats water in terms of the tariffs paid by water users.

Thereafter, in 1995, Morocco formulated a rural development strategy, aiming to accelerate growth and poverty alleviation in the context of a transition toward a more open and liberal economy. To support this policy-making work, a simulation model was developed and was used as an instrument to test proposed changes of policy and other exogenous conditions by measuring the impact of these changes in the model's results. At the base of this model was the computation of a SAM which is disaggregated in such a way as to capture the key aspects of the economy as they are linked to agriculture and rural activities. This 1995 Moroccan Government model is based on information from the Golden-adapted World Bank analysis (including the table A3-1), and from the OECD 1990 Input-Output table, and on data and information from the Moroccan government, the World Bank, FAO, IMF, and others.

This Moroccan Government 1995 model is distinguished from the OECD 1990 table, by the detailed treatment of agriculture, which is disaggregated into rainfed and irrigated areas. Table A3-2 shows the Moroccan Government model's disaggregation of factors, institutions, activities, and inputs. The matrix includes ten factor types, and each resource is allocated among

TABLE   A3-1

1990 OECD SAM for Morocco as adapted by I. Golden (World Bank)

	Rainfed Agriculture	Irrigated Agriculture	Manu-facturing	Services	Labour	Capital	Water	Tariff
Rainfed Agriculture	199	244	2,829	15	0	0	0	0
Irrigated Agriculture	348	298	3,458	18	0	0	0	0
Manufacturing	1,318	1,611	47,376	22,625	0	0	0	0
Services	525	642	9,516	11,542	0	0	0	0
Labour	1,555	1,901	11,219	32,258	0	0	0	0
Capital	5,125	6,264	11,599	14,437	0	0	0	0
Water	590	722	1,497	1,863	0	0	0	0
Tariff	598	731	7,719	0	0	0	0	0
Export Tax	9	10	314	1,863	0	0	0	0
Industrial Tax	55	68	2,683	463	0	0	0	0
Rural Household	0	0	0	0	7,782	12,832	0	0
Urban Household	0	0	0	0	50,151	24,593	0	0
Government	0	0	0	0	0	0	4,672	9,047
Enterprise	0	0	0	0	0	0	0	0
CapAcct	0	0	0	0	0	0	0	0
Rest of the World	1,867	34,527	34,527	4,131	0	0	0	0
Total	12,189	14,772	132,737	89,215	57,933	37,425	4,672	9,047

Source: Goldin and Winters, 1994

the 42 different activities, including 33 in agricuture. The matrix also covers the main livestock activities. For households, rural and urban areas have been distinguished. Other sectors with strong links to agriculture are singled out, such as fertilizer and energy. Also, labor is separated between rural and urban to assess the effect of irrigated activities, which touch primarily farmers and rural labor. This emphasis in the Moroccan Government 1995 model was essentially aimed at exploring rural development strategies.

Lofgren et al. at IFPRI have simulated a Social Account Matrix for 1994, which includes a set of activities as described in Table A3-2. The large number of rows and columns of this matrix makes it difficult to manipulate. In order to illustrate the methodology developed in this thesis, this large table has been aggregated to a smaller table that represents 15 sectors, summarized

Export Tax	Industrial Tax	Rural Household	Urban Household	Govern-ment	Enterprise	CapAcct	Rest of the World	Total
0	0	3,062	4,277	0	0	1,430	134	12,190
0	0	3,062	5,277	0	0	1,748	613	14,822
0	0	11,074	23,273	0	0	13,273	12,186	132,736
0	0	7,591	24,851	16,399	0	23,500	3,785	98,351
0	0	0	0	0	0	0	0	46,933
0	0	0	0	0	0	0	0	37,425
0	0	0	0	0	0	0	0	4,672
0	0	0	0	0	0	0	0	9,048
0	0	0	0	0	0	0	0	2,196
0	0	0	0	0	0	0	0	3,269
0	0	0	0	306	0	0	8,589	29,509
0	0	0	0	436	0	0	1,200	76,380
333	32,690	583	6,420	31	0	806	663	55,245
0	0	0	0	0	0	0	0	0
0	0	4,137	12,331	3,020	0	0	21,269	40,757
0	0	0	0	5,631	0	0	0	48,437
333	32,690	29,509	76,429	25,823	0	40,757	48,439	

in Table A3-3. The system developed for these 15 sectors could be generalized to much bigger models of the economy.

The SAM presented in this book and used as a component of MEIAH is also based in its design on the 1990 OECD matrix as updated to 1995. However, the OECD matrix contained about a hundred sectors, which for the purposes of MEIAH was far too detailed, and was therefore aggregated to 15 sectors. To aggregate the table, we have used the traditional method used in regional economic planning. This consists in the grouping of the same family of activities together by summing the cells corresponding to the rows, as well as the ones corresponding to the columns. This aggregated Social Account Matrix, as used in MEIAH and this book, is represented in Table A3-4.

TABLE   A3-2

Moroccan Government 1995 Model: Disaggregation of Activities, Factors, Other Inputs and Institutions

Set	Elements
Activities	Irrigated Agriculture
	Hard Wheat, Soft Wheat, Barley, Maize, Other Cereal, Legumes, Fodder, Sugarbeet, Sugarcane, Sunflower, Other Industrial Crops, Vegetables, Olives, Citrus, Other Fruit, Cows, Sheep-Goats
	Rainfed Agriculture
	HardWheat, Soft Wheat, Barley, Maize, Other Cereal, Legumes, Fodder, Sugarbeet, Sunflower, Other Industrial Crops, Vegetables, Olives, Other Fruit, Cow, Sheep-Goat
	Other, Other Animal Production, Rural Services, Forestry, Petrol, Electricity, Food processing, Sugar Processing, Fertilizers/Chemicals, Public Administration, Other Urban
Factors of Production	Resources
	Water, Irrigated Land, Rainfed Land, Pasture Land
	Labor
	Rural, Urban
	Capital
	Crop Machinery, Livestock (by animal type and irrigated/rainfed), Other Rural, Urban
Intermediate Inputs	Commodities produced by above-mentioned activities (including disaggregated treatment of animal commodities—manure, fodder products, etc.)
Institutions	Households
	Irrigated Farmer, Rainfed Farmer, Rural Worker, Other Rural, Urban
	Government
	Rest of the World

TABLE A3-3

Aggregated Set of Activities in Lofgren/IFPRI Social Account Matrix for 1994

Set	Elements
Activities	Irrigated Agriculture
	Wheat, Barley, Maize, Other Cereal, Legumes, Fodder, Sugarbeet, Sugarcane, Sunflower, Other Industrial Crops, Vegetables, Olives, Citrus
	Rainfed Agriculture
	Livestock
	Industry and Services
Factors of Production	Resources
	Water, Land
	Labor
	Capital
Intermediate Inputs	Commodities produced by abovementioned activities (including disaggregated treatment of animal commodities—manure, fodder products, etc.)
Institutions	Households
	Workers
	Government
	Rest of the World

TABLE A3-4

Aggregated 1995 SAM for Morocco

	WHT-AI	BARLEY-AI	MAIZE-AI	OTHCER-AI	LEGUME-AI	FODDER-AI	SGRBT-AI
WHT-AI	1.052	—	—	—	—	—	—
BARLEY-AI	—	0.341	—	—	—	—	—
MAIZE-AI	—	—	0.169	—	—	—	—
OTHCER-AI	—	—	—	0.051	—	—	—
LEGUME-AI	—	—	—	—	0.079	—	—
FODDER-AI	—	—	—	—	—	0.420	—
SGRBT-AI	—	—	—	—	—	—	0.382
SGRCN-AI	—	—	—	—	—	—	—
SNFLW-AI	—	—	—	—	—	—	—
OINDCRI-AI	—	—	—	—	—	—	—
VEGET-AI	—	—	—	—	—	—	—
PLANT-AI	—	—	—	—	—	—	—
RAINFED	6.411	4.544	0.873	0.207	1.069	0.217	0.115
LVST	—	—	—	—	—	—	—
INDSRV	0.093	—	0.003	—	—	—	—
LABOR+INCOME	0.169	0.088	0.083	0.012	0.044	0.229	0.174
CROPCAP	0.392	0.100	0.026	0.010	0.011	0.030	0.043
LAND	0.661	0.265	0.104	0.019	0.058	0.264	0.136
WATER	0.329	0.154	0.092	0.041	0.018	0.232	0.080
FAC-NTB	—	—	—	—	—	—	—
GOV	—	—	—	—	—	—	—
ROW	1.029	0.131	0.007	—	0.006	—	—
SAV-INV	—	—	—	—	—	—	—
WATTAR	—	0.024	—	—	—	—	—
DIRTAX	—	—	0.003	—	—	—	—
INDTAX	—	—	—	0.007	—	—	—
SUBSIDY	—	—	—	—	0.011	—	—
TARIFF	—	—	—	—	—	0.005	—
NTB	—	—	—	—	—	—	0.033
TOTAL	2.287	0.740	0.355	0.107	0.174	0.839	0.808

SGRCN-AI	SNFLW-AI	OINDCRI-AI	VEGET-AI	PLANT-AI	RAINFED	LVST	IND-SRV
—	—	—	—	—	1.052	0.054	0.929
—	—	—	—	—	0.341	0.050	0.161
—	—	—	—	—	0.169	0.053	0.139
—	—	—	—	—	0.051	0.098	—
—	—	—	—	—	0.079	—	0.027
—	—	—	—	—	0.420	0.817	—
—	—	—	—	—	0.382	—	0.728
0.146	—	—	—	—	0.146	—	0.283
—	0.019	—	—	—	0.019	—	0.021
—	—	0.222	—	—	0.222	—	0.918
—	—	—	2.471	—	2.471	—	0.337
—	—	—	—	2.867	—	—	1.690
—	0.292	0.195	0.921	2.066	14.843	2.090	10.349
—	—	—	—	—	—	—	24.717
—	—	—	—	—	0.771	11.960	909.101
0.065	0.005	0.068	1.100	1.362	5.690	2.635	119.265
0.005	0.004	0.015	0.104	0.152	2.543	4.671	72.418
0.059	0.012	0.082	0.481	0.831	16.329	1.676	—
0.114	0.014	0.086	0.300	1.511	—	—	—
—	—	—	—	—	—	—	—
—	—	—	—	—	—	—	—
—	0.059	0.764	0.224	0.031	2.221	—	71.610
—	—	—	—	—	—	—	—
—	—	—	—	—	—	—	—
—	—	—	—	—	0.027	—	—
—	—	—	—	—	0.012	0.615	22.255
—	—	—	—	—	0.142	—	—
—	—	—	—	—	0.029	—	18.350
—	—	—	—	—	0.015	—	6.322
0.292	0.039	0.464	5.029	5.733	14.056	24.717	569.920

continued

TABLE A3-4

Aggregated 1995 SAM for Morocco *(continued)*

	HOUSEHOLD	CROPCAP	LAND	WATER	FAC-NTB	GOV	ROW
WHT-AI	1.623	—	—	—	—	—	0.019
BARLEY-AI	0.430	—	—	—	—	—	0.066
MAIZE-AI	0.144	—	—	—	—	—	—
OTHCER-AI	—	—	—	—	—	—	—
LEGUME-AI	0.110	—	—	—	—	—	0.012
FODDER-AI	—	—	—	—	—	—	—
SGRBT-AI	—	—	—	—	—	—	—
SGRCN-AI	—	—	—	—	—	—	—
SNFLW-AI	0.027	—	—	—	—	—	0.005
OINDCRI-AI	0.536	—	—	—	—	—	0.103
VEGET-AI	2.177	—	—	—	—	—	2.279
PLANT-AI	2.965	—	—	—	—	—	0.934
RAINFED	19.542	—	—	—	—	—	2.170
LVST	—	—	—	—	—	—	—
INDSRV	171.602	—	—	—	—	40.781	54.394
LABOR+INCOME	—	74.585	19.300	2.971	9.593	7.501	21.396
CROPCAP	—	—	—	—	—	—	—
LAND	—	—	—	—	—	—	—
WATER	—	—	—			—	—
FAC-NTB	—	—	—				
GOV	1.871	5.938	—				
ROW	4.674	—	—			7.947	—
SAV-INV	44.959	—	—			7.772	6.684
WATTAR	—	—	—			—	—
DIRTAX	15.214	—	—				
INDTAX	—	—	—			—	—
SUBSIDY	—	—	—			3.195	—
TARIFF	—	—	—				
NTB	—	—	—				
TOTAL	416.270	80.556	18.004	2.971	9.593	67.196	88.735

SAV-INV	WATTAR	DIRTAX	INDTAX	SUBSIDY	TARIFF	NTB	TOTAL
—	—	—	—	0.267	—	—	3.014
—	—	—	—	—	—	—	0.707
—	—	—	—	—	—	—	0.341
—	—	—	—	—	—	—	0.102
—	—	—	—	—	—	—	0.160
—	—	—	—	—	—	—	0.839
—	—	—	—	—	—	—	0.764
—	—	—	—	—	—	—	0.292
—	—	—	—	0.003	—	—	0.058
—	—	—	—	—	—	—	1.592
—	—	—	—	—	—	—	5.285
—	—	—	—	—	—	—	5.785
—	—	—	—	1.678	—	—	18.367
—	—	—	—	—	—	—	24.717
59.415	—	—	—	1.247	—	—	1,263.930
—	—	—	—	—	—	—	416.303
—	—	—	—	—	—	—	80.523
—	—	—	—	—	—	—	20.975
—					—	—	2.971
					—	9.593	9.593
	0.196	15.214	23.528	—	20.449	—	67.196
—	—	—	—	—	—	—	88.735
—					—	—	59.415
—					—	—	0.196
					—	—	15.214
—					—	—	23.528
—					—	—	3.195
	—	—	—	—	—	—	20.449
					—	—	9.593
59.415	0.196	15.214	23.528	3.195	20.449	9.593	2,220.010

Appendix *4*

Dealing with Uncertainty
in Policy Decisions

Uncertainty of many kinds must be taken into account in planning for water resources. A central uncertainty is the amount of rain from year to year, which is particularly important for countries where water is scarce, rainfall is highly variable, and a still-agriculturally reliant economy is highly dependent on water. Floods and droughts have long had the attention of water resource planners worldwide, partly because they translate themselves into economic swings. In this book, we have applied MEIAH to a water-stressed country, Morocco, where water scarcity and frequent drought shape the whole economy and are always among the most important factors jeopardizing national growth.

MEIAH was developed and was used to investigate Scenarios A through D in the stipulated environment of a normal rainfall year, that is to say a year at about the fiftieth percentile of rainfall. This can also be described as the level of rainfall, which, if the future follows the patterns of the past, can be counted on to be met or exceeded in half of future years, which is often expressed as the level of 50% reliability. MEIAH has not yet been used for extensive investigation of markedly dry or wet years, although such variable rainfall years remain important realities confronting Morocco and similar countries. Nonetheless, by its capacity to link hydrologic phenomena to each other and to their economic effects, MEIAH has the potential to elucidate many of the consequences of drought, and to offer guidance in developing policies to mitigate, or to adapt to, pronounced variability in the water resource from one year to the next.

At the end of this annex, brief indications are given from preliminary informal application of the model to situations specified as "wet" years and "dry" years, of what trends should be expected in such non-average rainfall years. For example, what will be the effect of drought on the shadow price of water for urban and agricultural uses? Initially, however, this annex provides a glance at the many kinds of uncertainty that can influence the analytical results of water modeling, and then offers a rapid summary of how greatly Morocco is affected by variable rainfall, most specifically drought.

Uncertainty in a Water Analytical System

Types of Uncertainty

Uncertainty in the inputs in optimizing models has long been handled by simple sensitivity analyses involving multiple runs of the model, with the uncertain variables specified at different values within their range of variation at the time of input. The model's output is then inspected to see the effects of the alternative inputs. Occasionally, advanced stochastic methods have been postulated for use in water management, but these are usually "for demonstration purposes only," covering simply one or two reservoir systems and without exploration of policy implications.

Although we will deal below primarily with the very large real-world factor of year-to-year rainfall variability, decision-makers need to consider many different kinds of uncertainty in assessing the robustness of their model outputs, and in incorporating the likelihood of fluctuations of key parameters into their decisions. Uncertainty pervades every part of the modeling process, from input data to the methods chosen.

The different types of uncertainty can be summarized in four groups:

■ *Catastrophic Events:* Unpredictable (perhaps unprecedented), but extreme events, such as droughts, floods, cyclones, famines, and earthquakes, which often lead to large emergency expenditures.

■ *Variability in Data:* In water resource systems, the collection of data used for future planning or for better management is often based on simplifying assumptions, which can in turn conceal or mask uncertainties. Economic parameters can fail to reflect the possibility of exogenous effects, such as changes in inflation or exchange rates. Climatic and precipitation variability, which we take up here, has a large effect on a water balance, and influences hydrologic conclusions, such as an appropriate groundwater pumping rate for sustainable extraction. Water demand is often based on estimations of demographic growth and population distribution, which are subject to several uncertainties. Relevant factors can be unreachable or neglected in the collection and monitoring of data, depending, for example, on the length, breadth and quality of the records.

■ *Methodology:* Within the approach undertaken by water resource analysts, the accuracy of results can be jeopardized by several limitations in the data management process, such as lack of shared information or of appropriate systems for data handling, e.g. Geographical Information Systems (GIS). Different results can be generated according to the methods chosen for the aggregation of data (spatial, temporal and sectoral) as well as the kinds of projections used. Many assumptions used in data collection and system modeling, such as demand elasticities, can prove to be inexact, even as they affect the results generated by a model. There are always many potential modeling approaches, and therefore inevitable uncertainty about which will most faithfully and usefully reflect the situation being studied.

■ *Policy/Decision-Making:* Many challenging uncertainties lie in the post-analytic decision-making process, due to such factors as institutional and functional problems, or unclear or unagreed objectives and constraints among the decision-makers and stakeholders.

Having noted these sources of uncertainty, which should not be forgotten in using model results, the focus in this appendix will be on taking into account the major hydrological factor of year-to-year rainfall uncertainty.

Methods to Address Uncertainty

A conceptually simple and useful method to address uncertainty is "sensitivity analysis". This means running the model for a given scenario multiple times, each time specifying at an alternative value the parameter which is considered to be uncertain. Such parameters which can be tested at different values include flows and flow multipliers (different flow regimes, e.g. dry, regular, or wet years), or different levels of constraints. (Although our focus is on annual levels of water availability, sensitivity analysis can be applied to any input parameter, such as objective weights, budgets, other economic information, water quality standards, upstream/downstream minimum flow or sectoral allocation constraints.) A re-run of the model with alternative input values will show us the effects upon the model's output of alternatives and variations (which taken together cover the range of uncertainties) in the values of various input parameters. The sensitivity method can be used with an existing deterministic model such as MEIAH. It is simple, as it involves just a few additional runs for each scenario. By indicating which data have the most pronounced effects on output results, such analysis can guide the prioritization of various forms of information collection,. Having made use of alternative sets of inputs, ranges of variation in the outputs can usually be estimated, and thus, the "sensitivity" of an analytical result, or of a decision to be made, to the variation in initial conditions, or givens, can be evaluated.

Additional techniques are applied by water resource planners to assess the effect of uncertainty, such as stochastic dynamic programming, used to examine the effect of reservoir release rules. Running the optimization of a generated synthetic streamflow can be used to determine how one would make advance decisions differently knowing variability in flows. Other new techniques are starting to spread in several domains: ordinal optimization (Ho and Kao, 1991), as a methodology to chose the best and worst solutions under various policy variables; and "fuzzy" programming (McNeill and Freiberger, 1993). A method investigated in the preparation of this study was a detailed statistical analysis of the historical record, with the creation of synthetic but representative time series, as worked out in the Thomas-Fiering analysis (Maass et al, 1962). However these methods are computationally intense, or offer only a marginal refinement of results above those achieved by sensitivity testing, and hence are not further pursued here.

Water availability fluctuations can also be evaluated by means of the water input-output structure, which was presented in MEIAH, using the set of multipliers and ratios that were developed. Using multipliers, we can evaluate the effects of a change in the water sector on the total output of the economy, including incomes, employment and water uses; and break these indicators down to see different types of effects: direct, indirect and consumption induced.

Hydrological Variability in Morocco

Frequency in Drought Occurrence

Morocco has high intra-year and inter-year variability in rainfall, reflected in a similar variation of runoff and river flows. Tree-ring analysis indicates that this rainfall variation has been part of Morocco's existence for centuries. With about a thousand years of such data, it is inferred that on the average, droughts occur every eight years and the probability of drought in any given year for at least one of the major regions is quite high (30-40%).

The agricultural sector, the major water user, is severely affected by drought periods, especially since about 65% of agricultural production, mainly cereals, is not irrigated but is dependent directly on rainfall. Figure A4-1 shows the variability in cereal production from 1975 to 1995, where years of very low production due to drought can be seen. Cereal production uses 85% of the cultivated land, and in the interval of one year has dropped from 9.6 million metric tons (MMT) in 1994 to 1.7 MMT in 1995, due to intense water shortage in the latter year. Such an overwhelming decline in agricultural production reverberates throughout the whole economy. Employment in rural areas, which represent 50% of the working population, is particularly badly affected, and of course, the growth rate of the economy is not immune: while 1994 showed a 12% increase in GDP, an estimated 4% contraction of the economy resulted from the drought in 1995.

Urban water supply also suffers from variability in rainfall, but in general a great deal less, in part because much of urban water demand is covered by pumping groundwater from aquifers, whose yield does not suffer greatly in at least a relatively short drought. Nonetheless, swings in the water availability, and in the economy as a whole, have forced the government of Morocco to make large expenditures to combat drought, including expensive shipping of water from the south to the city of Tangier in the north and importing a large quantity of food and feed. Drought emergency measures in 1995 cost the government more than US$565 Million.

Flow Variability in the Oum Er Rbia, Bou Regrag and Sebou Basins

This intensely populated and cultivated region of Morocco, which was studied in the development of MEIAH, has a very complex water system. Its

---

FIGURE A4-1

Cereal Production in Morocco

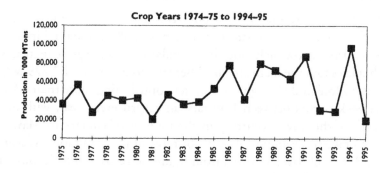

rivers are regulated by 17 dams, and 12 more dams are planned to be completed by 2020, based on the national plan to construct a dam per year for the next period to defend the nation against drought. For the five considered rivers: Oum Er Rbia, Bou Regrag, N'fifikh, Mellah and Sebou, there are 53 hydrometric stations, located downstream or upstream of the dams, from which streamflows have been observed for more than 50 years of record from 1934 to 1986. These multiple data points do not remove all difficulties from the analysis; for example, issues of incomplete coverage and human-caused flows (e.g., dam releases) remain to be dealt with.

To model the hydrology of such a complex system, streamflows were reconstructed to fit the schematic of the basins shown in Figure A4-2. Here the inflow nodes in the system are labeled: Oum Er Rbia from SO1 to SO9, Mellah and N'fifikh, respectively S1 and S2, Bou Regrag, from SB1 to SB3, and Sebou, from SS1 to SS8.

Sebou River Basin

We will provide details on the Sebou river basin among the three, since it has the largest water endowment, and both its annual pattern of rising and falling flow throughout the year, and its historical record of high water years and drought years is representative of all three rivers.

The Sebou flows from the Middle Atlas through the Guigou tributary (SS4), and is 500 km long, discharging into the ocean after receiving several tributaries:

- from the Medium Atlas: tributaries Zloul (SS8) and Mikkes (SS3),
- from the Medium Atlas and the Rif: tributary Inaouene (SS5),
- from the Rif: tributaries Lebene (SS6) and Ouergha (SS7),
- from the Central Plain: tributaries Beht (SS1) and Rdom (SS2).

The hydrological regime of the Sebou river depends on the regimes of a number of tributaries. The upstream tributary (12.5% of the total inflow) is quite regular from snow melt, and the irregularity of the regime increases as more tributaries join the main stream. There is a total inflow of 7,279 MCM per year, the Zloul and Ouergha tributaries contributing more than 63% of this. The peak occurs between February and April every year, with about three fourth of the flows occurring in the months of January to May. The lowest flows take place around August for most of the tributaries, as seen in Figure A4-3. (Zloul River, omitted from figure for reasons of scale, has same annual pattern as tributaries shown.)

FIGURE A4-2
Simplified Schematic of the Basin

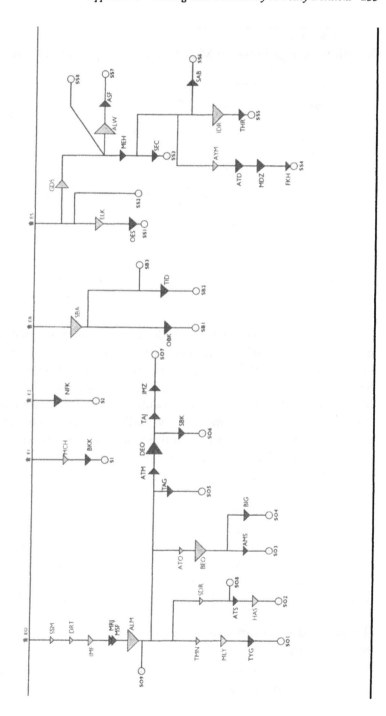

FIGURE   A 4 - 3

Monthly Average Flows in MCM by Tributary—Sebou Basin

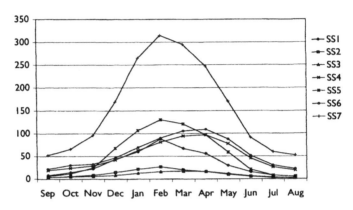

Source: Based on data from the Direction de l'Hydraulique, Ministry of Public Works, 1994

Based on records from 1934 to 1986, Figure A4-4 shows that there is a lot of inter-annual variation in flows in the Sebou basin. We see flood peaks as high as 10,286 MCM for 1962, interspersed by droughts where flows could be as low as the 1068 MCM in 1944. The recent six year drought from 1978 to 1984 was a devastating Morocco-wide episode which affected the Sebou along with other basins of the country. Earlier flows show a rough drought or a flood periodicity of about four to five years, but the pattern has been more confused of late. The flows of the tributaries of the Sebou basin seem to be highly correlated to each other. With several important cities located in the basin, such as Fez, Kenitra and Meknes, which take around 228 MCM per year, there is a large urban demand for water in the Sebou watershed. Industry demands 31 MCM per year, but is a heavy source of pollution of the river, as tanneries, and sugar and paper industries are concentrated here. Also there are large demand nodes for agriculture, both small scale irrigated areas and large scale ones, such as Gharb. Under the existing cropping pattern, the average agricultural demand for the Sebou is around 1,876 MCM per year.

Three Studied Basins Taken as a Whole: Dryness Increases to the South

The more one goes south in Morocco, the dryer the climate becomes and the more arid the soil. The Atlas Mountains give way to the widely spread Sahara.

FIGURE A4-4

Total Annual Historical Flows in MCM—Sebou Basin

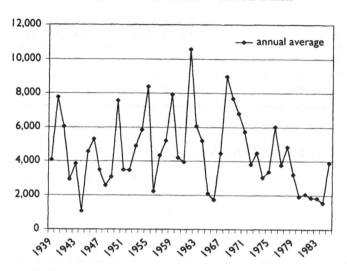

Source: Based on data from the Direction de l'Hydraulique, Ministry of Public Works, 1994

A comparison among the three studied river basins illustrates this climate change and explains the interest of water planners in the cross-basin transfer of water from the Sebou to the Bou Regrag, and mainly to the Oum Er Rbia watershed.

Based on the historical data, a comparison of the yearly and monthly averages of the total flows in the basin, as showed in Table A4-1, highlights the endowment of the north-located Sebou, which has greater flows than the rivers of the south, although Oum Er Rbia has the largest watershed of the country.

Table A4-2 illustrates the deficit and the surplus positions of the three river basins for the year 2020, as forecast by Moroccan water planners, based on demand projections taking into account both expected growth of the urban population and planned expansion of irrigated areas. It is clear that there is a deficit today in the Oum Er Rbia, which will deepen to reach 153 MCM in year 2020, but which could still be overcome through inter-basin transfers. There is a considerably greater prospective deficit in the Bou Regrag system, on which important cities depend.

TABLE   A4-1
Cross Basin Comparison of Average Flow

Basins	Average Annual Flow (MCM)	Average Monthly Flow (MCM)
Sebou	7,024	607
Bou Regrag & Coastal Area	796	62
Oum Er Rbia	3,815	318

TABLE   A4-2
Water Balance for the Three Basins in 2020

Basins	Water Supply (MCM)	Water Demand (MCM)
Sebou	4,890	4,120
Bou Regrag & Coastal Area	970	1,890
Oum Er Rbia	4,127	4,281

Analyzing Multi-year Records

A method to express hydrological uncertainty involves the computation of reliabilities of flows. A flow which is 75% reliable is one which was equaled or exceeded in three years out of four on average in the historical record, meaning that it is a relatively low flow. It is assumed that the past record can be used as a reasonable expectation of rainfalls in the future. Let us imagine a more abundant, water-rich year, bringing a relatively high level of water that comes only in one year out of four. That is therefore a year of only 25% reliability. For planning purposes, it can be less counted on than a lower amount of water, say an annual volume at the low 10th percentile, which has an 90% reliability, meaning that at least that much water can be expected nine years out of ten.

A 99% reliability corresponds to the set of flows that are exceeded 99% of the time. It will be a very low flow, but getting at least that much can be considered almost a "sure thing." Using such a low level as the 99% reliability as an assumption for designing a water system will result in a very conservative planning. Using a 50% reliability in the planning would be risky, as the system will be short of that amount of water half of the time. Water resource planners traditionally use 75% reliability in making decisions for irrigation water supply, but 90% or higher reliability is often used in municipal water supply. The choice of a water reliability as the basis of planning should not be arbitrary but should reflect economic and political judgment. However, it is important to see what kinds of decisions would be taken at different levels of reliability, and to be aware of the robustness, or the sensitivity, of decisions to hydrologic risk.

Flow records give us some idea of the hydrologic uncertainty in a basin. We see intra-year (month-to-month) and inter-year variability for each of the major tributaries to the rivers in the river basins considered. Although flow variations translate into economic variations, especially through their effects on agricultural production and farm product imports and exports, there is much that can be done, and is done, by water resource planners and others, to adapt to flow variations. The challenge for water resource professionals is to incorporate this knowledge of "certain uncertainty" into the planning process. Often, they use rules of thumb created by the accumulated knowledge of past experiences. However, it is important to build upon these experiences and to advance to handling uncertainty in a systematic manner.

Preliminary Indications from MEIAH of Trends in a Water-short Situation

To evaluate the effect of fluctuation in water availability on the local economy of the Oum Er Rbia, Bou Regrag and Sebou region, a preliminary application of MEIAH was made by varying the amount of available water specified, in effect creating a new scenario, or set of scenarios.

It was found that as long as water shortages are not of extreme, multi-year duration, cities in the Sebou, Bou Regrag, Oum Er Rbia region could generally meet their water needs through the use of groundwater, extracted at sustainable volumes in the region, and did not need to greatly curtail water consumption. Shortages in water, however, will lead to a reduction in both rainfed and irrigated agricultural production. In order to satisfy internal food consumption needs, agriculture imports increase, and due to a decrease in the agricultural goods exported, there is a negative change in the balance of trade.

The net benefit of water use to the economy as a whole decreases sharply with increasing scarcity. When an annual flow drops from the above average 65th percentile (35% reliability) to the level of an average year (50th percentile, 50% reliability), rainfed agriculture is impeded by water shortages, and substantial domestic demand for agricultural products would have to be met through international imports. This affects negatively the economic welfare of the region. The pattern is the same for the agricultural net benefits as calculated by MEIAH. For example, if the design reliability is increased from 50% to 75% (meaning a reduction in expected flow from the 50th to the 25th percentile), the net benefit from farming declines sharply from 820 Million DH to 250 Million DH.

Testing water quantity variations by sensitivity analysis shows changes in the shadow prices of water for both urban and agricultural sectors. The most important point is that shadow prices always remain higher for urban water use than for agricultural. Shadow prices change tremendously for agriculture from 2.62 DH/m3 at the low flow that is 75% reliable, to less than third of that, 0.80 DH/m^3, in the more abundant water year of 35% reliability. For the urban sector, the shadow price is far less affected: in the same circumstance of going from a low flow (75% reliability) to the much higher one of a 35% reliability, the shadow price of water drops only by 0.02 DH from 4.50 DH/m^3.

In both wet years and dry ones, the model indicates that overall national groundwater usage is approximately constant and almost always equal to the sustainable extraction yield. For the urban sector, however, the quantity pumped varies from 32 MCM in a 75% reliability situation to 79 MCM in 35% one. From an environmental point of view, due to the higher quantity of water in the river, the pollution concentration of BOD gets diluted from 0.427 mg/l to 0.401 mg/l with a decrease in flow reliability from 75% to 50%. As more water becomes available, more sugarbeet, fodder and vegetables are grown, and imports are generally decreased (fodder) and exports increase (sugarbeet, vegetables, wheat). Also, under extreme water scarcity, as rainfed crops suffer, irrigated wheat is grown to compensate.

Interpretations and Conclusion

Water availability greatly affects agricultural production, as well as agricultural imports and exports. Overall economic net benefit are sharply affected by water scarcity, not only due to a lower local agriculture production, but also due to an increase in agricultural imports.

A stochastic simulation of the flows, which has not been described here, confirms that the shadow price for urban water remains higher than that of agricultural water, no matter which scenario is considered, and for all levels of inflows. The standard deviation is lower for urban water allocation than it is for agriculture, as the priority is given to urban users because of their higher economic return. Urban areas should be given the priority in designing a strategy for water resources development. During frequent drought periods, for example, a national plan for water should be flexible to allow shifts of the water to neighboring cities when they suffer from a lack of water.

Finally, depending on how much risk policy makers are willing to take, the design of water systems can be based on different flow reliabilities: either 75% reliability, as traditionally practiced by water planners, or a 50% reliability, for a more risk-tolerant type of analysis.

Bibliography

Alaoui, Mohamed Ben El Hassan. 1994. *La Cooperation Entre l'Union Europeene et les Pays du Maghreb*. Editions Nathan. Paris.

Asad M. et al. 1999. *Management of Water Resources: Bulk Water Pricing in Brazil.* The World Bank. Washington, D.C.

Baumol, William J. and Alan S. Blinder. 1994. *Economics: Principals and Policy.* Harcourt Brace and Company.

Bergman, Lars, Dale W. Jorgenson and Erno Zalai. 1990. *General Equilibrium Modeling and Economic Policy Analysis*. Basil Blackwell, Inc.

Bhatia, Ramesh, Rita Cestti, and James Winpenny. 1995. *Water Conservation and Reallocation: Best Practice Cases in Improving Economic Efficiency and Environmental Quality*. The World Bank.

Biswas, Asit K. 1976. *Systems Approach to Water Management*. McGraw-Hill, Inc.

Bouhia, Hynd. 1996. *Water Losses: Technical and Economic Considerations*. Working Paper for the Technical Department of the Middle East and North Africa. The World Bank. Washington.

————. 1998. *Water in the Economy: Integrating Water Resources into National Economic Planning*. Ph.D. Thesis. Harvard University.

———— and Peter P. Rogers. 1997a. *Decision Support System for Integrated Water Resource Planning and Management: Application to Three Major Moroccan River Basins*. Fourth International Conference on Computer Methods and Water Resources, Byblos, Lebanon.

———— and Peter P. Rogers. 1997b. *Water in the Economy*, Water Resources Systems Program, Working Paper, 1997-1, Harvard University.

Briscoe, John. 1996. *Water as an Economic Good: The Idea and What it Means in Practice*. Paper presented at the World Congress of the International Commission on Irrigation and Drainage. The World Bank.

Brooke, A., D. Kendrick and A. Meeraus. 1988. *GAMS: A User's Guide*. The Scientific Press.

Bulmer-Thomas, Victor. 1982. *Input-Output Analysis in Developing Countries: Sources, Methods and Applications*. New York, John Wiely and Son, Ltd.

Buras, Nathan. 1976. *Scientific Allocation of Water Resources*. McGraw-Hill. New York.

Bussolo, M. and D. Roland-Holst. 1993. *A Detailed Input-Output Table for Morocco, 1990*. Technical Paper No. 90. Organization for Economic Co-operation and Developement.

Carson, Rachel. 1962. *Silent Spring*. Houghton Mifflin Company Boston.

Chvatal, Vasek. 1983. *Linear Programming*. W.H. Freeman and Company.

Ciriacy-Wantrup, S.V. 1954. *The Role of Benefit-Cost Analysis in Public Resource Development*. Water Resource and Economic Development of the West, Report no.3, Committee on the Economics of Water Resources Development of the Western Agriculture Economic Research Councli. Berkeley, California.

Dantzig, George. 1963. *Linear Porgramming and Extensions*. Princeton, N.J.: Princeton University Press.

DeHaan, M, S.J. Keunig and P.R. Bosch. 1993. *Integrating Indicators in a National Accounting Matrix Including Environmental Accounts (NAMEA)*. Statistics Netherlands, Occasional Paper n. NA-60.

Deichman, Uwe. 1989. *An Integrated Multiregional Input-Output Model for Water Policy Analysis*. Thesis submitted in partial satisfaction of the requirements for the degree of Master of Arts. University of California, Santa Barbara.

Delors, Jacques. 1996. *Learning: The Treasure Within*. Report to the United Nations Educational, Scientific and Cultural Organization (UNESCO) of the International Commission on Education for the Twenty-first Century.

DeNeufville, Richard and Joseph Stafford. 1971. *Systems Analysis for Engineers and Managers*. McGraw-Hill Book Company.

Dervis, Kemal, Jaime De Melo and Sherman Robinson. 1982. *General Equilibrium Models for Development Policy*. A World Bank Research Publication. Cambridge University Press.

Devarajan, Shantayanan, Jeffrey Lewis and Sherman Robinson. 1994. *Getting the Model Right: The General Equilibrium Approach to Adjustment Policy*. Draft Manuscript.

Dingman, S.Lawrence. 1996. *Physical Hydrology*. Prentice Hall.

DiPasquale, Denise and Karen Polenske. 1980. *Output, Income, and Employment Input-Output Multipliers*. In Economic Impact Analysis: Methodology and Applications, edited by Saul Pleeter. Boston, MA. Martinus Nijhoff Publishing.

Dixon, J.A. et al. 1994. *Economic Analysis of Environmental Impacts*. Earthscan Publications.

Dorfman, Robert and Nancy S. Dorfman. 1993. *Economics of the Environment—Selected Readings*. W. W. Norton & Company, Inc.

Dorfman, R., H.D. Jacoby and H.A. Thomas. 1972. *Models for Managing Regional Water Quality*. Harvard University Press.

Dufournaud, C.M., J.J. Harrington and P.P. Rogers. 1988. *Leontief's Environmnetal Repercussions and the Economic Structure... Revised: A General Equilibrium Formulation*. Geographical Analysis, Vol.20, No.4, Ohio State University Press.

Dunne, T. and L.B. Leopold. 1978. *Water in Environmental Planning*. W.H. Freman and Co. San Francisco, Ca.

Eckstein, O. 1958. *Water Resource Development and the Economics of Project Evaluation*. Cambridge. Harvard University Press.

Edwards et al. 1990. *Sustainable Agricultural Systems*. The Soil and Water Conservation Society.

Emsellem, Yves and Jean-Piere Bordet. 1985. *Model for the Seine-Normandy Basins, France*. Edited by Asit K. Biswas. Models for Water Quality Management. McGraw-Hill International Book Company.

Europa, 1994. *The Middle East and North Africa 1994*. 40th Edition. Europa Publications Limited.

Fossati, Amedeo. 1996. *Economic Modeling Under the Applied General Equilibrium Approach*. Avebury.

Freeze, Allan R. and John A. Cherry. 1979. *Groundwater*. Prentice-Hall, New Jersey.

Garn, Mike, 1990. *Water Supply Investments in Developing Countries: some Technical, Economic, and Financial Implications of Experience*. The World Bank, Washington.

Gibbons, D.C. 1986. *The Economic Value of Water*. Resources for the Future.

Gillis, Perkins, Roemer and Snodgrass. 1996. *Economics of Development*. W.W. Norton and Company.

Gleick, Peter H. 1993. *Water in Crisis: A Guide to the World's Fresh Water Resources*. Oxford University Press.

Goldin, Ian and L. Alan Winters. 1994. *The Economics of Sustainable Development*. Center for Economic Policy Research. Organization for Economic Co-operation and Developement. Cambridge University Press.

Goodman, A. 1984. *Principles of Water Resources Planning*. Prentice-Hall, Inc. New Jersey.

Grindle, Merilee S. and John W. Thomas. 1991. *Public Choices and Policy Change: The Political Economy of Reform in Developing Countries*. The Johns Hopkins University Press.

Grover, Nathan C. and Arthur W. Harrington. 1966. *Stream Flow: Measurements, Records and Their Uses*. Dover Publications, Inc.

Hall, Robert and John Taylor. 1986. *Macro-Economics: Theory, Performance, and Policy*. W.W. Norton & Company, Inc.

Hanke, S.H. 1978. *A Method for Integrating Engineering and Economic Planning*. Journal of American West Works Association. Vol.70, No 9.

Harshadeep, Nagaraja. 1995. *Comprehensive Multi-Objective River Basin Planning: Fuzzy and Game-Theoretic Approaches*. Thesis submitted in partial fulfillment of the Doctor of Philosophy, Division of Engineering and Applied Sciences, Harvard University. Cambridge, MA.

Henry, MS and E Bowen. December 1981. *A method of estimating the value of water among sectors of regional economy*. Southern Journal of Agriculture Economics.

Henry, Glynn and Gary Heinke. 1986. *Environmental Science and Engineering*. Prentice Hall.

Hillier, Frederick S. and Gerald J. Lieberman, 1980. *Introduction to Operation Research*. Holden-Day, Inc.

Ho, Y.C. and X. Cao. 1991. *Perturbation Analysis of Discret Event Dynamic System*. Kluwer Academic Publisher.

Isard, Walter, T.W. Langford, Jr. and E. Romanoff. 1967. *Philadelphia Region Input-Output Study: Working Papers*. Regional Science Research Institute. Cambridge Office.

Isard, Walter and Eliahu Romanoff (a). August 1967. *Water Utilization: Input-Output Coefficients*. Regional Science Research Institute. Cambridge Office.

Isard, Walter and Eliahu Romanoff (b). November 1967. *Water Use and Water Pollution Coefficients: Preliminary Report*. Regional Science Research Institute. Cambridge Office.

James, Douglas L. and Robert R. Lee. 1971. *Economics of Water Resources Planning*. Tata McGraw-Hill Publishing Company.

Jensen, R.C. 1986. *Australian Regional Development. Input-Output for Practitioners: Theory and Applications*. Australian Government Publishing Service.

Jordan, Peter and Karen Polenske. 1986. *A Multiplier Impact Study of Fishing Activities in New England and Nova Scotta*. Discussion Papers. Resources for the Future. Washington, D.C.

Kahn, R.F. 1931. *The Relation of Home Investment to Employment*. Economic Journal. 41.

Katz, Michael and Harvey Rosen. 1994. *Microeconomics*. Richard D. Irwin, Inc.

Keynes, John Maynard. 1936. *The General Theory of Employment, Interest, and Money*. London: MacMillan.

Kirsten, J.F. and J. Van Zyl. 1990. *Economic Impact of Irrigation Agriculture: Methodological Aspects and an Empirical Application*. Development Southern Africa. Vol. 7, p. 209–24.

Konijn, P.J.A, A de Boer and J. Van Dalen. 1994. *Materials Flows and Input-Ouput Analysis: Methodological Description and Empirical Results*. Sector National Accounts. Statistics Netherlands.

Krugman, Paul R. and Maurice Obstfeld. 1997. *International Economics: Theory and Policy*. Addison-Wesley Longman, Inc.

Kutcher, G.P. 1980. *The Agro-Economic Model*. Technical Report no.16. Master Plan for Water Resources Development. UNDP-EGY-73/024, Cairo.

Leontief, Wassily. 1986. *Input-Output Economics*. Oxford University Press.

Linsley, Ray K. 1976. *Rainfall-Runoff Models*. Published by Asit K. Biswas in Systems Approach to Water Management.

Lofgren, H. and S. Robinson. 1997. *The Mixed-Complementarity Approach to Specifying Agricultural Supply in Computable General Equilibrium Models*. TMD Discussion Paper No.20. International Food Policy Research Institute. Washington.

Lofgren, H. et al. 1997. *Rural Development in Morocco: Alternative Scenarios to the Year 2000*. TMD Discussion Paper No.17. International Food Policy Research Institute. Washington.

Lofting, E. M. and P. H. McGauhey, 1968. *Economic Evaluation of Water—Part IV: AN Input-Output and Linear Programming Analysis of California Water Requirements*. Water Resource Center. Contribution no.116. University of California. Berkeley.

Loucks, Daniel P., Jery R. Stedinger and Douglas A. Haith. 1981. *Water Resource Systems Planning and Analysis*. Prentice-Hall, Inc. New Jersey.

Maass, Arthur et al., Maynard M. Huschmidt, Robert Dorfman, Harold A. Thomas, Jr., Stephen A. Marglin, and Gordon Maskew Fair. 1962. *Design of Water-Resource Systems: New Techniques for Relating Economic Objectives, Engineering Analysis, and Government Planning*. Harvard University Press. Cambridge.

Major, David C. and Roberto L. Lenton. 1979. *Applied Water Resource Systems Planning*. Prentice-Hall.

Major, David and Harry Schwarz. 1990. *Large-Scale Regional Water Resources Planning*. Kluwer Academic Publishers.

Mankiw, Gregory N. 1998. *Macroeconomics*. Fourth Edition. Worth Publishers.

McBeill, D. and P. Freiberger. 1993. *Fuzzy Logic: the Revolutionary Computer Technology that is Changing our World*. Simon and Schuster for Touchstone.

Metzel, Jeff. 1992. *The Impact of Cereals Market Reform on the Feed and Livestock Sectors*. Moroccan Cereal Market Reform Project. Associates for International Resources and Development. Cambridge. MA.

Miller, Irwin, John Freund and Richard Johnson. 1990. *Probability and Statistics for Engineers*. Prentice Hall, Inc.

Miller, Ronald E. and Peter D. Blair. 1985. *Input-Ouput Analysis: Foundations and Extensions*. Prentice-Hall, Inc. New Jersey.

Mirrilees, Ronald. 1991. *Economics Project Evaluation. Value of Water in South Africa.* Draft.

Moore, Frederick T. and James W. Peterson. 1955. "Regional Analysis: An Interindustry Model of Utah". *Review of Economics and Statistics*, 37, 368–363.

Munasinghe M. February 1990. *Water Supply Policies and Issues in Developing Countries.* Natural Resources Forum. Butterworth & Co Ltd.

OECD. 1993. *A Detailed Input-Output Table for Morocco, 1990.* Prepared by Maurizio Bussolo and David Roland-Holst. OECD Technical Paper no.90. Paris.

————. 1994. *Environmental Accounting for Decision-Making Summary Report of an OECD Seminar.* OECD Environment Monograph no.113. Paris.

————. 1995. *Natural Resource Accounts: Taking Stock in OECD Countries.* OECD Environment Monograph no.84. Paris.

Office National de l'Eau Potable. 1996. *Besoins en Eau en Milieu Urban pour les Regions Economiques.* Maroc.

Panayotou, Theodore. 1993. *Green Market: The Economics of Sustainable Development.* Harvard Institute for International Development.

Pearce, David W. and R. Kerry Turner. 1990. *Economics of Natural Resources and the environment.* The John Hopkins University Press.

Polensky, Karen R. and Stephen F. Fournier 1993. *Conceptual Input-Output Accounting and Modeling Framework.* In Spreadsheet Models for Urban and Regional Analysis, edited by Richard E. Klosterman and Richard K. Brail. New Brunswick, NJ: Center for Urban Policy Resarch pp.205–228.

Postel, Sandra. 1992. *Last Oasis: Facing Water Scarcity.* The Worldwatch Environmental Alert Series. W.W. Norton & Co.

Postel, Sandra. 1997. *Dividing the Waters.* Technology Review. April 97.

Pyatt, Grahan and Jeffery Round. 1985. *Social Accounting Matrices: A Basis for Planning.* The World Bank. Washington, D.C.

Raghunath, H.M. 1996. *Hydrology: Principles-Analysis-Design.* New Age International Publishers.

Ray, Debraj. 1998. *Development Economics.* Princeton University Press.

Resnick, Sidney I. 1992. *Adventures in Stochastic Processes.* Birkhauser Boston.

Robinson, S.. 1989. *Multisectoral Models.* In Hollis B. Chenery and T.N. Srinivasan (eds.), Handbook of Development Economics, Vol. 2. Amsterdam: North-Holland, 1989, pp. 885–947.

Rogers, Peter P.. 1986. *Water: Not as Cheap as you Think.* Technology Review. Vol.89, No.8, Nov/Dec, 1986.

————. 1992. *Comprehensive Water Resource Management: A Concept Paper.* Working Paper Series 879. Infrastructure and Urban Development Department. World Bank. Washington, D.C.

————. 1993. *America's Water: Federal Roles and Responsibilities.* The Twentieth Century Fund Book. The MIT Press. Cambridge.

————. 1995. *La Grande Secheresse: Strategic Considerations.* Report prepared for the USAID. Rabat, Morocco.

————. 1997. *Hydroeconomics: Getting Water into National Economic Planning.* Stockholm Water Symposium.

————, Ramesh Bhatia and Annette Huber. 1996. *Water as a Social and Economic Good: How to Put the Principle into Practice.* Paper presented to the Global Water Partnership meeting in Namibia.

———— and Hynd Bouhia. May 1997a. *Integrating Water into National Planning: Macro-Economic Analysis of Hydrology for Morocco.* Newsletter. Division of Engineering and Applied Sciences. Harvard University.

————, Christopher Hurst and Nagaraja Rao Harshadeep. 1993. *Water Resources Planning in a Strategic Context: Linking the Water Sector to the National Economy.* Water Resources Research. Vol.29, no.7, pp. 1895–1906.

———— and Nagaraja Rao Harshadeep. 1996. *Industry and Water: Options for Management and Conservation.* UNIDO. Vienna. Austria.

————, Kazi F. Jalal et al. 1997. *Measuring Environmental Quality in Asia.* The Division of Engineering and Applied Sciences, Harvard University and the Asian Development Bank.

———— and Fiering M.B. August 1986. *Use of Systems Analysis in Water Management.* Water Resources Research, Vol.22, No.9, pp.146S–158S.

———— and Peter Lydon, 1994. *Water in the Arab World.* Harvard University Press.

Rogers, S. et al.. 1981. *Application of the Brookhaven Energy-Economic Assessment Model in the Portugal–U.S. Cooperative Assessment.* Brookhaven National Laboratory.

Roland-Holst, David and Dominique Van der Mensbrugghe. 1994. *A General Equilibrium Modeling Facility for Morocco.* OECD Development Center.

Romer, David. 1996. *Advanced Macroeconomics.* McGraw-Hill Company.

Royaume du Maroc. 1989a. *Etude Plan Directeur Integre d'Amenagement des Eaux des Bassins du Sebou, Bou-Regrag Oum-Er-Rbia—Avenant no.2 Souss Mission.* Ministere des Travaux Publics. Rabat, Morocco.

————. 1989b. *Etude National de Tarification de l'Eau Potable.* Ministere des Affaires Economiques. Rabat, Morocco.

————. 1992. *Plan Directeur Integre d'Amenagement des Eaux des Bassins du Sebou, Bou-Regrag Oum-Er-Rbia*. Ministere des Travaux Publics. Rabat, Morocco.

————. 1993a. *Plan Directeur Integre d'Amenagement des Eaux des Bassins du Loukkos, du Tangerois et des Cotiers Mediterraneens*. Conseil Superieur de l'Eau. Rabat, Morocco.

————. 1993b. *Plan Directeur Integre d'Amenagement des Eaux du Bassin de Moulouya*. Conseil Superieur de l'Eau. Rabat, Morocco.

————. 1993c. *Plan Directeur Integre d'Amenagement des Eaux du Bassin de Tensift*. Conseil Superieur de l'Eau. Rabat, Morocco.

————. 1993d. *Plan Directeur Integre d'Amenagement des Eaux des Bassins du Souss-Massa*. Conseil Superieur de l'Eau. Rabat, Morocco.

————. 1994a. *Etude Plan Directeur Integre d'Amenagement des Eaux des Bassins du Sebou, Bou-Regrag Oum-Er-Rbia—27 reports of the study details*. Ministere des Travaux Publics. 1985–1994. Rabat, Morocco.

————. 1994b. *Enquete Agricole: Productions Vegetales Principales*. Campagne 1992–93. Ministere de l'Agriculture et de la Mise en Valeur Ajoute. Direction de la Plannification et des Affaires Economiques.

————. 1995. *Annuaire Statistique du Maroc*. Premier Ministere Charge de la Population. Direction de la Statistique. Rabat, Morocco.

————. 1996. *Etude du Secteur de l'Eau*. *Theme 1 to 11*. Ministere des Travaux Publics. 1995–1996. Nedeco-Holinger-CID.

————. 1997. *Developpement des Resources en Eau au Maroc*. Premier Forum Mondial de l'Eau. Marrakech. Ministere des Travaux Publics.

Russell, Clifford, David Arey and Robert Kates. 1970. *Drought and Water Supply: Implications of the Massachusetts Experience for Municipal Planning*. The John Hopkins Press.

Salman, Salman M.A. 1997. *The Legal Framework for Water Users' Associations: A Comparative Study*. World Bank Technical Paper no. 360. The World Bank. Washington, D.C.

Schaible, Gleen D., Noel R. Gollehon, Mark S. Kramer, Marcel P. Aillery, and Michael R. Moore. 1995. *Economic Analysis of Selected Water Policies Options for the Pacific Northwest*. Agricultural Economic Report, no. 720. US Department of Agriculture.

Serageldin, I. 1995. *Toward Sustainable Management of Water Resources*. The World Bank, Washington, D.C.

Serghini, Hassan, Kevin McNamara and Paul V. Preckel. 1996. *1994–1995 Drounght in Morocco: An Input-Output Analysis*. Paper submitted to the Interconference Symposium of the International Association of Agricultural Economists and the Moroccan Association of Agro-Economy, June 24–26. Rabat, Morocco.

Shaw, Malcolm N. 1997. *International Law*. Grotius. Cambridge Press.

Shen, Hsieh W. 1976. *Stochastic Approaches to Water Resources*. Volume I and II. Colorado State University.

Shoven, John B. and John Whalley. 1992. *Applying General Equilibrium*. Cambridge University Press.

Simmons, Donald M.. 1975. *Non-Linear Programming for Operations Research*. Englewood Clifs, N.J.: Prentice-Hall, Inc..

Sohn, Ira. 1986. *Readings in Input-Output Analysis: Theory and Applications*. Oxford University Press.

Solanes, Miguel. 1997. *Integrated Water management: Water Planning and Water Legislation—From the Perspective of the Dublin Principles*. Draft. ECLAC/ONU.

Stephan, Gunter. 1989. *Pollution Control, Economic Adjustment and Long-Run Equilibrium: A Computable Equilibrium Approach to Environmental Economics*. Springer-Verlatg Berlin Heidelberg.

Stryker, Dirck. 1991. *Groupe Charge de l'Aspect Consommation des Cereales au Maroc—Recherche sur les Fonctions de Demande*. Associates for international Resources and Development. Cambridge, MA.

Swearingen, Will D. 1987. *Moroccan Mirages: Agrarian Dreams and Deceptions, 1912–1986*. Princeton University Press.

Thiessen, E.M. and D.P. Louks. February 1992. *Computer Assisted Negociation of Multiobjective Water Resources Conflicts*. Water Resources Bulletin. Vol.28, no.1.

Thrall, Robert M. et al. 1979. *Economic Modeling for Water Policy Evaluation*. Volume 3. North-Holland/TIMS Studies in the Management Sciences. North-Holland Publishing Company.

Titetenberg, Tom. 1996. *Environmental and Natural Resource Economics*. Fourth Edition. Harper Collins College Publishers.

Tsakok, Isabelle. 1990. *Agriculture Price Policy*. Cornell University Press.

United Nations. 1992. *The Dublin Statement and Report of the Conference*, International Conference on Water and the Environment: Development Issues for the 21st Century, 26–31 January 1992, Dublin.

United Nations Department of Development Support and Management Services (UN/DDSMS). 1996. *Towards an Action Plan for Water Resources Management in Ta'iz Region, Yemen*. Prepared by Jac A.M. Van der Gun.

Young, Robert A.. 1996. *Measuring Economic Benefits for Water Investments and Policies*. World Bank Technical Paper no.338. World Bank.

Viessman, Warren and Garry L. Lewis. 1989. *Introduction to Hydrology*. Harper and Row Publishers.

Wagner, Harvey M. 1969. *Principles of Operations Research.* Englewood Cliffs, N.J.: Prentice-Hall, Inc..

Walpole, Ronald E. and Raymond H. Myers. 1993. *Probability and Statistics for Engineers and Scientists.* Macmillan Publishing Company.

Waterbury, John. 1979. *Hydropolitics of the Nile Valley.* Syracuse University Press.

Weimer, David L. and Aidan R. Vining. 1992. *Policy Analysis: Concepts and Practice.* Prentice Hall, New Jersey.

Winpenny, J.T. 1991. *Values for the Environment: A Guide to Economic Appraisal.* Overseas Development Institute.

Winston, Wayne L. 1996. *Introduction to Mathematical Programming: Applications and Algorithms,* PWS-Kent Publishing Co.

World Bank. 1990. *Arab Republic of Egypt: An Agricultural Strategy for the 1990s.* A World Bank Country Study. Washington, D.C.

———. 1993. *Water Resources Management.* A World Bank Policy Paper.

———. 1994a. A Strategy for Managing Water in the Middle East and North Africa. Washington, D.C.

———. 1995a. *Deuxieme Projet de Protection de l'Environment: Depollution Industrielle du Bassin du Sebou.* Rapport de Mission.

———. 1995b. *From Scarcity to Security: Averting a Water Crisis in the Middle East and North Africa.* Report no. 14750-MOR. Washington, D.C.

———. 1996a. *Kingdom of Morocco—Water Sector Review.* Report no. 14750-MOR. Washington, D.C.

———. 1996b. *Social Indicators of Development.* Washington, D.C.

———. 1997. The Kingdom of Morocco. *Rural Development Strategy: Integrating the Two Morocco (1997–2000).* Report No. 16303-MOR. Washington.

———. 1998. *Kingdom of Morocco—Water Resources Management Project.* Staff Appraisal Report no. 15760-MOR. Washington, D.C.